3:00
.Mr Ewald

# THE BAHÁ'Í FAITH

The shrine of the Báb, Mount Carmel, Haifa, Israel

# THE BAHÁ'Í FAITH

## The Emerging Global Religion

William S. Hatcher
and J. Douglas Martin

1817

Harper & Row, Publishers, San Francisco

Cambridge, Hagerstown, New York, Philadelphia
London, Mexico City, São Paulo, Singapore, Sydney

Library of Congress Cataloging in Publication Data

Hatcher, William S.
    THE BAHÁ'Í FAITH

    Bibliography: p.
    Includes index.
    I. Bahai Faith. I. Martin, J. Douglas (James Douglas) II. Title.
BP365.H335 1984        297'.89        84-42743
ISBN 0-06-065441-4

85  86  87  88  10  9  8  7  6  5  4

Dedicated to the men and women who have given their lives
for the Bahá'í Faith in Iran, 1844–1984.

*This people have passed beyond the narrow straits of names, and pitched
their tents upon the shores of the sea of renunciation.*

—BAHÁ'U'LLÁH

# Contents

# Preface

In 1974, with the encouragement of the National Spiritual Assembly of the Bahá'ís of Canada, a group of scholars and students created an association to promote the systematic study of the Bahá'í Faith at the university level. The group flourished, producing lectures, conferences, and a series of publications. Today the Association for Bahá'í Studies, with headquarters in Ottawa, Canada, boasts national affiliates in several countries around the world.

As the organization grew, it was recognized that no one of the existing sources would meet the need for a textbook on which courses of undergraduate study could be based. The outcome was the commissioning of the present work. Consequently, the authors feel a particular sense of gratitude to the Association not only for the initiative that launched the project, but also for the consistent support given to its realization.

We would like also to express our gratitude to Todd Lawson of the Institute for Islamic Studies at McGill University, who reviewed the chapter on the Islamic background; to Brownlee Thomas, who generously contributed her professional services as technical editor; and to Marion Finley at Université Laval who was kind enough to do the transliteration of Persian and Arabic terms. Thanks are owed, too, to Larry Bucknell and Betty Fisher of the United States Bahá'í Publishing Trust for the many kinds of practical assistance they provided. Both of us feel deeply indebted to Susan Lyons, who stayed with the manuscript through its several versions.

Finally, we are grateful to the many Bahá'í friends who encouraged us to undertake the project; and particularly to our wives, whose understanding and support made possible its completion.

W.S.H., J.D.M.

*Toronto, July 8, 1984*

# Note on the Transliteration of Persian and Arabic Names

The system of transliterating Persian and Arabic names used in this work is one of several such systems currently in use. It differs from the Cambridge system primarily by its use of accents ("á" and "í") instead of overlining ("ā" and "ī"), though there are some other differences as well.

Generally speaking, we have avoided transliterating geographical names which have either current or well-established English language forms. We have applied this same principle to the names of persons of Oriental origin who subsequently established themselves in the West under a particular English language form of their name, and to names of historical figures (e.g., Muhammad) with established English language forms. Also, names of titles ("Shah" or "Imam") with established English equivalents are not transliterated unless they occur as part of a transliterated name ("Náṣiri'd-Dín Sháh").

Two particular cases should be mentioned. First, we have avoided use of the common "Koran" and used instead the transliterated "Qur'án" which appears to us a more dignified form to designate the holy book of the Muslim faith. Second, we have used the established form "Shiah" throughout to designate the Twelver (Imami) branch of Islam, consistently avoiding such other hybrid forms as "Shiite" which are in current use.

In all, we have tried to achieve the greatest possible simplicity consistent with clarity and accuracy.

Seat of the Universal House of Justice, Mount Carmel, Haifa, Israel.

# Introduction

The Bahá'í Faith is the youngest of the world's independent religions. From its obscure beginnings in Iran during the mid-nineteenth century, it has now spread to virtually every part of the world, has established its administrative institutions in over two hundred independent states and major territories, and has embraced believers from virtually every cultural, racial, social, and religious background.

The new faith is a distinct religion, based entirely on the teachings of its founder, Bahá'u'lláh. It is not a cult, a reform movement or sect within any other faith, nor merely a philosophical system. Neither does it represent an attempt to create a new religion syncretistically by bringing together different teachings chosen from other religions. In the words of Arnold Toynbee:

> Bahaism is an independent religion on a par with Islam, Christianity, and the other recognized world religions. Bahaism is not a sect of some other religion; it is a separate religion, and it has the same status as the other recognized religions.[1]

This text attempts to examine a wide range of Bahá'í teachings. It will be helpful at the outset to note the pivotal concept of the Bahá'í Faith: the oneness of humankind. Bahá'u'lláh's central message is that the day has come for the unification of humanity into one global family. He asserts that God has set in motion historical forces that are bringing about worldwide recognition that the entire human race is a unified, distinct species. This historical process in which, Bahá'ís believe, their faith has a central role to play, will involve the emergence of a global civilization.

---

[1] From a letter to Dr. N. Kunter, Avakat, Istanbul, Turkey, dated 12 August 1959. Published in *British Bahá'í Journal*. No. 141, p. 4, November 1959. The correct name of the religion is the Bahá'í Faith, not "Bahaism."

Entirely separate from this breathtaking vision, the Bahá'í Faith holds a particular interest for students of the history of religion. This is because the empirical data is so accessible. It would be difficult or perhaps impossible to establish precisely the generating impulses that gave rise to the birth and development of any of the earlier major religions of the world. An explanation of the nature of the teachings of the Buddha, the actual events of the life of Jesus, the era in which Zoroaster lived and the nature of his influence, even substantiating the historical existence of "Krishna"—all remain seemingly insoluble problems. The life and person of Muhammad are more accessible, but even here controversy exists on many matters of vital detail.

One of the earliest Western historians to become interested in Bahá'í history was Edward Granville Browne, a noted Cambridge orientalist.[2] It was Browne's view that the then little-known faith afforded a unique opportunity to examine in detail how a new and independent religion comes into existence. He said:

for here he [the student of religion] may contemplate such personalities as by lapse of time pass into heroes and demi-gods still unobscured by myth and fable; he may examine by the light of concurrent and independent testimony one of those strange outbursts of enthusiasm, faith, fervent devotion, and indomitable heroism—or fanaticism, if you will—which we are accustomed to associate with the earlier history of the human race; he may witness, in a word, the birth of a faith which may not impossibly win a place amidst the great religions of the world.[3]

The same point has been made by modern observers from outside the Bahá'í community:

The Bábí-Bahá'í movement provides the historian of religion with invaluable sources for studying its origin and development as with no other religion. There are at least two reasons for this. First, the Bahá'í Faith is the most recent religion. Other religions began hundreds or thousands of years ago. Of the so-called eleven major, living religions of the world, only Islam

---

[2] For a fuller discussion of Browne's contribution see Appendix.

[3] Edward G. Browne, *A Traveller's Narrative Written to Illustrate the Episode of the Báb*, p. viii. *Note:* Complete bibliographical information for this book and all other works cited in this text will be found in the bibliography.

(seventh century A.D.) and Sikhism (sixteenth century A.D.) are centuries old: the others—Hinduism, Buddhism, Jainism, Taoism, Confucianism, Shinto, Zoroastrianism, Judaism, and Christianity—date back thousands of years. The Bahá'í Faith originated only in the last century (1844 A.D.), and only since 1963 has it reached possibly the last phase of its formative development, which incidentally makes the present time most appropriate for making a study of that development. The Bahá'í Faith is, therefore, a religion of modern times and is naturally more accessible for study and understanding than the older religions.[4]

Most recently, the intensification of the persecution of Iranian Bahá'ís by the Islamic regime in their country has attracted international attention. Since it is principally the religious affiliation of the victims which has occasioned the attacks, interest has increasingly focused on the Bahá'í Faith itself. The beliefs that distinguish Bahá'ís from Muslims, particularly, and the sequence of historical events that has led up to the current outbreak, have been the subject of considerable discussion in Western information media.

For all of the reasons mentioned above, the Bahá'í Faith is increasingly included for study in university and college course curricula on world religions. The writings of the founder of the Bahá'í Faith, together with in depth expositions by his appointed interpreters, are readily available in compilations published as English-language translations. Apart from these primary sources, literature on the Bahá'í Faith represents two main types of secondary material: commentaries by its adherents written to educate Bahá'ís and attract support, and a number of attacks by antagonists from among the Christian clergy. Neither type of secondary source publication can be considered adequate or appropriate to the objective exposition of the history and teachings of the Bahá'í Faith.

The present text covers four main areas of study: (1) the history of the Bábí and Bahá'í Faiths; (2) Bahá'u'lláh's basic teachings; (3) the institutional structure of the Bahá'í Faith; and (4) the development of the Bahá'í community. A final chapter suggests some of the new challenges facing the young religion as a consequence of the

---

[4] Vernon Elvin Johnson. "The Challenge of the Bahá'í Faith" in *World Order*. Vol. 10, No. 3, 1976, p. 39.

dramatic success it has enjoyed during its 140 years of growth.

The study of any religion poses special challenges. Unlike most of the phenomena science studies, religion claims to comprehend human beings themselves. Religion demands not only attention, but ultimately devotion and commitment. So it is that many religious thinkers have insisted that there is a fundamental conflict between faith and science and that the realm of the former lies essentially beyond the explorations of the latter.

Here the Bahá'í Faith comes to the aid of those who undertake to study it. One of the teachings of its founder, Bahá'u'lláh, is that God's greatest gift to humankind is reason. Bahá'ís accept that reason must be applied to all the phenomena of existence, including those which are spiritual, and the instrument to be used in this effort is the scientific method.[5] 'Abdu'l-Bahá, the son of Bahá'u'lláh and the appointed interpreter of his writings, asserted that: "Any religion that contradicts science or that is opposed to it is only ignorance—for ignorance is the opposite of knowledge."[6]

To an unusual degree, therefore, one who studies the Bahá'í Faith finds the subject laid open to examination. The mysteries one encounters, like those in the physical universe, reflect no more than the recognized limitations of human knowledge. That is to say, they do not represent assertions about the natural world which contradict science and reason. The minimum of ritual and the absence of a priestly elite endowed with special powers or knowledge also afford relatively easy access to the central features of the Bahá'í Faith.

Nevertheless, the study of religion is not paleontology. It is an examination of living phenomena which must be penetrated, to the fullest extent possible, not only by the mind but also by the heart, if a clear understanding is to result. The Bahá'í Faith is a subject which represents the deepest beliefs of several million people, beliefs which govern the most important decisions in hu-

---

[5] "The Revelation proclaimed by Bahá'u'lláh, His followers believe is . . . scientific in its method . . . religious truth is not absolute, but relative." Shoghi Effendi, *The World Order of Bahá'u'lláh, Selected Letters,* p. xi (1938 ed.).

[6] 'Abdu'l-Bahá, *Paris Talks,* pp. 130–141. For a detailed treatment of the subject of science and religion in a Bahá'í context, see William S. Hatcher, *The Science of Religion.*

man life, and for which many thousands of Bahá'ís have accepted and are today accepting persecution and death.

The authors of the present work have sought to balance these demands of mind and heart which the study of religion imposes on those who pursue it.

# 1. The Islamic Background

To assert that a religion is independent of other faiths is not to argue that it began in a religious vacuum. Buddhism emerged from a traditional Hindu background, and only after it had crossed the Himalayas did it assume its full character as a separate faith destined to become a major cultural force in China, Japan, and the lands of Southeast Asia. Similarly, Jesus Christ and his immediate followers began their mission within the context of Judaism and for some two centuries the movement was regarded by neighboring peoples as a reformed branch of the parent religion. Christianity did not appear as a separate religion with its own scriptures, laws, and institutional and ritual forms until it had begun to attract large numbers of adherents from the many non-Semitic races in the Mediterranean world.

The religious matrix of the Bahá'í Faith was Islam. Much as Christianity was born out of the messianic expectations of Judaism, the religion that was to become the Bahá'í Faith arose from eschatological tensions within Islam. In the same way, however, the Bahá'í Faith is entirely independent of its parent religion. The validity of this view has most recently again been acknowledged by one of the most prolific scholars of modern Islam. 'Allámah (an honorific meaning "very learned") Siyyid Ṭabáṭabá'í states categorically, "the Bábí and Bahá'í sects . . . should not in any sense be considered as branches of Shi'ism."[1]

---

[1] 'Allámah Siyyid Muḥammad Ḥusayn Ṭabáṭabá'í, *Shi'ite Islam*, p. 76. Sunni Islam has also disavowed any connection between itself and the Bahá'í Faith. As early as 1925, the religious court of Beba, Egypt, issued the following decision: "The Bahá'í Faith is a new religion, entirely independent, with beliefs, principles and laws of its own, which differ from, and are utterly in conflict with, the beliefs, principles and laws of Islam. No Bahá'í, therefore, can be regarded a Muslim or vice-versa, even as no Buddhist, Brahmin, or Christian can be regarded as Muslim or vice-versa." Cited by Shoghi Effendi, *God Passes By*, p. 365.

For a study of the relationship of the Bahá'í religion with Islam, see Udo

The new faith first appeared in Persia, a predominantly Muslim country.[2] It then spread to neighboring Muslim lands in the Ottoman and Russian Empires and to northern India. Though some early followers were of Jewish, Christian, or Zoroastrian background, the vast majority had been followers of Islam. Their religious ideas were drawn from the Qur'án, and they were primarily interested in those aspects of their new belief system that represented the fulfillment of Islamic prophecies and the interpretation of Muslim teaching. Similarly, the Islamic clergy initially saw those who followed the new faith as Muslim heretics.

Because of the Bahá'í Faith's Islamic background, it is important to begin our study with a consideration of the Islamic matrix out of which the Bahá'í Faith arose. Such an examination is important for a second reason as well: Islam fits into a concept of both religious history and the relationship between religions which is central to Bahá'í teaching. The Bahá'í Faith is perhaps unique in that it unreservedly accepts the validity of the other great faiths. Bahá'ís believe that Abraham, Moses, Zoroaster, the Buddha, Jesus, and Muhammad are all equally authentic messengers of one God. The teachings of these divine messengers are seen as paths to salvation which contribute to the "carrying forward of an ever-advancing civilization".[3] But Bahá'ís believe that this series of interventions by God in human history has been progressive, each revelation from God more complete than those which preceded it, and each

---

Schaefer, "The Bahá'í Faith and Islam," in *The Light Shineth in Darkness, Five Studies in Revelation after Christ,* pp. 113–132. As to the question of the Bahá'í Faith being a "sect" (above), see Schaefer's discussion of this question as it pertains to the model of the religious sect constructed by its modern fathers, Weber and Troeltsch, in this essay, pp. 113–114. Schaefer, in the course of this discussion, remarks: "The Bahá'í Faith, according to its own interpretation, does not aim to be a reform or a restoration of Islam, but rather claims its origin in a new act of God, in a new outpouring of the divine spirit and in a new divine covenant. The foundation of belief and of law is the new divine word revealed by Bahá'u'lláh. This is why the Bahá'í is not a Muslim." Ibid., p. 114.

[2] Under the Pahlavis (1925–1979), the ancient name Iran replaced the designation Persia. This text has used "Persia" in describing events of the nineteenth and early twentieth centuries, and "Iran" in reference to more recent ones.

[3] "All men have been created to carry forward an ever-advancing civilization." Bahá'u'lláh, *Gleanings from the Writings of Bahá'u'lláh,* p. 215.

preparing the way for the next. In this view, Islam, as the most recent of the prior religions, constituted the immediate historical preparation for the Bahá'í Faith. Not surprisingly, therefore, one finds in the Bahá'í writings a great many Quranic terms and concepts.

Some tenets of Islam are especially important to a clear understanding of the Bahá'í Faith. Like Muslims, Bahá'ís believe that God is One and utterly transcendent in his essence. He "manifests" his will to humanity through the series of messengers whom Bahá'ís call "Manifestations of God." The purpose of the Manifestation is to provide perfect guidance not only for the spiritual progress of the individual believer, but also to mold society as a whole. An important difference between the two faiths in this respect is that while, among the existing religions, the Qur'án designates only Judaism, Christianity, and Islam itself as divinely inspired, Bahá'ís believe that all religions are integral parts of one divine plan:

There can be no doubt whatever that the peoples of the world, of whatever race or religion, derive their inspiration from one heavenly Source, and are the subjects of one God. The difference between the ordinances under which they abide should be attributed to the varying requirements and exigencies of the age in which they were revealed. All of them, except a few which are the outcome of human perversity, were ordained of God, and are a reflection of His Will and Purpose.[4]

There is yet another aspect of Islam which influenced the development of the new religion and which dictated Muslim reaction to it. Like Christianity before it, Islam gradually divided into a number of major sects. One of the most significant of these is the Shiah sect, which believes that it was Muhammad's intention that his descendants inherit the spiritual and temporal leadership of the faithful. These chosen ones, called Imams, or "leaders," were believed to be endowed with unqualified infallibility in the discharge

---

[4] Bahá'u'lláh, *Gleanings from the Writings of Bahá'u'lláh*, p. 217. For a discussion of this subject see: Juan Ricardo Cole, *The Concept of Manifestation in the Bahá'í Writings*.

of their related responsibilities. However, the great majority of Muslims rejected such claims believing that the *sunna*—the "way" or mode of conduct attributed by tradition to the Prophet Muhammad—was a sufficient guide. Those who subscribed to this latter belief became known as Sunni. Although Sunni Muslims vastly outnumber the Shiah today, and are usually referred to by Western scholars as "orthodox" as opposed to the "heterodoxy" of the Shiah, Shiah Islam has a long and respected tradition, a tradition that only recently has become the object of serious study among a growing group of non-Muslim scholars.[5]

By A.D. 661, only twenty-nine years after Muhammad's death, power in the Muslim world fell into the hands of the first of a series of dynastic rulers, theoretically elected by the faithful, but in fact representing the dominance of various powerful families. The first two of these Sunni dynasties, the Umayyads and the Abbasids, saw the Imams as a challenge to their own legitimacy. Consequently, according to Shiah accounts, one Imam after another was put to death, beginning with Ḥasan and Ḥusayn, grandsons of Muhammad. These Imams, or descendants of the Prophet, came in time to be regarded by Shiah Islam as saints and martyrs.

Although Shiah Islam began among the Arabs, it reached its greatest influence in Persia. From the beginning, the Persian converts to Islam were attracted by the idea of the Imam as a divinely appointed leader. Unlike the Arabs, the Persians possessed a long heritage of government by a divinely appointed monarch, and the devotion that gathered around this figure in time came to focus on the person of the Prophet's descendants and appointed successors.[6] After centuries of oppression by Sunni caliphs, the tradition of the

---

[5] Why this attribution of orthodoxy to the Sunni branch of Islam should have been so fostered by non-Muslim authors is itself a question of some significance. The most frequently cited reason for it stems from the fact that, for a long time, Shiah Islam was simply unheard of in the West because of the geographic remoteness of its major centers from Europe and the European colonies established during the Crusades. For the Shiah point of view, see Ṭabáṭabá'í, *Shi'ite Islam*, pp. 9–16. A more complete discussion is in Seyyed Hossein Nasr, *Ideals and Realities of Islam*.

[6] For a brief but excellent introduction to the themes of pre-Islamic Iranian religion, see Geo. Widengren, "Iranian Religion," in *Encyclopedia Britannica*, pp. 867–872.

Imamate eventually triumphed in Persia through the rise of a strongly Shiah dynasty, the Safavids, in the sixteenth century.

By this time, however, the line of Imams had ended. One of the features of Iranian Shiah tradition is that, in the year 873, the twelfth and last appointed Imam—only a child at the time—withdrew into "concealment" in order to escape the fate of his predecessors. It is believed that he will emerge "at the time of the end" to usher in a reign of justice throughout the world. This eschatological tradition (doctrine of "last things") has much in common with the Christian expectation of the return of Christ and Mahayana Buddhism's promise of the advent of Maitreya Buddha, "the Buddha of universal righteousness." Among other titles Muslims have assigned to this promised deliverer, the "Hidden Imam," are *Mahdi* (the Guided One) and *Qá'im* (He Who Will Arise—i.e., from the family of the Prophet).

For a period of sixty-nine years following his disappearance, the twelfth or Hidden Imam was said to have communicated with his followers through a series of deputies. These intermediaries took the title *báb* (gate), because they were the only way to the Hidden Imam. There had been four bábs up to the year 941, when the fourth one died without naming a successor.

The refusal of either the Imam or the final báb to name a successor implied that the matter was to be left by the faithful entirely in the hands of God. In time, a messenger or messengers of God would appear, one of whom would be the Imam Mahdi, or Qá'im, and who would again provide a direct channel for the Divine Will to human affairs. It was out of this tradition that the Bahá'í religion and its forerunner, the Bábí Faith, appeared in the mid-nineteenth century.

# 2. The Bábí Faith

The early nineteenth century was a period of messianic expectation in the Islamic world as well as in the Christian world. In Persia, two influential theologians, S͟hayk͟h Aḥmad–i–Aḥsá'í and his disciple and successor, Siyyid Káẓim-i-Ras͟htí, taught a doctrine that departed radically from orthodox Shiah belief. In addition to interpreting the Qur'án in an allegorical rather than a literal manner, the "S͟hayk͟hís", as their followers were known, proclaimed that the return of the Imam Mahdi, the appointed deliverer and successor of Muhammad, was imminent.[1] Their teachings attracted widespread interest and aroused an air of expectancy reminiscent of contemporary Christian groups like the Millerites[2] in Europe and America, which at the same time were eagerly awaiting the return of Jesus Christ.

Before Siyyid Káẓim died in 1843, he urged his disciples to scatter in search of the Promised One who would shortly be revealed. He pointed out that the year, according to the Islamic calendar, was 1260 A.H., or exactly one thousand lunar years since the disappearance of the Hidden Imam.

For one of the leading S͟hayk͟hís, a man called Mullá Ḥusayn, the search ended abruptly in the city of Shiraz on the evening of May 23, 1844, when he encountered a young man named Siyyid (a title referring to the descendants of Muhammad) 'Alí-Muḥammad, who announced that he was the Promised One whom the S͟hayk͟hís were seeking. The claim was set forth in a lengthy document entitled Qayyúmu'l-Asmá', which the young Siyyid began that same night,

---

[1] For recent scholarship on this doctrine, see Vaḥíd Ráfatí, *The Development of S͟hayk͟hí Thought in S͟hí'i Islam* and Henri Corbin, *En Islam iranien; aspects spirituels et philosphiques.* Vol. 4

[2] See, for example, Whitney R. Cross, *The Burned-over District* and Ira V. Brown, "Watchers for the Second Coming, the Millenial Tradition in America" in *Mississippi Valley Historical Review.* Vol. 39, No. 3, 1952, pp. 441–458.

and which became the foundation stone of the Bábí Faith. The document identifies its author as a Messenger of God, in the line of Jesus, Muhammad, and those who had preceded them. In subsequent statements, Siyyid 'Alí-Muhammad also referred to himself by the traditional Muslim title "Báb" (Gate), although it was apparent from the context that he intended by this term a spiritual claim very different from any which had previously been associated with it.[3]

The charm and force of the Báb's personality, together with his extraordinary capacity to reveal the meaning of the most abstruse passages in the Qur'án, prompted Mullá Husayn to declare his faith.[4] He became the first believer of the Bábí Faith. Within a few weeks, seventeen other seekers accepted the Báb's claim to be the promised messenger. He appointed these first eighteen believers as the "Letters of the Living," and dispatched them throughout Iran to announce that the Day of God heralded in the Qur'án and all earlier religious scriptures had dawned.

Siyyid 'Alí-Muhammad, who became known to history as the Báb, was born in Shiraz on October 20, 1819, to a family of merchants.[5] Both his father and his mother were descendants of the

---

[3] It has been argued, usually by opponents of the Bahá'í Faith, that the Báb's conception of his mission only gradually "evolved" in his mind, presumably as a consequence of a series of successes. This clearly is not correct. The statement made by the Báb in first disclosing his claim to Mullá Husayn describes himself not only as the Messenger of God, but specifically as the "Remembrance of God" and the "Proof of God," titles which unequivocally referred to the long-expected advent of the Hidden Imam. That his audacious claim was understood by both his followers and the Muslim clergy was at once made clear. One of the first of those to accept the Báb, Mullá 'Alíy-i-Bastámí, left Persia almost immediately upon accepting the Báb in 1844, taking with him a copy of the Qayyúmu'l-Asmá', and was arrested on a charge of heresy shortly after his arrival in neighboring Baghdad. In January 1845, he was formally condemned on this charge by an edict (fatvá) of the assembled Shiah and Sunni clergy. The condemnation was based on his belief in one who claimed to be the source of a revelation like that of the Qur'án, and the Báb as author was also condemned. For a full discussion of the subject, see Muhammad Afnán and William S. Hatcher, "Western Islamic Scholarship and Bahá'í Origins," forthcoming in Religion, vol. 15, 1985.

[4] Shoghi Effendi, The World Order of Bahá'u'lláh, Selected Letters, pp. 123–128.

[5] The four principal sources used for the history of the Bábí religion are Shoghi Effendi, God Passes By; Hasan Balyuzi, The Bab, The Herald of the Day of Days; Nabíl-i-A'zam (Muhammad-i-Zarandí), The Dawn-breakers, Nabíl's Narrative of

Prophet Muhammad. The Báb's father died while his son was still a child and the Báb was raised by a maternal uncle, Hájí Mírzá Siyyid 'Alí, who in later years became one of the Báb's most devoted followers and one of the early martyrs of the new faith. All surviving accounts agree that the Báb was an extraordinary child. Although he received only elementary training in reading and writing, as was customary for the minority of Persian children who received any education at all, he exhibited an innate wisdom that astonished both his teacher and other adults with whom he came in contact. To these qualities of mind was added a profoundly spiritual nature. Even as a young boy he spent long periods in meditation and prayer. On one occasion, when his teacher protested that such lengthy devotions were not required of a child, the Báb is reported to have said that he had been in the house of his "Grandfather" whom he was trying to emulate. The reference was to the Prophet Muhammad, who was occasionally spoken of in this fashion by those who could claim direct descent from him.

The Báb left school some time before his thirteenth birthday, and at fifteen years of age he joined his uncle in the family business in Shiraz. Shortly thereafter he was sent to take over the management of the family trading house in Búshihr. While pursuing a business career that won him a reputation for integrity and ability, he continued his meditations, some of which he wrote down. In the spring of 1841, he left Búshihr to undertake a series of extended visits to various Muslim holy cities associated with the shrines of the martyred Imams. During his visit to Karbilá, the Báb met Siyyid Káẓim who greeted him with a reverence and enthusiasm which the Siyyid did not choose to explain to others, and which greatly surprised his students. The Báb stayed briefly with the group around Siyyid Káẓim and then returned to Iran where he married Khadíjih, the daughter of another merchant family, to whom he was distantly related. Less than two years later, his declaration to Mullá Ḥusayn in Shiraz took place.

---

*the Early Days of the Bahá'í Revelation;* Joseph Arthur, Comte de Gobineau, *Les Religions et les Philosophies dans l'Asie Centrale.*

The next step was publicly to proclaim the new faith. This began with a visit by the Báb to the center of pilgrimage for the Muslim world, the twin cities of Mecca and Medina in Arabia. On Friday, December 20, 1844, standing with his hand on the door-ring of the Kaaba, the holiest shrine in all the Islamic world, the Báb publicly declared: "I am that Qá'im Whose advent you have been waiting." He also addressed a special "tablet," or letter, to the Sharíf of Mecca, guardian of the shrines, in which he made the same claim. On neither occasion, although he was treated with great respect, was any serious attention given to his claims by the authorities of Sunni Islam. Undeterred, the Báb set sail for Persia, where the teaching activities of the Letters of the Living were beginning to raise a storm of excitement among both the clergy and the general public.

To the Shiah Muslim clergy, the claims made by the Báb were not merely heretical, but a threat to the foundations of Islam. Orthodox Islam holds that Muhammad was the "Seal of the Prophets" and thus the bearer of God's final revelation to humankind until the "Day of Judgment." Only Islam has remained pure and undiminished because its repository, the Qur'án, represents the authentic words uttered by the Prophet himself. From this baseline, Muslim theology had gone on to assert that Islam contains all that humanity will ever need until the Day of Judgement and that no further revelation of the divine purpose could or would occur.

The Báb's declaration of his mission was, therefore, a challenge to the central pillar of this theological system. For the Shiah, the dominant branch of Islam in Persia, the challenge was especially acute. Over the centuries, Shiah dogma had accorded unlimited authority over all human affairs to the person of the "Hidden Imam," whose advent was to signal the Judgment Day. Indeed, it had been argued that the shahs themselves reigned merely as the Imam's trustees. Accordingly, throughout Persia, mullas arose in violent opposition to the Báb almost as soon as they heard his claim. This opposition was greatly intensified by the Báb's denunciation of the prevailing ignorance and degeneracy of the clergy, which he saw as the principal obstacle to the progress of the Persian people.

The mullas' opposition went far beyond denunciations from the pulpit. In nineteenth-century Persia the Shiah clergy represented a system of power and authority parallel to that of the shah. Much of daily life was regulated by Islamic religious law under the juris-diction of mujtahids or doctors of theology. In theory, the judg-ments of these ecclesiastical courts depended on the support of the secular government for their enforcement. In practice, the Shiah clergy had resources of their own by which they could compel submission to their decrees. A leading modern authority on the subject describes the conditions prevailing in Persia at the time the Báb announced his mission:

Throughout most of the Qájár period, we encounter cases of mujtahids, particularly in Isfahan and Tabriz, surrounded by what can only be called private armies. Initially they consisted more of straightforward brigands *(lútí's)* than of mullas. The lútís, who originally formed chivalrous broth-erhoods similar to those of their counterparts, the *fatí's* in Anatolia and the Arab lands, acted to support clerical power by defying the state and by enforcing fatvás. In return they were permitted to engage in plunder and robbery, taking sanctuary, when threatened with pursuit, in the refuge known as *bast* which mosques and residences of the 'ulamá provided.[6]

These private armies served as the spearhead of an even more powerful resource available to the mullas. By declaring an enemy to be an infidel, the clergy could arouse mobs of the fanatical and largely ignorant population of towns and villages to stream into the streets in defense of what was regarded as the one true faith. Not only heterodox groups, but even the state itself had frequent-ly felt the power of this clerical weapon.

Despite the growing threat from this source, the period from 1845 to 1847 witnessed a great expansion in the number of people who declared themselves to be "Bábís," or followers of the Báb. Indeed, this number included many people drawn from the clergy. One of the new believers was a brilliant and extremely influential theologian named Siyyid Yaḥyáy-i-Darabí, later given the name "Vaḥíd" (Unique). The Báb had been placed under house arrest by

[6] Hamid Algar, *Religion and State in Iran, 1784–1906*, p. 19.

the governor of Shiraz, at the instigation of Muslim clergy in the area. Vaḥíd had been sent to interrogate him on behalf of Muhammad Shah, the ruler of Persia, who had heard rumors of the new movement and wished to secure reliable firsthand information. Not surprisingly, upon learning of Vaḥíd's conversion, the Shah sent orders that the Báb be brought immediately to the capital—Tehran —under escort, but treated as an honored guest. The Báb had earlier indicated his own desire to meet the ruler and fully explain his mission.

Unfortunately, the plan miscarried. Muhammad Shah was a weak and vacillating man, already experiencing the later stages of an illness that would kill him within the year. Moreover, he was completely dominated by his prime minister, Ḥájí Mírzá Áqásí, one of the most bizarre figures in Iranian history.[7] The prime minister had been the Shah's childhood tutor and was implicitly trusted by him. Fearing that his own influence might be fatally undermined should the Shah meet the Báb, the prime minister ordered that the Báb be taken in great secrecy to the fortress of Máh-Kú, in the northern province of Ádhirbayján, on the Russian frontier. The excuse given to the Shah was that the Báb's arrival in the capital might produce a confrontation between his followers and those of the orthodox clergy, and could possibly lead to public disorder of the kind which was common to this period.[8]

---

[7] Gobineau said of Muhammad Shah and his chief minister: "Muhammad Shah, of whom I have already spoken, was a prince with quite a special disposition—one which is quite common in Asia but which Europeans have hardly seen, let alone understood. . . . His health had always been deplorable; gouty to the last degree, he suffered continual pain and had very little relief from it. His character which was naturally weak, had become melancholy and, as he was in great need of affection but seldom experienced feelings of this kind within his family among his wives and children, he concentrated all his affection on the old mulla, his tutor. He made him his only friend, his confidant, then his all-powerful prime minister, and finally, with no exaggeration, his god. . . . The Ḥájí, for his part, was a god of a very special kind. It is not absolutely certain that he did not himself believe what Muhammad Shah was convinced of. In all situations, he professed the same general principles as the king, and had in good faith instilled them into him." *Les Religions et les Philosophies,* pp. 160–162, author's own translation.

[8] Nicolas writes: "An anecdote shows which sentiments the prime minister obeyed when he determined the will of the Shah. Prince Farhád Mírzá, still a young man, was the pupil of Ḥájí Mírzá Áqásí. He further related: 'One day as I was strolling

However, the prime minister, who came from Ádhirbayján, almost certainly chose that area because he hoped that its wild Kurdish mountain people would be totally unsympathetic to the Báb and his message. To his chagrin, the contrary proved true. The new faith spread even to Ádhirbayján, and the governor and other officials of the fortress of Máh-Kú were disarmed by the captivating sincerity of their prisoner. In a final effort to contain what he saw to be a mounting threat, Ḥájí Mírzá Áqásí had the Báb transferred from Máh-Kú to the equally remote castle of Chihríq. The same process was repeated and the Kurdish chieftain in charge of the fortress, Yaḥyá Khán, became another of the Báb's devoted admirers.

Realizing that the Shah was about to die and fearing the antagonism which his own misrule had aroused among influential groups in Persia, Ḥájí Mírzá Áqásí attempted to ingratiate himself with the powerful Muslim clergy who were bitterly opposed to the Báb and who had urged a formal condemnation of the new movement. At their urging, the prime minister ordered that the Báb be taken to the city of Tabriz and tried before a panel of leading ecclesiastics.

The trial took place in the summer of 1848 and by all accounts proved a farcical event. Its only purpose, it was clear, was to humiliate the prisoner.[9] The meeting ended with a decision to inflict corporal punishment on the Báb, and he was subsequently subjected to the bastinado.[10] The resulting injuries had an unexpected result: they put the Báb in contact with the only Westerner who has left an account of meeting him. During the course of the infliction of the bastinado, one of the mullas struck the Báb across the face and an English physician, Dr. William Cormick, was asked to provide treatment. The following is his account:

with him in the garden and he seemed in a good mood, I went so far as to ask him, "Ḥájí, why did you send the Báb to Máh-Kú?" He replied, "you are still young and there are certain things you cannot understand, but you should know that if he had come to Tehran, you and I would not be walking about at this moment free from all care in these shady surroundings." ' " Siyyid 'Alí–Muḥammad, Dit le Báb, cited in Nabíl-i-A'zam, The Dawn-Breakers, pp. 231–232.

[9] Shoghi Effendi, God Passes By, p. 21. Balyuzi provides a detailed description of the trial in The Báb, pp. 139–145. See also Browne, A Traveller's Narrative, pp. 277–290.

[10] Caning on the soles of the feet as punishment or torture.

[The Báb] was a very mild and delicate-looking man, rather small in stature and very fair for a Persian, with a melodious soft voice, which struck me much. . . . In fact his whole look and deportment went far to dispose one in his favour. Of his doctrine I heard nothing from his own lips, although the idea was that there existed in his religion a certain approach to Christianity. . . . Most assuredly the Musselman [sic] fanaticism does not exist in his religion, as applied to Christians, nor is there that restraint of females that now exists [in Islam].[11]

While the Báb was being held in prison his followers were experiencing growing attacks from mobs instigated by the Shiah mullas. This raised for them the question of self-defense. Islam, unlike Christianity, contains a much-misunderstood doctrine of *jihád* (holy war), which permits the conversion of pagan populations by force of arms. It also allows Muslims to defend themselves when attacked, but forbids any form of aggressive warfare and the forced conversion of other "Peoples of the Book" (i.e., followers of another revealed religion, generally interpreted as Jews and Christians).[12] Raised in this Muslim value system, the Bábís felt fully justified in defending themselves and their families against the attacks of the mullas. Some may even have expected that the Báb would reveal his own doctrine of *jihád*.

If so, they were disappointed. In the *Qayyúmu'l-Asmá'* the Báb reviewed in detail the basic principles of the Quranic concept of *jihád* and called on his followers to observe this governing order of the society in which they lived. Attacks on Muslims, as one of the peoples of the book, were therefore prohibited to them. The Báb made any form of aggressive *jihád* contingent upon his own approval, an approval which was not given despite the increasingly violent character of the conflict with the Shiah clergy.

These restrictions proved to be the first step in the gradual dismantling of a concept which had been one of the fundamental doctrines of the Islamic religion. When the *Bayán* (the *Exposition),* the book containing the laws of the Báb's faith, was subsequently

---

[11] Cited in Balyuzi, *The Báb,* pp. 146–147.
[12] For a full discussion of this subject see Muḥammad Afnán and William S. Hatcher, "Western Islamic Scholarship and Bahá'í Origins."

revealed, no *jihád* doctrine was included. The Bábís were thus left free to defend themselves if attacked, but were precluded from proclaiming the Bábí dispensation through the use of the sword, as the prophet Muhammad had permitted his followers to do under the barbaric conditions prevailing in pre-Islamic Arabia. The protection and ultimate triumph of his faith, the Báb said, were in the hand of God.

While the Báb was undergoing imprisonment and trial in northern Iran, his following continued to grow in other parts of the country. At about the time of his public declaration at Tabriz, a large group of leading Bábís met in the village of Badasht. This conference proved of great significance to the development of the Bábí Faith. One of the most prominent Bábís present was an extraordinary woman named Qurratu'l-'Ayn, known to Bahá'í history as Ṭáhirih (the Pure One).

Born into a family of scholars and theologians, Ṭáhirih had become recognized as one of the most gifted poets of Persia. To appreciate the magnitude of this achievement, it is necessary to consider how secluded and restricted Muslim women of this period were. Through the influence of an uncle and a cousin who had become disciples of Shaykh Aḥmad, Ṭáhirih came in contact with some of the early Bábís. Although she never met the Báb, she corresponded with him, declared her faith, and was named by him one of the original Letters of the Living.

One of the primary reasons for holding the Badasht conference was to decide on what steps might be taken to free the Báb from the castle of Chihríq. However, the gathering was unexpectedly electrified by a daring exposition by Ṭáhirih of some of the implications of the Báb's message. Some of the Bábís may have regarded the founder of their faith as a religious reformer; others may have been confused by traditional connotations of the term *báb*. Ṭáhirih explicitly clarified the implications of the Báb's own statements about his mission, uttered first on the night he had declared himself to Mullá Ḥusayn: he was the long-awaited Imam Mahdi, he who was to arise from the house of Muhammad. Thus he was a messenger of God, the founder of a new and independent religious dispensation. Just as early Christians had to free themselves from the laws and ordinances of the Torah, so were the Bábís called upon to free themselves from the requirements of the Islamic Sharí'ah (canon law). New social teachings had been revealed by the Báb and it was these to which Bábís should look for guidance.

To dramatize this exposition, Ṭáhirih appeared at one of the sessions of the conference without the veil required by Muslim tradition. Her action, and others like it, proved a severe test of faith for many of the more conservative Bábís and further aroused the antagonism of orthodox Muslims. Wild stories that the Bábís were atheists who believed in sexual promiscuity and community of property were eagerly spread by mullas determined to portray the movement as the enemy of both decency and public order.[13]

The situation was made even more unstable in September 1848, when Muhammad Shah finally succumbed to his many illnesses. His death precipitated the usual period of political upheaval while the question of the succession was being settled.[14] Ḥájí Mírzá Áqásí was overthrown by his political enemies and the mullas took advantage of the ensuing disorder to intensify their campaign for eradication of the Bábí heresy.

---

[13] Fragmentary early accounts by Western commentators in Persia repeat many of these stories gleaned, it must be assumed, from the Muslim contacts on whom these observers were almost entirely dependent for their understanding of the Persian language and their interpretation of religious issues in the country. Momen has brought together (*The Bábí and Bahá'í Religions,* pp. 3–17) a number of these reports, which include references to rebellion, nihilism, atheism, and community of wives and property. It was only after scholarly study by Gobineau, Browne, Nicolas, and others who could communicate directly with followers of the new faith, that these impressions were corrected.

[14] Gobineau wrote: A change of reign is always a very critical time in Central Asia. In Persia, in Turkestan, in the Arab States, a period of anarchy sets in which can last for a long time, which takes on a rather violent and turbulent character, but which always manages to keep law enforcement in abeyance, according to the principle that the will of the sovereign has, for a greater or lesser period, disappeared. . . . It is a watch which has stopped; the springs are not and should not be changed; but, until it is wound up again by hand, it no longer works.

Moreover, there are many passions and interests to arouse, stir up, and fan the flame of general discord. If there are several claimants to the throne, they want disorder so as to increase their chances of success and find themselves active supporters." *Les Religions et les Philosophies,* pp. 175–176, author's own translation)

In the province of Mázindarán, a group of some three hundred Bábís, under the leadership of Mullá Ḥusayn and the Báb's leading disciple, a young man named Quddús (who had accompanied the Báb on his pilgrimage to Mecca), found themselves besieged in a small fortress which they had hastily erected at the isolated shrine dedicated to a Muslim saint, Shaykh Ṭabarsí. They had enthusiastically swept through the province proclaiming that the promised Qá'im had appeared, and called on all who heard them to arise and follow. The local Shiah clergy had denounced them as heretics and aroused the population of several villages to attack them. No sooner were the Bábís penned up behind the palisade they had put together at Shaykh Ṭabarsí than the mullas accused them of responsibility for the civil disorder which the clergy's own fulminations against heresy and apostasy had aroused. In the highly charged atmosphere surrounding the struggle for power among Muhammad Shah's heirs, this reckless new accusation served as a spark to gunpowder. Mírzá Taqí Khán, a man of great ability, but ruthless and intensely suspicious had replaced Ḥájí Mírzá Áqásí as grand vizier. Deciding that the Bábi movement must be crushed, the new vizier dispatched an armed force to support the efforts of the mullas and their partisans.

The siege at the fort of Ṭabarsí turned, however, into an occasion of humiliation for the opponents of the Bábís. Over the following year, one army after another, numbering finally thousands of men, was sent to overcome the few hundred defenders of the fort, and all in turn suffered decisive defeat. Eventually, the small garrison, which had already lost a large percentage of its members—including Mullá Ḥusayn—was enticed to surrender under a solemn promise, witnessed on a copy of Qur'án, that they would be freed. However, no sooner did they leave the protection of the fortress than they were set upon by the besiegers. Many were killed outright, others were tortured to death, and the remainder were stripped of their possessions and sold into slavery. Quddús was given over into the hands of a leading ecclesiastic of the area who had him dragged through the streets, mutilated, and finally killed.

Similar events took place in two other major centers, Nayríz and Zanján. In both places, armed forces of the Qájár princes came to the support of mobs that had been stirred into a state of fanatic frenzy by the Shiah clergy, who were determined to exterminate all the followers of the new religion. In Nayríz, not even the fact that the Bábís were led by so preeminent a figure as Vaḥíd succeeded in calming the rage of local authorities and the aroused and angry mob. Vaḥíd perished in the massacre that followed the capture of the small fort in which the beleaguered Bábís had taken refuge. At Zanján, as at Fort Shaykh Ṭabarsí, the surrender of the Bábí defenders was secured by false pledges of peace and friendship signed and sealed on a copy of the Qur'án, following which the prisoners were similarly massacred.

Scenes of violence occurred throughout the country. Advised by the mullas that the property of the "apostates" was forfeit, many local authorities joined in hunting down Bábís. Social position offered no protection. In the capital of Tehran, at about the time of the massacre of Zanján, seven prominent and highly respected leaders of the merchant and academic communities were publicly put to death with great cruelty when they refused to recant their newly proclaimed faith. It is indicative of the public fury which had been aroused that one of these murdered men, Mírzá Qurbán 'Alí, regarded as a person of unusual saintliness, had served as spiritual mentor to the royal family as well as to several members of the government.[15]

Responsibility for the majority of these atrocities and those that were to follow must be attributed not only to the Shiah clergy, but also to the new prime minister, Mírzá Taqí Khán. The new ruler, Náṣiri'd-Dín Shán, was still a boy of sixteen; thus, once again, the monarch's authority fell into the hands of a chief minister. Mírzá Taqí Khán had been head of the faction that had installed the new ruler after overcoming the partisans of two other heirs to the throne. Concluding that his own power as well as the general stability of the regime could be best assured by suppressing the Bábí movement, he had collaborated in the horrors of Fort Shaykh Ṭabarsí,

---

[15] Shoghi Effendi, *God Passes By*, p. 47.

Nayríz and Zanján, and also in the deaths of the "Seven Martyrs of
Tehran," as they became known. Now he determined to strike the
movement at its heart.

While the siege of Zanján was still in progress, Mírzá Taqí Khán
ordered the governor of Ádhirbayján to take the Báb to Tabriz and
there conduct a public execution.[16] Mírzá Taqí Khán had no
personal authority to issue such an order, nor did he consult the
other members of the government. Because of this, the governor
of Ádhirbayján, who had come to respect his captive, refused Mírzá
Taqí Khan's order. The latter was therefore finally compelled to
send his own brother, Mírzá Ḥasan Khán, to execute the task. The
Báb was hastily taken to Tabriz where the leading mujtahids were
asked to decide the case as a matter of religious rather than civil law.
As Mírzá Taqí Khán had anticipated, the clergy readily cooperated
in signing a formal death warrant on a charge of heresy. On July
9, 1850, in the presence of a crowd of thousands who thronged
rooftops and windows of a public square, arrangements were made
to carry out the sentence. What followed was a most extraordinary
event.

The Báb and one of his disciples were suspended by ropes
against the wall of a military barracks and a regiment of 750 Armenian Christian troops were drawn up to form a firing squad.
The colonel of the regiment, a certain Sám Khán was reluctant to
carry out the order of execution, which he feared would bring down
the wrath of God on his head. The Báb is reported to have given
him the following assurance: "Follow your instructions, and if your
intention be sincere, the Almighty is surely able to relieve you of
your perplexity."[17]

Many eye-witnesses testified to what followed.[18] The regiment
was drawn up and 750 rifles were discharged. The smoke from these

---

[16] Several Western diplomatic representatives sought, unsuccessfully, to dissuade
the prime minister from his course, arguing that persecution could only further
spread the teachings he feared. (Momen, *The Bábí and Babáí Religions,* pp. 71–72,
103).

[17] Momen, *Bábí and Bahá'í Religions,* p. 52.

[18] Momen, *Bábí and Bahá'í Religions,* (pp. 77–82) has brought together a number of
eye witness accounts of the event, transmitted by Western commentators.

muzzle-loading rifles shrouded the square in darkness. When the smoke cleared, incredulous onlookers saw the Báb's companion standing unscathed beside the wall; the Báb had vanished from sight! The ropes by which the pair had hung had been severed by the bullets. A frenzied search ensued, and the Báb was found unhurt in the room he had occupied the night before. He was calmly engaged in completing his final instructions to his secretary.

The crowd was in a state of near pandemonium and the Armenian regiment refused to take any further part in the proceedings. Mírzá Ḥasan Khán was faced with the real possibility that the fickle mob, which had first hailed the Báb and then denounced him, might view his deliverance as a sign from God and rise up in his support. A Muslim regiment was thus hastily assembled, the Báb and his companion were once again suspended from the wall, and a second volley was discharged. This time the bodies of the two prisoners were riddled with bullets. The last words of the Báb to the crowd were:

O wayward generation! Had you believed in Me every one of you would have followed the example of this youth, who stood in rank above most of you, and would have willingly sacrificed himself in My path. The day will come when you will have recognized Me; that day I shall have ceased to be with you [19]

The extraordinary circumstances of the Báb's death provided a focal point for a new wave of interest in his message. The story spread like wildfire, not only among the Persians, but also among the diplomats, merchants, military advisers, and journalists who made up the substantial European community in Persia at the time. The words of a French consular official, A. L. M. Nicolas, suggest the impact the drama in Persia made on educated Westerners:

This is one of the most magnificent examples of courage which mankind has ever been able to witness, and it is also an admirable proof of the love which our hero had for his fellow countrymen. He sacrificed himself for mankind; he gave for it his body and his soul, he suffered for it hardships,

---

[19] Momen, *Bábí and Bahá'í Religions*, p. 53.

insults, indignities, torture and martyrdom. He sealed with his blood the pact of universal brotherhood, and like Jesus he gave his life in order to herald the reign of concord, justice and love for one's fellow men.[20]

For the Bábí community, however, the effect of the Báb's death, occurring so soon after the extermination of most of the faith's leaders, including the majority of the Letters of the Living, was a devastating blow. It deprived the community of the leadership it needed, not only to endure the intensifying persecutions it was experiencing, but also to maintain the integrity of the standards of behavior taught by the Báb.

The Bábís had continuously emphasized that their sole concern was to proclaim the new spiritual and social teachings revealed by the Báb. At the same time, because their basic religious attitudes and ideas were built upon the foundations of their Islamic background, they believed they had every right to defend themselves and their families, provided they did not engage in aggression to secure their religious ends. Once the guiding hands of those who understood the Báb's message were withdrawn by the brutal repression exercised by Mírzá Taqí Khán, it was predictable that volatile elements among the Bábís might prove unable to maintain the original discipline.

This proved to be the case when on August 15, 1852, two Bábí youths, obsessed by the sufferings they had witnessed and driven to despair by the attitude of the authorities, fired a pistol at the Shah. The king escaped serious injury because the pistol was loaded only with birdshot; but the attempt on the monarch's life triggered a new wave of persecutions on a scale far surpassing anything the country had yet witnessed. A reign of terror ensued.

One account has been left by Captain Alfred von Goumoens, an Austrian military attaché in the Shah's employ. Horrified by the cruelties he was compelled to witness, he tendered his resignation and subsequently wrote in a letter published in a Viennese newspaper, the following:

---

[20] A. L. M. Nicolas, *Siyyid 'Alí-Muḥammad, Dit le Báb,* cited in Shoghi Effendi, *God Passes By,* p. 55, author's own translation.

Follow me, my friend, you who lay claim to a heart and European ethics, follow me to the unhappy ones who, with gouged-out eyes, must eat, on the scene of the deed, without any sauce, their own amputated ears; or whose teeth are torn out with inhuman violence by the hand of the executioner; or whose bare skulls are simply crushed by blows from a hammer; or where the bazaar is illuminanted with unhappy victims, because on right and left the people dig deep holes in their breasts and shoulders, and insert burning wicks in the wounds. I saw some dragged in chains through the bazaar, preceded by a military band, in whom these wicks had burned so deep that now the fat flickered convulsively in the wound like a newly extinguished lamp. Not seldom it happens that the unwearying ingenuity of the Oriental leads to fresh tortures. They will skin the soles of the Bábí's feet, soak the wounds in boiling oil, shoe the foot like the hoof of a horse, and compel the victim to run. No cry escaped from the victim's breast; the torment is endured in dark silence by the numbed sensation of the fanatic; now he must run; the body cannot endure what the soul has endured; he falls. Give him the coup de grâce! Put him out of his pain! No! The executioner swings the whip, and—I myself have had to witness it—the unhappy victim of hundredfold tortures runs! This is the beginning of the end. As for the end itself, they hang the scorched and perforated bodies by their hands and feet to a tree head downwards, and now every Persian may try his marksmanship to his heart's content from a fixed but not too proximate distance on the noble quarry placed at his disposal. I saw corpses torn by nearly one hundred and fifty bullets.[21]

The most prominent victim of the new persecutions was the poetess, Ṭáhirih, who for some time had been kept under house arrest. One of the features of the new age, which she proclaimed the revelation of the Báb would bring about, was the removal of the restrictions that kept women in a position of inferiority. Advised that she had been condemned to death, Ṭáhirih said to her jailer:

---

[21] Cited in Shoghi Effendi, *God Passes By*, p. 65. The Russian ambassador, Prince Dolgoroukov, who likewise witnessed these cruelties, denounced them in a personal interview with the Shah as "barbarous practices" which "did not even exist among the most savage nations." The British chargé d'affaires likewise protested to the Persian authorities against practices which "Her Majesty's Government had imagined to be confined to the barbarous tribes of . . . Africa." (Momen, *Bábí and Bahá'í Religions*, pp. 100–101).

"You can kill me as soon as you like, but you cannot stop the emancipation of women."[22]

Thus ended what Bahá'ís call "the Dispensation of the Báb," the first phase of Bahá'í history. For a brief period, the whole of Persia had hovered on the brink of sweeping social change. Had the Báb entertained designs to seize political power, as his enemies imputed, few doubted that he could have established himself as master of the country. The extraordinary ability of his leading followers, the demonstrated susceptibility of the public to a new religious message, the demoralization and factionalism rife amongst both civil and ecclesiastical leadership, and the temporary period of civil disorder which accompanied the final illness and death of Muhammad Shah, combined to create a situation in which the Báb would have merely had to take advantage of the offers of help so urgently pressed upon him.

Late in 1846, the governor-general of Isfahan, Manúchihr Khán, one of the most powerful men in the kingdom, had offered the Báb the full resources of his army and vast wealth, urging a march on Tehran and confrontation with both the clergy and the Shah. Such an action would have been entirely justified under Shiah belief. The fundamental principle underlying the Persian monarchy was that the Shah served merely as a vice-regent who held the kingdom in trust for the Imam Mahdi. Since the central claim of the Báb was that he was this long-awaited spiritual authority, and since some of the finest minds and spirits of the kingdom accepted him as such, fidelity to Shiah teaching would have required that Muhammad Shah and Náṣiri'd-Dín Sháh examine his claims with utmost respect and care. That they did not do so was the result only of the intervention of religious and political leaders, who feared that the Báb would threaten the authority which their positions conferred upon them.

By refusing to force the issue, even at the cost of his own life, the Báb gave conclusive evidence of the peaceable character of his mission and his complete reliance on the spiritual forces which he had said from the beginning were his sole support.

---

[22] Cited in Shoghi Effendi, *God Passes By,* p. 65.

What were the teachings which provoked so violent a reaction and for which the Báb and so many thousands of others willingly gave their lives? The answer is far from simple. Because the Báb's message related so specifically to the theological concerns of Shiah Islam, it is very difficult for Western minds to grasp many of the issues with which his writings deal. Indeed, an important reason for the success which the Báb experienced in converting distinguished theologians and a host of young seminarians was his apparently effortless mastery of the most abstruse and controversial questions of Islamic jurisprudence, prophecy, and belief.

It seemed to his hearers extraordinary that a young man, little versed in fields of learning which were the primary preoccupation of the Persian intellectual class, should so easily be able to confound venerable theologians who spent their lives at this study and established their public careers on it. Early historical accounts by Bábís draw extensively on the details of these elucidations and the effects which they produced on listeners. For the European or North American reader, these subjects often appear quite obscure.[23]

Despite this mastery, the Báb did not encourage the pursuit of such learning by the scholars, clergy, and seminarians who joined his cause. His reasons can perhaps best be appreciated by noting the assessment of Shiah theological studies expressed by the British orientalist Edward Granville Browne. Browne has described the treatises, commentaries, super-commentaries, and notes that passed for intellectual activity in nineteenth-century Persia as unreadable "rubbish," whose very existence serious scholars "must deplore," adding that his opinion was shared by leading thinkers in Islam:

Shaykh Muḥammad 'Abduh late Grand Muftí of Egypt and Chancellor of the University of al-Azhar, than whom perhaps no more enlightened thinker and no more enthusiastic lover of the Arabic language and literature has been produced by Islam in modern times, used to say that all this stuff should be burned, since it merely cumbered book shelves, bred maggots

---

[23] A French translation of the *Bayán, Le Béyan Persan,* was made by A. L. M. Nicolas, consular representative of the government of France, who spent considerable time in Persia.

and obscured sound knowledge. This was the view of a great and learned Muhammadan theologian, so we need not scruple to adopt it. . . .[24]

These views had already been strongly expressed by the Báb. His principal book, the *Bayán,* envisioned a time when Persia's accumulated legacy of misspent energy would be entirely destroyed and the intellectual capacities of its people liberated from superstition. He spoke of a coming age in which entirely new fields of scholarship and science would emerge and in which the knowledge of even young children would far surpass the learning current in his own time.[25]

Far more interesting than his extensive theological commentaries, therefore, was the Báb's social message. Among the important differences between Islam and Christianity is the emphasis the former places on revelation as the guide to the detailed organization of society. The Qur'án envisioned the establishment of a fully Muslim society. Muhammad took the first step in this direction when he established the first Muslim state in the city of Medina. It is no doubt significant that, whereas the Christian calendar begins with the supposed date of the birth of Jesus, the Islamic calendar dates from the Hijrah and the establishment of the Muslim state in Medina. Far from rendering unto Caesar "the things that are Caesar's," Islamic teaching contains a wide range of moral instruction relating to the state's administration of human affairs. Shiah Muslims fully expected that, when the Imam Mahdi appeared, he would not only open the way to salvation for the individual soul, but would reaffirm the concept of a "nation summoning mankind unto righteousness."[26]

It is against this background that the Báb's message must be understood. The minds and hearts of his hearers were locked in a mental world that had changed little from medieval times, except

---

[24] E. G. Browne, *A Literary History of Persia,* pp. 415–416.

[25] Cited in Nabíl, *The Dawn-Breakers,* pp. 92–94. This is the source of the story, circulated by Muslim opponents of the new faith, that a Bábí state would destroy all books. Once the separation from Shiah Islam had been accomplished, Bahá'u'lláh rescinded bans of this type (see pages 76–77).

[26] Qur'án, III, 104. See also II, 143.

to become more obscurantist, isolated, and fatalistic.[27] The Báb's way of overcoming this problem was to create the concept of an entirely new society, one that retained a large measure of cultural and religious elements familiar to his hearers, but which, as events were to show, could arouse powerful new motivation. He called upon the Shah and the people of Persia to follow him in the establishment of this society. During the brief period still left him, he elaborated a system of laws for the conduct of public affairs; for the maintenance of peace and public order; for the direction of economic activity; for such social institutions as marriage, divorce, and inheritance; and for the relationship between the Bábí state and other nations. Prayers, meditations, moral precepts, and prophetic guidance were revealed for the individual believer. These teachings have been described by a Bahá'í historian as intentionally "rigid, complex and severe." Their aim was to effect a break with the believers' Muslim frame of reference and to mobilize them for a unique role in human history.[28]

This role was the theme that runs through every chapter of the *Bayán* and for which the spiritual and social transformation of Persia was intended to serve as a prelude. The Báb proclaimed that the central purpose of his mission was to prepare for the coming of the universal Manifestation of God. The Báb referred to this promised deliverer as "He Whom God Will Make Manifest." The Báb himself, although an independent messenger of God in the line of Moses, Jesus, and Muhammad, was the herald of the one whom all the religions of the world were awaiting. The term *báb* had far greater implications in the new revelation than any it held in Islam; the Báb was the "gateway" to the Manifestation of God whose message would be carried throughout the world.

Passages of the *Bayán* and other writings of the Báb deal at length with this central subject. They make it clear that the Báb saw his religious dispensation as a purely transitional one. When the

---

[27] The extent of this regression can be seen in the regime established in Iran by the Islamic Republic after 1979, in which full effect was given to the Shiah mullas' conceptions of human nature and human society.

[28] Shoghi Effendi, *God Passes By,* Foreword, xvii. See also pp. 24–25.

Promised One appeared, he would reveal the teachings for the coming age and would decide what, if any, part of the Bábí system was to be retained:

A thousand perusals of Bayán cannot equal the perusal of a single verse to be revealed by "Him Whom God Shall Make Manifest." . . . Today, the Bayán is in the stage of seed; at the beginning of the manifestation of "Him Whom God shall make manifest," its ultimate perfection will become apparent. . . . The Bayán deriveth all its glory from "Him Whom God shall make manifest."[29]

The Báb refused to state precisely when the Promised One would appear, but indicated that it would be very soon. Several of his followers were informed that they would see with their own eyes him whom God shall make manifest and have the privilege of serving him. The *Bayán* and other writings contain cryptic references to "the year nine" and "the year nineteen." Moreover, the Báb categorically stated that no one could falsely claim to be he whom God shall make manifest, and succeed in such a pretension. The Bábís were warned not to oppose anyone who advanced such a claim, but rather to hold their peace so that God might accomplish his own will in the matter. To the faithful and distinguished Vaḥíd, for example, the Báb wrote:

By the righteousness of Him Whose power causeth the seed to germinate and Who breatheth the spirit of Life into all things, were I to be assured that in the day of His manifestation thou wilt deny Him, I would unhesitatingly disown thee and repudiate thy faith. . . . If, on the other hand, I be told that a Christian, who beareth no allegiance to My Faith, will believe in Him, the same will I regard as the apple of Mine Eye."[30]

The Bábí state, therefore, had it come into existence, was to have served chiefly as a receptive agent for the message of the Promised One to come, and for its rapid diffusion throughout the

---

[29] Shoghi Effendi, *The Dispensation of Bahá'u'lláh,* p. 8. For more complete texts of statements the Báb made on this subject, see: Báb, *Selections from the Writings of the Báb,* pp. 3–8 and pp. 153–168.

[30] Cited in Shoghi Effendi, *The World Order of Bahá'u'lláh,* p. 101.

world. The martyrdoms of the Báb and the majority of his closest disciples, together with the massacre of several thousands of his followers, aborted this vision before it could be realized. Indeed, by 1852, the Báb's mission appeared to have ended in failure and his faith hovered on the verge of extinction.

# 3. Bahá'u'lláh

Prominent among the handful of Bábí leaders who escaped the massacres of 1848–1853 was a nobleman named Mírzá Ḥusayn 'Alí. [1] His family, from among Persia's oldest landed gentry, held extensive estates in the area of Núr in the province of Mázindarán. [2] Mírzá Ḥusayn 'Alí was one of the first of those to declare his faith in the Báb, in 1844, when Mullá Ḥusayn delivered a message from the Báb at the family's mansion in Tehran. From Mullá Ḥusayn's account of the incident, it is clear that he had sought out Mírza Ḥusayn 'Alí on special instructions from the Báb. Indeed, the Báb delayed a long-planned pilgrimage to Mecca, where he publicly announced his mission for the first time, until he received Mullá Ḥusayn's letter advising him of the outcome of his visit to Mírzá Ḥusayn 'Alí. Four brothers of the convert followed him into the new faith, including a younger half-brother named Mírzá Yaḥyá. Since the vast majority of the Báb's followers were drawn from the ecclesiastical, merchant, and peasant classes, the conversion of members of an influential family from the governing caste was a significant development.

For the first three to four years, the social position of Mírzá Ḥusayn 'Alí, who became an active teacher of the new faith, shielded him to some extent from the physical attacks his correligionists were experiencing. His activities were also protected by a reputation for personal integrity highly unusual in government circles of his

---

[1] The principal authority used for the events of the life and mission of Mírzá Ḥusayn 'Alí, known as Bahá'u'lláh, is Shoghi Effendi, *God Passes By*, chapters 5–8. A major biography has also been completed by H. M. Balyuzi, *Bahá'u'lláh*. Another valuable source is the series of studies of the writings of Bahá'u'lláh produced by Adib Taherzadeh, *The Revelation of Bahá'u'lláh*, Vols. 1, 2, 3.

[2] The family was descended from one of the great dynasties of Persia's pre-Islamic period of high culture, the Sásánián. Balyuzi, *Bahá'u'lláh*, pp. 9–11, provides details.

day, where bribery was a national institution and all advancement depended upon it. For several generations, members of his family had held positions of considerable political influence. His father, Mírzá 'Abbás, had been chief minister for the province of Mázindarán. Born on November 12, 1817, Mírzá Husayn 'Alí was only twenty-two at the time of his father's death in 1839, but had nonetheless been offered his father's post in the government. To the astonishment of his family and associates, he declined this lucrative appointment. Instead, for the next several years he devoted his efforts to management of the family's estates, raising and training the younger members of the family, and to a wide range of charities, which earned him the popular title of "Father of the Poor" from the people of the region.

Upon becoming a follower of the Báb at the age of twenty-seven, Mírzá Husayn 'Alí threw himself energetically into the affairs of the young faith, which was beginning to experience the first tremors of the persecutions that were to follow. He traveled widely, was responsible for the conversion of a significant number of people of ability, including some of his own relatives, and provided financial support for much of the Bábí teaching activity in various parts of the country.

Very early after his declaration of faith, Mírzá Husayn 'Alí entered into a correspondence with the Báb, which lasted until the Báb's execution in 1850. Through this correspondence and through intimate association with such leading Bábís as Vahíd, Quddús, Mullá Husayn, and Táhirih, he was increasingly looked to by his fellow believers as a guide in their understanding of their faith's teachings. Mírzá Husayn 'Alí's influence as a Bábí leader culminated with the conference of Badasht in 1848, which he personally organized and indirectly guided. The conference dramatically revealed the revolutionary scope of the Báb's teachings.[3]

A second occurrence that took place at Badasht would also have far-reaching significance. In recognition of the new Day of God that had dawned, Mírzá Husayn 'Alí conferred upon each of the eighty-one participants a new name related to that individual's particular

---

[3] For a detailed report of the events of the conference see Nabíl-i-A'zam, *The Dawn-Breakers*, pp. 292–298.

spiritual qualities. It was at Bada<u>sh</u>t that the great poetess of Qazvín, Qurratu'l-'Ayn, was given the name Ṭáhirih (the Pure One), an act which silenced those who objected to her appearing in the meeting unveiled. For himself, Mírzá Ḥusayn 'Alí chose the title Bahá (Splendor, or Glory). Shortly after the conference ended, his authority to confer such designations was endorsed when the Báb wrote a series of letters to the Bada<u>sh</u>t participants, in which he formally addressed each by the name given by Mírzá Ḥusayn 'Alí at the conference. To Bahá, the Báb sent an extraordinary document penned in the form of a star by his own hand. It contained over three hundred brief verses, all consisting of derivatives of the word "Bahá," including the title Bahá'u'lláh, "Glory of God."

The art of calligraphy was a particularly prized cultural attainment of Persian men of letters, and the manuscript in question was regarded as a masterpiece which no trained calligraphist could equal—"so fine and intricate," in the words of one writer, "that viewed at a distance, the writing appeared as a single wash of ink on the paper."[4] It was by the name Bahá'u'lláh that Mírzá Ḥusayn 'Alí became known to his Bábí associates and to history.

New waves of violence aroused as a result of the conference at Bada<u>sh</u>t and its aftermath created a situation in which no member of the new faith was immune from attack. When Bahá'u'lláh intervened to protect Ṭáhirih and some of her companions who had been arrested following the conference, he was himself imprisoned and bastinadoed. He suffered the same abuse some time later, when he was again arrested while en route to meet Quddús and Mullá Ḥusayn at <u>Sh</u>ay<u>kh</u>-Ṭabarsí. While at liberty, he made repeated efforts to convince friends and relatives in positions of authority (who remonstrated with him concerning his activities) that the Bábís were both peaceful and law-abiding. He warned these officials that if the government did not carry out its responsibility to check the persecutions the clergy were inciting, the kingdom would find itself thrown into mass violence and public disorder.

The warning proved all too accurate with the attempt on the life

---

[4] Nabíl-i-A'ẓam, *The Dawn-Breakers*, p. 505.

of the Shah by two young Bábís in the summer of 1852. Along with other prominent Bábís, Bahá'u'lláh was arrested, taken to Tehran, and incarcerated in a notorious prison known as "Síyáh-Chál" (Black Pit). It is described as "a subterranean dungeon in Tehran—an abominable pit that had once served as a reservoir of water for one of the public baths of the city."[5]

Bahá'u'lláh spent four months in the Síyáh-Chál, during which time the anti-Bábí conflagration raged throughout Persia. The prisoners in the Síyáh-Chál lived under threat of imminent death. Each day the executioners would descend the steps, select a victim, and conduct him to execution. Several of the condemned were murdered on the spot. In some instances, a hammer and peg were used to drive a heavy wooden gag down the throat of the victim, whose body might then be left lying for hours or days chained to those still alive.

One of the victims from the Síyáh-Chál, whose stories have become immortalized in Bahá'í history, was a young man named Sulaymán Khán a former cavalier in the imperial army. Fearing no danger, Sulaymán Khán had already risked his life to recover the remains of the Báb, which had been left on the edge of a moat following his execution in Tabriz. When his own turn came to die, the executioners dug a number of holes in Sulaymán Khán's body with sharp knives and inserted in each a lighted candle. In this manner he was led through the streets to his death. Persian culture prized nothing so highly as style, and it is a testimony to the combination of spiritual exaltation and sense of drama that Sulaymán Khán strode through the streets of the capital, smiling at acquaintances and reciting passages from the great Persian classical poets. When asked why, if he was so happy, did he not dance, he obliged his tormentors by twirling slowly through the stately movements of a dance created by the Mawlaví mystics.[6]

Such dramatic displays in death exercised an irresistible attraction on the imaginations of Western scholars and artists. People as

---

[5] Shoghi Effendi, *God Passes By*, p. 100.
[6] Shoghi Effendi, *God Passes By*, pp. 77–78.

different as the Comte de Gobineau, Sarah Bernhardt, Leo Tolstoy, and Ernest Renan were captivated by the tragic history of the youthful Báb and his band of heroes. Edward Browne first encountered the story in the writings of the Comte de Gobineau and subsequently devoted a large part of his life to a study of the Bábí and Bahá'í Faiths. Browne described the young martyrs in this way:

It is the lives and deaths of these, their hope which knows no despair, their love which knows no cooling, their steadfastness which knows no wavering, which stamp this wonderful movement with a character entirely its own. For whatever may be the merits or demerits of the doctrines for which these scores and hundreds of our fellow-men died, they have at least found something which made them ready to

"leave all things under the sky,
And go forth naked under sun and rain,
And work and wait and watch out all their years."

It is not a small or easy thing to endure what these have endured, and surely what they deemed worth life itself is worth trying to understand. I say nothing of the mighty influence which, as I believe, the Bábí faith will exert in the future, nor of the new life it may perchance breathe into a dead people; for, whether it succeed or fail, the splendid heroism of the Bábí martyrs is a thing eternal and indestructible. . . .

But what I cannot hope to have conveyed to you is the terrible earnestness of these men, and the indescribable influence which this earnestness, combined with other qualities, exerts on any one who has actually been brought into contact with them. That you must take my word for. . . .[7]

Bahá'u'lláh miraculously survived this worst of the successive waves of persecution. The civil authorities were loath to release him because they were aware of the influential role he played in the Bábí community. Yet, because of his family's social position and a personal intervention by the Russian ambassador, Prince Dolgorukov, it would have been extremely unwise to have executed him without a trial. A trial was impossible. The would-be assassin of the Shah had confessed at his own arraignment, in the presence of a representative sent by the Russian Government, and had completely ex-

---

[7] Edward G. Browne, "Bábism" in *Religious Systems of the World*, pp. 352–353.

onerated the Bábí leaders, including Bahá'u'lláh, of complicity in his act.[8]

The new prime minister, a relative of Bahá'u'lláh was eventually able, therefore, to persuade the members of the royal family who wished to execute their prisoner that it would be preferable to banish him from Persia.[9] The banishment was pronounced, but not before Bahá'u'lláh's properties had been confiscated by the Shah, his mansion in Tehran looted, his country home razed to the ground, and the works of art and manuscripts he owned had found their way into the hands of Persian government officials (including the prime minister himself).

In this state, despoiled of his possessions, weakened and permanently scarred by the physical abuse he had experienced in the Síyáh-Chál, Bahá'u'lláh was exiled from his native land without trial and without recourse. Those who saw him were astonished that so devastating an experience appeared rather to have left him with renewed assurance and power. In fact, it was there, in the dark pit of the Síyáh-Chál, that the most significant event in Bábí and Bahá'í history had occurred. It was there that Bahá'u'lláh received the mantle of "Him Whom God Will Make Manifest." Bahá'u'lláh described the experience in the dungeon of the prison which conveyed to him the first intimation of his mission:

One night in a dream, these exalted words were heard on every side: "Verily, We shall render Thee victorious by Thyself and by Thy pen.

---

[8] The Persian government's own account, published in the official Gazette, *Rúznámiy-i-Vaqáyi'-i-Ittifáqíyyih*, naively admits the innocence of Bahá'u'lláh and several other persons who had been arbitrarily arrested, but states that they will be punished anyway: "Among the Bábís who have fallen into the hands of justice there are six whose culpability not having been well established have been condemned to perpetual imprisonment." Bahá'u'lláh's name is the second listed in the Gazette statement. (Momen, *Bábí and Bahá'í Religions* p. 141.) Equally representative of conditions in nineteenth-century Persia is the satisfaction the statement takes in describing the barbarous tortures practiced on those victims who had been executed.

[9] Mírzá Taqí Khán, the prime minister who had taken the lead in the anti-Bahá'í pogroms, had himself been executed in 1853 at the order of the young Shah, who was jealous of his growing power. This was a not-infrequent fate of able administrators in the Qájár period of Persian history.

Grieve Thou not for that which hath befallen Thee, neither be Thou afraid, for Thou art in safety. Ere long will God raise up the treasures of the earth—men who will aid Thee through Thyself and through Thy Name, wherewith God hath revived the hearts of such as have recognized Him." . . . During the days I lay in the prison of Ṭihrán, though the galling weight of the chain and the stench-filled air allowed Me but little sleep, still in those infrequent moments of slumber I felt as if something flowed from the crown of My head over My breast, even as a mighty torrent that precipitateth itself upon the earth from the summit of a lofty mountain. Every limb of My body would, as a result, be set afire. At such moments My tongue recited what no man could bear to hear.[10]

Bahá'u'lláh was thus the object of the Báb's revelation and the center of truth for those who had followed him. There is considerable evidence that the Báb had, from the beginning, regarded Bahá'u'lláh as the one for whom he himself had come to prepare the way. He had strongly intimated this to a few of his closest disciples, and stated in a remarkable passage in the *Bayán:*

Well is it with him who fixeth his gaze upon the Order of Bahá'u'lláh and rendereth thanks unto his Lord! For he will assuredly be made manifest. God hath indeed irrevocably ordained it in the *Bayán.*[11]

After four months of confinement in the Síyáh-Chál, Bahá-'u'lláh was released in the same arbitrary fashion in which he had originally been confined and was informed that, by a formal decree of the Shah, he was to be sent into exile with his family and any who wished to accompany him. It is significant that he did not choose this occasion to announce his mission to his followers. Offered a refuge in Russia, he instead chose as his place of exile the city of Baghdad in what is now Iraq, then a province of the neighboring Ottoman Turkish Empire. Gradually, over the next three years, a small colony of Bábís gathered around him as well as the members of his family who accompanied him into exile. One of these was his younger half-brother, Mírzá Yaḥyá, who fled Persia in disguise and joined the family shortly after their arrival in Iraq in 1853. It was

---

[10] Cited in Shoghi Effendi, *God Passes By,* p. 101.
[11] Cited in Shoghi Effendi, *The World Order of Bahá'u'lláh,* pp. 146–147.

from this unexpected source that a new form of hardship and opposition arose.

The story of Mírzá Yaḥyá is at once intriguing and pathetic. Yaḥyá's activities posed a grave threat to Bahá'u'lláh's mission, and the effects have continued to provide fuel for attacks on the Bahá'í community to the present day.

Mírzá Yaḥyá was thirteen years younger than Bahá'u'lláh, and his education was largely supervised by the latter. Being a talented calligraphist, he served for a time as Bahá'u'lláh's personal secretary. He was described by those who knew him as a timorous and impressionable individual, easily swayed by stronger personalities. He eagerly followed his brother into the Bábí Faith and even accompanied him on some of his early travels on its behalf.

Mírzá Yaḥyá, amiable by nature, was respected by the Bábí community because of this close relationship to Bahá'u'lláh and also because of his family's social position. At about the time of the conference of Badasht, the Báb, after consultation with Bahá'u'lláh and another leading Bábí, wrote a statement nominating Yaḥyá as the titular head of the Bábí community in the event of the Báb's death. In retrospect, it is apparent that the aim of the nomination was to create a channel through which Bahá'u'lláh could continue to guide the affairs of the new faith, while avoiding the risk of adding a formal designation to the personal prominence he had gained.[12] Yaḥyá, at the time of the nominal appointment, was in little personal danger, as he remained for the most part in seclusion on family estates in the north and fled when the troubles reached that area.[13]

Hardly had the group of exiles settled in Iraq, however, than Yaḥyá succumbed to a proposal urged on him by a persuasive personality, a student of Muslim theology named Siyyid Muḥammad. Siyyid Muḥammad, who appears to have wanted to make himself a doctrinal authority in the Bábí community, urged Yaḥyá to throw off his brother's tutelage and assume the leadership of the

---

[12] Even so, the order banishing Bahá'u'lláh from Persia (the original of which has survived) mentions him alone, making no reference to Mírzá Yaḥyá.

[13] Shoghi Effendi, *God Passes By*, chapters 7 and 10. See also 'Abdu'l-Bahá, *A Traveler's Narrative*, p. 53.

Bábí religion for himself.[14] Yaḥyá wavered for a period of time; but, encouraged by Siyyid Muḥammad, he eventually separated himself from Bahá'u'lláh and claimed the powers and prerogatives of a successor to the martyred Báb.

The response of Bahá'u'lláh to Yaḥyá's action provides an illuminating insight into his character. Rather than enter into a dispute that would endanger the unity and survival of the already demoralized Bábí community, Bahá'u'lláh left without warning for the mountains near Sulaymáníyyih in neighboring Kurdistán. For nearly two years he remained totally out of touch with the Bábí community. This self-imposed exile in the wilderness of Kurdistán is reminiscent of similar periods in the lives of the founders of other great religions. As later became apparent, it was a time of great creativity for him. His mission began to take definite form in his mind, and to be articulated in meditations, prayers, and poems, which he composed during the months of isolation. A few of these early intimations of his message to the world have survived in the original Persian.

While Bahá'u'lláh was in Sulaymáníyyih, the affairs of the Bábí religion were left entirely in the hands of Yaḥyá, who was assisted by his new mentor, Siyyid Muḥammad. The result was near anarchy in the small community of Bábí exiles. Within less than twenty-four months, nearly a score of desperate souls advanced various claims of their own in attempts to usurp the unstable leadership, and Mírzá Yaḥyá withdrew into seclusion, leaving Siyyid Muḥammad to settle the theological questions that arose as best he could. The would-be leader had demonstrated his incapacity for the position he had sought so vigorously. The lesson was not lost on the majority of his fellow Bábís.

As conditions rapidly deteriorated, several of the exiles made energetic efforts to locate Bahá'u'lláh and induce him to return. Eventually, one of the more zealous found Bahá'u'lláh as a result of rumors he had heard regarding a "saint" living in the mountains. Even Yaḥyá joined with the family and other Bábís in an appeal to

---

[14] See Shoghi Effendi, *God Passes By,* chapter 10; Balyuzi, *Bahá'u'lláh,* pp. 112–114.

Bahá'u'lláh to return and assume the direction of the community. On March 19, 1856, he acceded to these requests.

The next seven years witnessed a startling transformation in the fortunes of the Bábí community. Through example, exhortation, and a vigorous discipline, Bahá'u'lláh restored the community to the moral and spiritual level it had attained during the Báb's lifetime. Mírzá Yaḥyá remained entirely withdrawn, and Bahá'u'lláh's reputation as a spiritual teacher spread throughout Baghdad and the neighboring regions. Princes, scholars, mystics, and government officials came to meet with him, including many individuals prominent in Persian public life.

In Baghdad, Bahá'u'lláh composed the *Kitáb-i-Íqán*, or *Book of Certitude*, in which he laid out the panorama of God's redemptive plan for humankind. The book contains a detailed presentation of Bahá'u'lláh's teaching on the nature of God, the function of the sequence of divine Manifestations, and the spiritual evolution of humankind. It concludes with a demonstration of the truth of his own mission. In subsequent years the *'Íqán'* became the most influential of Bahá'u'lláh's writings and the foundation for much of the work of disseminating Bahá'í belief.

Bahá'u'lláh's growing influence, however, excited intense fear and suspicion in the minds of the Shah and his government, who in turn made representations to the Ottoman government. Suddenly, without warning, in April 1863, Bahá'u'lláh and his family were advised that the Ottoman government had acceded to the Persian demands that the refugees be moved further from the borders of their native land. They were to be moved to and settled in Constantinople (now Istanbul).

As preparations for departure were being made, Bahá'u'lláh temporarily transferred his residence to a garden on an island in the Tigris River, since known to Bahá'ís by the name he gave it at that time, the Garden of Riḍván ("Paradise"). It was in the garden that he announced to a selected handful of his closest followers that he was "He Whom God Will Make Manifest," the universal messenger of God promised by the Báb and by scriptures of earlier religions. Bahá'í history refers to Bahá'u'lláh's experience in the Síyáh-

<u>Ch</u>ál as the dawning of his revelation. In the Riḍván declaration, his claim was explicitly stated to others and the course of Bábí history thereby permanently altered. The event is today celebrated around the world as the chief festival of the Bahá'í Faith, although the impact of the declaration was to be felt only after the public declaration of Bahá'u'lláh's mission four years later.[15]

On August 16, 1863, the party of exiles arrived in the Ottoman capital of Constantinople after a journey of over three months; their stay there was to be very brief. Relations between the Ottoman and Persian Empires had long been strained and were marked by frequent minor wars, endless intrigues, and the constant annexation of territories. Fearing that the Bábí exiles, through their conections in Persia, might become an instrument of Turkish policy, the Shah's government became increasingly uneasy over the decision to settle the group in the Ottoman capital. The Persian ambassador, Mírzá Ḥusayn <u>Kh</u>án, thus began a campaign to pressure the Turkish authorities to move the Bábís to a more remote part of the Empire.[16] He coupled this pressure with a warning that Bábís were enemies of all established order and a special menace to a society as cosmopolitan and unstable as the Ottoman Empire. His efforts succeeded. Early in December 1863, Bahá'u'lláh, his family, and his companions were suddenly banished, again without prior warning, to Adrianople (now known as Edirne) in European Turkey.[17]

In Adrianople a new stage in Bahá'í history began. Already the impact of Bahá'u'lláh's personality on a constant stream of visitors who sought him out, the seemingly miraculous transformations in the Baghdad community that he had accomplished, and his wide-

---

[15] The Feast of Riḍván lasts twelve days, from April 21 to May 2, with the first, ninth, and twelfth days being regarded as Bahá'í holy days. Bahá'í elections are held during this period.

[16] The Turkish authorities at first resisted this pressure. 'Alí Pá<u>sh</u>á, the prime minister, is quoted by the Austrian ambassador, Count von Prokesch-Osten, as saying he had "great veneration" for Bahá'u'lláh, considering him to be a "man of great distinction, exemplary conduct, great moderation and a most dignified figure": Momen, *Bábí and Bahá'í Religions*, p. 187.

[17] For examples of the correspondence on the Bahá'í exiles between the Persian Foreign Office and their ambassador in Istanbul, see Edward G. Browne, *Materials for the Study of the Bábí Religions*, pp. 278–287.

ranging correspondence and influence with and among persecuted groups of Bábís throughout Persia made him the focal point of the Bábí Faith. Intimations of his declaration in the Garden of Riḍván were openly discussed among the Bábís. With the community in a state of receptivity, Bahá'u'lláh decided that the time had come for the public declaration of his mission.

The first step in this proclamation was to acquaint Mírzá Yaḥyá, as nominal trustee of the Bábí faith, with the nature of his mission. Accordingly, in a statement known as the Súriy-i-Amr,[18] Bahá'u'lláh announced his claim to be "He Whom God Will Make Manifest" and called upon Yaḥyá to recognize and support him as the Báb had explicitly instructed him to do. Such a response, however, was not forthcoming. Shortly after the exiles reached Adrianople, Yaḥyá, encouraged again by Siyyid Muḥammad, began a series of machinations designed to restore his lost prominence. When these failed, Yaḥyá made two attempts to have his brother assassinated. It was shortly after the second of these two attempts that Bahá'u'lláh's announcement was read to him.

Yaḥyá wavered briefly, and then astonished the Bábí community by proclaiming that he, rather than Bahá'u'lláh, was the Manifestation of God promised by the Báb. His reaction at least clarified a situation that his previous behavior had made a source of confusion and distress. Yaḥyá was abandoned almost overnight by virtually all of the Bábís in Adrianople, and by the vast majority of those in Persia and Iraq, including the surviving members of the Báb's family who were believers. Edward Browne estimated that no more than three or four in every hundred clung to Yaḥyá, all the remainder acknowledging Bahá'u'lláh's claim. It is from this point on that Bábís began to describe themselves as "Bahá'ís," and the Bahá'í Faith emerged as a distinct religion.[19]

Having established his authority among the Báb's followers, Bahá'u'lláh turned his attention to his mission. Beginning in Sep-

---

[18] See Adib Taherzadeh, *The Revelation of Bahá'u'lláh*. Vol. 2, pp. 161–162.

[19] Taherzadeh, *The Revelation of Bahá'u'lláh*. Vol. 1, Those who followed Mírzá Yaḥyá became known as "Azalís" after a designation given to Yaḥyá by the Báb, Ṣubḥ-i-Azal.

tember 1867, he wrote a series of letters which rank among the most remarkable documents in religious history. They were addressed collectively to the "Kings of the earth" and individually to specific monarchs. In them he declared himself to be the One promised in the Torah, the Gospels, and the Qur'án, and he called on the kings to arise and champion his faith. The letters contained dramatic warnings that the nineteenth-century world would be torn apart; that a world civilization was to be born. The keynote of the new age was the oneness of the entire human race. Bahá'u'lláh called specifically upon the powerful rulers of Europe to subordinate all other aims to the task of achieving world unity:

The time must come when the imperative necessity for the holding of a vast, an all-embracing assemblage of men will be universally realized. The rulers and kings of the earth must needs attend it, and, participating in its deliberations, must consider such ways and means as will lay the foundations of the world's Great Peace amongst men. . . . It is not for him to pride himself who loveth his country, but rather for him who loveth the whole world. The earth is but one country, and mankind its citizens.[20]

The letters asserted that God had set in motion historical forces which no human schemes could resist. The rulers were told that power was entrusted to them by God in order to serve the needs of humankind and to establish international peace, social justice, and world unity. Governments that attempted to use their powers to resist the process of the unification of humankind would bring disaster on themselves and on their nations.

Hardly did the public proclamation begin when the new faith received another serious blow whose effects linger even today. It again came from Mírzá Yaḥyá. Yaḥyá's rejection of Bahá'u'lláh's mission had ended his influence among the followers of the Báb. Yaḥyá later told Professor Browne that he had been so abandoned by the other exiles that he was compelled on occasion to go himself to the marketplace in order to shop for food. However, he still

---

[20] Bahá'u'lláh, *Gleanings,* p. 249. Bahá'u'lláh's letters to the secular and religious leaders of the world, both collectively and individually, have been compiled by the Universal House of Justice as *The Proclamation of Bahá'u'lláh.*

maintained the support of Siyyid Muḥammad and two other exiles in Adrianople. This small group appears to have cast about for some means to interfere with the complete conversion of the Báb's followers, which was taking place throughout Persia and the Ottoman territories. Bahá'u'lláh's letters to the kings suggested a means for serving this end.

At this point in history, the ramshackle Ottoman Empire was on the brink of disintegration. Pressure from the many minorities that comprised the empire was particularly acute and unremitting in the European territories beyond Adrianople, where such new states as Greece, Bulgaria, Serbia, and Montenegro were breaking away from it. The Persian ambassador to Constantinople, Mírzá Ḥusayn Khán, was exerting every effort to convince the Turkish authorities that the group of Bahá'í exiles constituted a political as well as a religious danger. Mírzá Yaḥyá and Siyyid Muḥammad therefore sought to picture Bahá'u'lláh's messages to the kings in this light. Anonymous letters warning of a political conspiracy were forwarded to Constantinople. The stories no doubt gained credence from the fact that a constant stream of visitors from all parts of the empire sought out Bahá'u'lláh in Adrianople, and the authorities there seemed equally under his spell.[21]

Bahá'u'lláh was known to have been offered the protection of both the British and Russian governments at earlier stages of the Bábí persecutions, and this may have added to the fears of the Ottoman government that Yaḥyá's accusations held some validity. It was decided to resolve the question of the exiled community once and for all. Sulṭán 'Abdu'l-'Azíz issued an imperial order, without recourse, committing the exiles in Adrianople to perpetual imprisonment in the penal colony at Acre in Palestine. On the morning of August 21, 1868, Bahá'u'lláh and some seventy to eighty members of his family and close companions boarded a steamer at Gal-

---

[21] Momen, *Bábí and Bahá'í Religions* (pp. 198–200) lists a number of documents in the Ottoman State Archives which relate to this campaign by Mírzá Yaḥyá. One of them is a report to the central authorities from Khurshíd Páshá, the Governor of Adrianople, who expresses the view that Bahá'u'lláh had just cause to complain of the activities of Yaḥyá and his supporters.

lipoli; and after a harrowing journey of ten days, were put ashore under heavy guard at the Sea Gate leading to the grim fortress of Acre.

Ironically, Mírzá Yaḥyá and Siyyid Muḥammad were caught in the net they themselves had prepared. Suspecting that Yaḥyá might himself be engaged in conspiracy, the Turkish authorities sent him as a prisoner to the island of Cyprus, together with three Bahá'í prisoners who, it was hoped, would hinder his activities.[22] Siyyid Muḥammad and a companion were sent with the party of Bahá'í exiles to Acre for much the same reason.

Acre was chosen because it was confidently believed that Bahá-'u'lláh could not survive the experience. In the 1860s the prison city was a pestilential place, a home for criminals from all parts of the empire, a warren of labyrinthine alleys and damp crumbling buildings. Prevailing winds and tides washed the refuse of the Mediterranean onto its shores, creating a climate so unhealthy that a popular saying held that a bird which flew over Acre would fall dead in the streets.

The first two years of the Bahá'ís' imprisonment was a period of intense deprivation and hardship. From Constantinople, the Persian ambassador issued orders that an agent of his government be installed in Acre to ensure that the local Ottoman authorities strictly enforced the harsh terms in the formal decree. A number of the exiles died from the treatment to which they were subjected, as did Bahá'u'lláh's second son, Mírzá Mihdí, who lost his life in a tragic accident occasioned by the conditions of the prison. A degree of relief arrived in 1870, when the fortress was required to serve as a military barracks during a period of tension between Turkey and

---

[22] Yaḥyá died in 1912, still an exile in Cyprus. The complete extinction of his fortunes is reflected in a letter written to Professor Browne by one of Yaḥyá's sons. Describing his father as bitterly deploring the oblivion into which he had fallen, the son complained that it had been necessary to arrange for Yaḥyá the customary Muslim burial under the direction of a local mulla as "none were to be found there of witnesses to the *Bayán*'" (i.e., followers of the Báb). This same son subsequently indicated his interest in selling the originals of a number of his father's writings, but Browne declined because "the prices demanded were, in my opinion, excessive . . ." E. G. Browne, *Materials,* pp. 317–315.

Russia and the prisoners were moved to confinement in rented houses and other buildings.

Gradually, in spite of initial public prejudice, Bahá'u'lláh's influence began to have the same effect it had exerted in Baghdad and Adrianople. Sympathetic governors reduced the number of guards and influential voices began expressing admiration and interest. Then a new blow fell. Siyyid Muḥammad and two companions, frustrated by the improvement of the prisoners' situation, began to agitate the lower classes of the city in order to provoke an attack on Bahá'u'lláh's house—an attack which, it was hoped, might lead to his death.

The new threat proved too great a provocation for some of the exiles to endure. Ignoring the principles of nonviolence and reliance on the Will of God which they professed, seven of them took matters into their own hands. After deliberately instigating a fight, they killed Siyyid Muḥammad and his accomplices.

The effect of these murders was a far greater setback for the new faith than anything Siyyid Muḥammad could himself have achieved. It added fuel to the dying fire of accusations leveled against the exiles by opponents among the Muslim clergy. For Bahá'u'lláh, the shock of the incident struck a blow far more severe than physical imprisonment because it tarnished the integrity of his work. In a letter written at the time, he said:

My captivity can bring on Me no shame. Nay, by My life, it conferreth on Me glory. That which can make Me ashamed is the conduct of such of My followers as profess to love Me, yet in fact follow the Evil One.[23]

In time, a civil court established that the outburst of violence had neither been countenanced by Bahá'u'lláh nor by the majority of the Bahá'ís in Acre, and the guilty parties alone were punished. Passions gradually cooled. In the meantime, Bahá'u'lláh had again taken up the series of letters to the kings and rulers which had been interrupted by his departure from Adrianople. Individual letters were addressed to Emperor Louis Napoleon, Queen Victoria, Kaiser Wilhelm I, Tsar Alexander II, Náṣiri'd-Dín Sháh in Persia,

---

[23] Cited in Shoghi Effendi, *God Passes By,* p. 190.

Emperor Franz Joseph of Austria, and the Ottoman Sultan, 'Abdu'l-'Azíz.

In these letters Bahá'u'lláh called on the monarchs to join together in the creation of an international tribunal that would have the authority to decide on disputes between nations. This embryonic world government, he said, should be supported by an international police force maintained by the member states and used to enforce peaceful resolution of all international disputes.

The letters also contained prescriptions for creating a sense of community among the peoples of the world. For example, Bahá'u'lláh called for the creation of an international auxiliary language, which would allow every society to maintain its own cultural identity while benefitting from the ability to communicate with all other races and nations. A compulsory educational system would assure worldwide literacy; an international system of weights and measures would create common standards for a global economic system; military expenditures would be sharply curtailed and taxation used for social welfare. The monarchs were urged to accept certain basic democratic principles of government in the conduct of their internal affairs.

Owing to the close confinement of the exiles, these extraordinary messages were smuggled out of the prison in the clothing of sympathetic visitors. The French consul personally delivered Bahá'u'lláh's first communication to the Emperor Louis Napoleon.

Powerful messages were also addressed to the leaders of the world's religions, including Pope Pius IX. Their principal theme was a challenge to ecclesiastical leaders to set aside dogma and attachment to their positions of secular leadership, and to examine seriously the claims Bahá'u'lláh put forward. It was primarily the clergy, the letters asserted, who had been the first to reject and persecute the founders of each of the world's religions.

The letter to Pope Pius IX is particularly interesting to students of institutional history, because it outlines a prescription for actions many of which the Pope's successors have since found it impossible to avoid taking. The pontiff was called upon to surrender his temporal sovereignty over the Papal States to a secular government, to leave the seclusion of the Vatican palaces to meet with the leaders of non-Catholic faiths, to present himself before the secular rulers of the world and summon them to peace and justice, to divest himself of the excessive ceremonialism that had grown about his person, and to "be as thy Lord hath been." Similarly, the Catholic clergy were urged to

Seclude not yourselves in churches and cloisters. Come forth by My leave, and occupy yourselves with that which will profit your souls and the souls of men. Thus biddeth you the King of the Day of Reckoning. Seclude yourselves in the stronghold of My love. This, verily, is a befitting seclusion, were ye of them that perceive it. . . . He that wedded not (Jesus) found no place wherein to dwell or lay His head, by reason of that which the hands of the treacherous had wrought. His sanctity consisteth not in that which ye believe or fancy, but rather in the things We possess.[24]

None of the letters received any significant response from those to whom they were addressed. Among the few recorded reactions was that of Queen Victoria, who is reported to have said merely: "If this is of God it will endure; if not, it can do no harm."[25]

In time, however, the letters attracted attention because of the startling fulfillment of the individual prophecies they contained.[26] Emperor Louis Napoleon, seemingly the most powerful European ruler of the time, was warned that because of his insincerity and the misuse of his power:

thy kingdom shall be thrown into confusion, and thine empire shall pass from thine hands, as a punishment for that which thou hast wrought . . . Hath thy pomp made thee proud? By my life! It shall not endure . . .[27]

Within two years the emperor had lost throne and empire in the

---

[24] Cited in Bahá'u'lláh, *The Proclamation of Bahá'u'lláh*, pp. 95–96.

[25] Cited in Shoghi Effendi, *The Promised Day Is Come*, p. 65.

[26] In 1870, the year after the above-mentioned letter to Pope Piux IX was delivered, the pontiff found himself stripped of his role as an independent monarch. The forces of the Italian national revolution compelled him to surrender the Papal States to King Victor Emmanuel. The pope then withdrew into self-imposed retirement as the "prisoner of the Vatican."

[27] Cited in Bahá'u'lláh and 'Abdu'l-Bahá, *Bahá'í World Faith,* p. 50.

entirely unforeseen debacle at Sedan, and was himself an exile from his native land.[28]

Subsequently, the conqueror of Louis Napoleon, Kaiser Wilhelm I, who had just been made Emperor of a united Germany, received a similar warning. Pride and desire for earthly domination would bring against Germany "swords of retribution" that would leave "the banks of the Rhine covered with blood." Similar warnings were addressed to the Tsar of Russia, Emperor Franz Joseph of Austria, and the Persian Shah.

Particularly explicit were the warning letters to the Turkish Sulṭán 'Abdu'l-'Azíz and his prime minister, 'Alí Páshá, who held the life of the prisoner of Acre in their hands. These letters predicted the deaths of both 'Alí Páshá and his colleague, Fu'ád Páshá, who was foreign minister, the loss of Turkey's European dominions, and the fall of the Sulṭán himself. The fulfillment of all of these predictions significantly enhanced the prestige which was steadily growing around Bahá'u'lláh's name.[29]

The ten-year period beginning in 1863, which constituted the formal declaration of Bahá'u'lláh's mission, culminated in the completion of the book that today serves as the core of what Bahá'ís regard as the revelation of Bahá'u'lláh, the *Kitáb-i-Aqdas* (literally, *The Most Holy Book).*

The *Kitáb-i-Aqdas* provides for the establishment and continuation of the authority Bahá'u'lláh called upon humankind to accept. It begins with a reiteration of his claim to be "the King of Kings" whose mission is none other than the establishment of the Kingdom of God on earth. Its two major themes are the proclamation of the laws which are to transform individual souls and guide humankind

---

[28] Alistair Horne, a leading scholarly authority on the events referred to, said "History knows of perhaps no more startling instance of what the Greeks called *peripateia,* the terrible fall from prideful heights. Certainly, no nation in modern times, so replete with apparent grandeur and opulent in material achievement, has ever been subjected to a worse humiliation in so short a time." *The Fall of Paris* (London; Macmillan, 1965), p. 34.

[29] Shoghi Effendi devoted an entire book to this subject, *The Promised Day Is Come.* A prominent Muslim academic who was to become the greatest scholar of the Bahá'í Faith in the Near East, Mírzá Abu'l- Faḍl, was converted on seeing the fulfillment of these predictions.

collectively, and the creation of institutions through which the community of those who recognize him is to be governed. A more complete discussion of these two themes may be found in chapters 7 and 8. It will be sufficient to note here that the system of the *Aqdas* entirely replaced, for Bahá'ís, both those Islamic laws which the Báb had left unabrogated and the strict code which the Báb himself had laid down. *Jihád,* the use of force, was explicitly forbidden, as was any form of religious contention.[30] With the separation from Islam fully achieved, even the Báb's harsh condemnation of theological studies was rescinded. Bahá'ís were encouraged to be open to truth wherever they might encounter it:

Warn . . . the beloved of the one true God not to view with too critical an eye the sayings and writings of men. Let them rather approach such sayings and writings in a spirit of open-mindedness and loving sympathy.[31]

The completion of the *Kitáb-i-Aqdas* opened the final period of Bahá'u'lláh's ministry. The isolation the Sultán's decree of banishment had sought to impose crumbled away. There followed nearly two decades of creative work devoted chiefly to the revelation of a vast body of writings that elaborated Bahá'u'lláh's vision of humankind's future. Dignitaries throughout Palestine became first warm admirers and later confirmed devotees. A leading Muslim ecclesiastic, the Muftí of Acre, became a convert to the new faith and the governor of the city would not enter Bahá'u'lláh's presence without first removing his shoes as a sign of respect. The doors of the prison city were opened to a constant stream of pilgrims whose recounted experiences and letters from Acre nourished the Bahá'í communities in Persia and Iraq. Public works such as the reconstruction, at Bahá'u'lláh's request, of an ancient aqueduct to provide Acre with fresh water, helped to overcome the antagonism of the general public, which had initially greeted the party of exiles on their arrival in 1868.

---

[30] Bahá'u'lláh, *Gleanings,* p. 303. For a brief resumé of the contents of the *Kitáb-i-Aqdas,* see Bahá'u'lláh, *A Synopsis and Codification of the Laws and Ordinances of the Kitáb-i-Aqdas.*

[31] Bahá'u'lláh, *Gleanings,* p. 330.

In 1877 Bahá'u'lláh agreed to move from Acre to a nearby country estate called Mazrá'ih, which had been prepared for his residence by his friends. Two years later the exiles obtained, for a nominal sum, the lease of a magnificent mansion on the outskirts of the city, because the wealthy owner had left the area out of fear of a threatening epidemic.

It was in this final residence, known as Bahjí (Joy), that Bahá'u'lláh received Professor Browne, one of the few Westerners who is known to have visited and written of him. Captivated by the story of the Bábí martyrs, Browne determined to record the story of the Bábí and Bahá'í Faiths. He thus describes his meeting at Bahjí with the founder of the Bahá'í Faith:

I found myself in a large apartment, along the upper end of which ran a low divan, while on the side opposite to the door were placed two or three chairs. Though I dimly suspected whither I was going and whom I was to behold (for no distinct intimation had been given to me), a second or two elapsed ere, with a throb of wonder and awe, I became definitely conscious that the room was not untenanted. In the corner where the divan met the wall sat a wondrous and venerable figure, crowned with a felt head-dress of the kind called *táj* by dervishes (but of unusual height and make), round the base of which was wound a small white turban. The face of him on whom I gazed I can never forget, though I cannot describe it. Those piercing eyes seemed to read one's very soul; power and authority sat on that ample brow. . . . No need to ask in whose presence I stood, as I bowed myself before one who is the object of a devotion and love which kings might envy and emperors sigh for in vain!

A mild dignified voice bade me be seated, and then continued:—"Praise be to God that thou hast attained! . . . Thou hast come to see a prisoner and an exile. . . . We desire but the good of the world and the happiness of the nations; yet they deem us as a stirrer of up strife and sedition worthy of bondage and banishment. . . . These strifes and this bloodshed and discord must cease, and all men be as one kindred and one family. . . . Let not a man glory in this, that he loves his country; let him rather glory in this, that he loves his kind. . . ."[32]

Later that year, Bahá'u'lláh "pitched his tent" on Mount Car-

---

[32] Browne, *A Traveller's Narrative*, pp. xxxix-xl.

mel, across the bay from Acre. There he pointed out the site he had chosen for the interment of the remains of the martyred Báb. This site has since become the focal point for the extensive shrines, administrative buildings, and gardens that comprise the international headquarters of the Bahá'í Faith.

During the closing years of his life, Bahá'u'lláh had increasingly withdrawn from contact with society so that he could devote himself to his writings and to his meetings with Bahá'í pilgrims. The practical affairs of the community had been left in the hands of his eldest son, 'Abbás, called by him 'Abdu'l-Bahá (literally, Servant of Bahá). Late in 1891 Bahá'u'lláh told those around him that his work was done and that he wished to "depart from this world." He was being called, he said, to "other dominions whereon the eyes of the people of names have never fallen." Shortly thereafter he contracted a fever and, following a brief illness, passed away at dawn on May 29, 1892, in his seventy-fifth year.

# 4. The Succession to Leadership

With the passing of Bahá'u'lláh, the Bahá'í Faith entered a stage in its development that marked the emergence of what Bahá'ís regard as the distinguishing feature of their religion. This was Bahá'u'lláh's explicit conveyance of authority for the establishment of an institutional system designed to guide, protect, and enlarge the emerging Bahá'í community. It is principally because of this system that the Bahá'í Faith, alone among the independent religions, has escaped division into sects.

The system was erected on the basis of a body of interrelated documents in which Bahá'u'lláh established a "Covenant" or solemn agreement with his followers. The Covenant named his eldest son, 'Abdu'l-Bahá, as the sole authoritative interpreter of his teachings and the source of authority in all affairs of the faith. One of the titles he gave to 'Abdu'l-Bahá was Ghuṣn-i-A'ẓam (The Most Mighty Branch). The documents of the Covenant made it clear that 'Abdu'l-Bahá was to be regarded not as a prophet or divine messenger, but rather as the perfect human example of Bahá'u'lláh's teachings. The conveyance of this authority was explicit and sweeping:

Whosoever turns to Him hath surely turned unto God, and whosoever turneth away from Him hath turned away from My beauty, denied My proof and is of those who transgress. Verily, He is the remembrance of God amongst you and His trust within you, and His manifestation unto you and His appearance among the servants who are nigh. Thus have I been commanded to convey to you the message of God, your Creator; and I have delivered to you that of which I was commanded.[1]

---

[1] For the full text of the documents involved see Bahá'u'lláh and 'Abdu'l-Bahá, *Bahá'í World Faith, Selected Writings of Bahá'u'lláh and 'Abdu'l-Bahá,* Wilmette, Bahá'í Publishing Trust, 1943, rev. edn., 1956, pp. 204–210. This quotation is on p. 205.

Bahá'u'lláh also took particular care to assure that the Bahá'í community would gradually become accustomed, during his own lifetime, to the role he intended 'Abdu'l-Bahá to play after his passing. Matters between the Bahá'í community and the civil authorities, as well as any relations with the general population of Palestine, were left almost entirely in the hands of 'Abdu'l-Bahá. Pilgrims from Persia were customarily received by "the Master" (another title Bahá'u'lláh gave exclusively to his eldest son), and meetings with the founder of the faith were arranged under 'Abdu'l-Bahá's supervision. The nature of the authority conferred on 'Abdu'l-Bahá and the demands presented by the growing Bahá'í community provided an opportunity for him to exercise his impressive personal capacities. Professor Browne, who initially met 'Abdu'l-Bahá in 1890 and later came to know him well, wrote:

Seldom have I seen one whose appearance impressed me more. A tall strongly-built man holding himself straight as an arrow, with white turban and raiment, long black locks reaching almost to the shoulder, broad powerful forehead indicating a strong intellect combined with an unswerving will, eyes keen as a hawk's, and strongly-marked but pleasing features—such was my first impression of 'Abbás Effendi, "the master" (Áqá) [sic] as he *par excellence* is called by the Bábís. Subsequent conversation with him served only to heighten the respect with which his appearance had from the first inspired me. One more eloquent of speech, more ready of argument, more apt of illustration, more intimately acquainted with the sacred books of the Jews, the Christians, and the Muhammadans, could, I should think, scarcely be found even amongst the eloquent, ready, and subtle race to which he belongs. These qualities, combined with a bearing at once majestic and genial, made me cease to wonder at the influence and esteem which he enjoyed even beyond the circle of his father's followers. About the greatness of this man and his power no one who had seen him could entertain a doubt.[2]

In retrospect, it is clear that 'Abdu'l-Bahá saw the task of firmly establishing the Bahá'í Faith on a very wide scale throughout Europe and North America as one of the most important challenges

---

[2] Browne, *A Traveller's Narrative,* p. xxxvi.

facing him.³ Opportunities opened up, encouraged to a significant degree by the attention which the Bábí epic had already attracted among intellectual and artistic circles, particularly in western Europe. In North America the first recorded public reference to the Bahá'í Faith occurred at the "Parliament of Religions" held in connection with the 1893 Chicago World's Fair, when a Christian spokesman concluded the paper he presented with the words Bahá'u'lláh had addressed to Edward Browne three years earlier.

At about the same time a Syrian merchant, Ibrahim Kheiralla, who had enrolled in the Bahá'í Faith in Cairo, Egypt, immigrated to the United States and began classes among interested enquirers. The first American Bahá'í was an insurance executive named Thornton Chase. By 1897, Kheiralla reported that there were Bahá'í believers numbering in the hundreds in the Chicago and Kenosha, Wisconsin areas. It became significant to the later development of the faith that all of these "declarants" were encouraged to write directly to 'Abdu'l-Bahá in the Holy Land, expressing their faith in the teachings of Bahá'u'lláh and seeking the Master's blessing.

Kheiralla's activities were important not only because of the large number of adherents his efforts attracted, but also because these included several individuals who later became some of the faith's leading exponents in the West. One of the new Western believers was a talented and energetic woman named Louisa Getsinger, who began traveling throughout the United States lecturing to interested groups in an attempt to extend the influence of the new movement beyond the immediate Chicago-Kenosha areas.

During the course of these travels she met with and was responsible for the enrollment of the philanthropist millionaire, Mrs. Phoebe Hearst. In 1898 the latter expressed her desire to meet 'Abdu'l-Bahá and he agreed to the visit. Mrs. Hearst then gathered together a party of fifteen pilgrims, the first group of whom arrived

---

³ The details of the life of 'Abdu'l-Bahá are taken from Shoghi Effendi, *God Passes By*, chapters 14–21 and also from a biography by H. M. Balyuzi entitled *'Abdu'l-Bahá, The Centre of the Covenant of Bahá'u'lláh*.

in Acre on December 10, 1898. Mrs. Getsinger, her husband, Dr. Edward Getsinger, and Ibrahim Kheiralla were among them. The meeting was attended with some degree of personal risk owing to the continuing political tensions in the Near East. Under those strained circumstances, the unexpected arrival of a group of Westerners necessarily aroused a good deal of suspicion.

Despite the handicaps, this brief visit proved critical to the early growth of the Bahá'í Faith in the West. The impact of 'Abdu'l-Bahá's mind and endearing personality on the first Western followers of Bahá'u'lláh was immediate and decisive. In him they believed they saw the spirit of Jesus Christ again moving among humanity. Indeed, in their enthusiasm they were prepared to put his station well beyond the bounds of that which Bahá'u'lláh had assigned to his son. Some, like Mrs. Hearst, believed that 'Abdu'l-Bahá was himself "The Messiah," the return of Jesus Christ.[4] It is revealing, therefore to note 'Abdu'l-Bahá's own words on the subject:

... what is meant in the prophecies by the "Lord of Hosts" and the "Promised Christ" is the Blessed perfection (Bahá'u'lláh) and His Holiness, the Exalted One (the Báb). My name is 'Abdu'l-Bahá (Servant of Bahá). My qualification is 'Abdu'l-Bahá. My reality is 'Abdu'l-Bahá. My praise is 'Abdu'l-Bahá. Thraldom to the Blessed Perfection is my glorious and refulgent diadem, and servitude to all the human race my perpetual religion. . . . No name, no title, no mention, no commendation have I, nor will ever have, except 'Abdu'l-Bahá. . . . This is my greatest yearning. This is my eternal life. This is my everlasting glory.[5]

The significance of the relationship between 'Abdu'l-Bahá and his father's followers in the West is outlined in a summary of the first century of Bábí-Bahá'í history, published in 1944:

The pilgrims brought back the sense of the early days of the faith, when the Prophet has been seen by human eyes and heard by human ears, and the world is filled with ecstasy like the golden light of perfect dawn. . . . All the activities of the Cause of Bahá'u'lláh in America emanated from

---

[4] Cited in Shoghi Effendi, *God Passes By*, p. 258.
[5] Cited in Shoghi Effendi, *The World Order of Bahá'u'lláh*, p. 139.

the few score souls who attained the goal of all earthly seeking in 'Akká and Haifa between the years 1894 and 1911.[6]

The visit of the Hearst party was the beginning of a continuous stream of Bahá'í visitors from Europe and North America that spanned a period of nearly twenty-three years and continued until 'Abdu'l-Bahá's death in 1921, interrupted only by the duration of World War I.

Communities were established throughout the United States and Canada. Public meetings and informal discussion groups were organized, and a modest production of booklet literature on the faith began. These publications consisted almost exclusively of excerpts from the Tablets of Bahá'u'lláh and 'Abdu'l-Bahá, together with accounts given by returning North American believers who had undertaken the pilgrimage to 'Akká (Acre). Informally organized groups also circulated carbon copies of typewritten manuscripts containing more extensive excerpts from the prayers and meditations of Bahá'u'lláh and excerpts from letters 'Abdu'l-Bahá had written to individual believers.

Hardly had this stage in the faith's development begun when it was subjected to a severe shock and setback that had several features of the Yaḥyá episode in Bábí history. A younger half-brother of 'Abdu'l-Bahá, named Muḥammad-'Alí, began to chafe under the authority conferred upon the new head of the faith. Unable to challenge the specific terms of his father's covenant, Muḥammad-'Alí sought first to impose limitations on 'Abdu'l-Bahá's exercise of his function in the Bahá'í community. When this failed Muḥammad-'Alí attempted to create a following of his own within the Bahá'í community. The resulting rupture occurred shortly before the arrival of the first group of Western pilgrims, and it quickly attracted the attention of Dr. Kheiralla.

The latter saw himself as both the most influential teacher of the faith in North America, and a leading exponent of its fundamental concepts. Browne later published notes from Kheiralla's lectures, which present a rather startling view of the kind of concepts which

6 *The Bahá'í Centenary, 1844–1944*, p. 139.

Kheiralla was teaching.[7] The only Bahá'í themes that had survived their migration from Persia to North America were the station of Bahá'u'lláh and the idea of the oneness of humankind. These two concepts were presented by Dr. Kheiralla in a mélange of esoteric doctrines that bore no relation to the teachings of the founder of the Bahá'í Faith.

During his visit to Acre in 1898, Kheiralla sought 'Abdu'l-Bahá's endorsement of his presentation of the Bahá'í Faith. 'Abdu'l-Bahá at that time corrected a number of Kheiralla's misconceptions and urged him to begin a serious study of the Bahá'í writings. He declined, and became progressively more and more estranged from Bahá'u'lláh's teachings. During the course of this same visit, Muhammad-'Alí sought him out; on his return to America the following year, Kheiralla stunned his Bahá'í friends and students by a rejection of 'Abdu'l-Bahá and an insistence on his own role as the arbiter of the faith's fortunes in the West. However, these efforts to usurp Bahá'í leadership failed, and Kheiralla eventually returned to Syria, bitterly disappointed. With his departure the danger of a schism passed, as Muhammad-'Alí was never able to attract a following of his own apart from a small handful of relatives and retainers.

The crisis and its outcome were critical to Bahá'í history. At this important juncture, the new faith took the one course that could lead to the realization of its claims to represent the birth of an independent world religion. There is little doubt that had Muhammad-'Alí and Kheiralla succeeded in their efforts to dominate the movement and seize control of its leadership, it would have quickly dwindled to the status of a cult.

Instead, the Bahá'í community in North America, though reduced in numbers and suffering from the shock of charges and counter-charges, turned to 'Abdu'l-Bahá for authoritative guidance on his father's teachings. In response, with more freedom and vigor than before, he expounded on the principal features of the Bahá'í revelation. Discouraging metaphysical speculation, 'Abdu'l-Bahá

---

[7] Browne, *Materials,* pp. 115–150.

set himself the task of explaining Bahá'u'lláh's social message to the world. In countless letters, table talks with pilgrims and expository writings, 'Abdu'l-Bahá insisted that not only the individual heart but also the entire social order must be transformed. The validity of all the world's religions, the need to abolish racial prejudices, the implications of the equality of man and woman, universal education, justice in social and economic systems, and a host of similar themes were emphasized. The social teachings of Bahá'u'lláh were related to the needs of contemporary society as revealed by the recurrent crises gripping the world.[8]

In 1908 the Young Turk Revolution freed all political and even religious prisoners of the Ottoman Empire. As a result, 'Abdu'l-Bahá was suddenly free to leave Palestine and take a more direct hand in the expansion and establishment of his father's faith in the West. Before doing so, however, he was able to realize one of the great desires of his life and fulfill one of the major responsibilities given to him by Bahá'u'lláh. On March 20, 1909, in the presence of a company of believers from both East and West, he laid the small wooden coffin containing the mortal remains of the Báb in a magnificent marble sarcophagus supplied by the Bahá'ís of Burma. The burial took place in a stone shrine erected on the slopes of Mount Carmel, on the spot chosen by Bahá'u'lláh many years earlier, and intended by him to serve as the central point for the complex of the various administrative institutions comprising the international headquarters of the Bahá'í Faith. The Bahá'í community regards the blood of the Bábí martyrs as the "seed" of the administrative institutions which Bahá'u'lláh called for and which Bahá'ís were beginning to establish around the world under the guidance of 'Abdu'l-Bahá. Now, at the heart of the Bahá'í community, the Báb's sacrifice was

---

[8] See 'Abdu'l-Bahá, *Some Answered Questions,* sections 1 and 5 in particular. Christian missionaries opposed to the Bahá'í Faith sought to argue that 'Abdu'l-Bahá had added these social teachings in consequence of his contact with the West. Browne, however, had already identified most of them in the writings of Bahá'u'lláh as early as the 1880's: Browne, "Bábism," pp. 351–352. Since then the translation and publication of major sections of Bahá'u'lláh's writings have demonstrated convincingly that it was from this source that 'Abdu'l-Bahá drew his themes.

intimately linked with the central institutions of that religious system, and the essential historical unity of the Bábí and Bahá'í Faiths was given compelling symbolic expression.

By 1910 'Abdu'l-Bahá was able to conclude that circumstances in the Holy Land would permit the departure which he had for so long yearned. The rigors of his long imprisonment had seriously undermined his health and the first stage of the journey was therefore a period of recuperation in Egypt. Then, on August 11, 1911, accompanied by a small group of attendants, he sailed on the *S.S. Corsica* for Marseille, to begin a twenty-eight month journey throughout the Western world. This journey included two trips to London, Paris, and Stuttgart, and briefer visits to other European centers, as well as a very demanding trip across North America.

On April 11, 1912, 'Abdu'l-Bahá arrived in New York City. During this North American tour he visited some forty cities and towns in the United States, from coast to coast. Among these was Chicago, where he laid the cornerstone of the building that was to become the "Mother Temple of the West." He also visited Eliot, Maine, where Sarah Farmer, founder of Green Acre, a center for adult education, had become a Bahá'í and opened her facility for the systematic presentation of the Bahá'í message.[9] In Canada, 'Abdu'l-Bahá visited Montreal, where he was the guest of the Canadian architect, William Sutherland Maxwell, and his wife, May Bolles Maxwell. Mrs. Maxwell became a Bahá'í as a very young woman and had been with the original Hearst party which visited in Acre in 1898.

'Abdu'l-Bahá's Montreal visit was in many respects typical of the receptions accorded to him in other major centers throughout the West.[10] He visited Notre-Dame Cathedral, was invited to speak at

---

[9] Green Acre served as the principal center of the Bahá'í Faith in North America until the election of the first national spiritual assembly in 1925. The assembly established its headquarters at Wilmette, Illinois, a suburb of Chicago and site of the house of worship which 'Abdu'l-Bahá had inaugurated.

[10] For a more complete description of his visit to Canada and the United States and the collected addresses and interviews given there see *'Abdu'l-Bahá in Canada;* Balyuzi, *'Abdu'l-Bahá;* and Allan L. Ward, *239 Days, 'Abdu'l-Bahá's Journey in America.*

the Church of the Messiah and St. James Church, addressed a large trades union meeting at their hall on St. Lawrence Street, and gave a great many informal talks both in his suite at the Windsor Hotel and at the Maxwell home on Pine Avenue, where he stayed as the family's houseguest during the first part of his visit. As elsewhere throughout North America and Europe, major newspapers gave the tour extensive coverage.

The effects of the tour were far-reaching. Western believers were directly exposed to the leader and acknowledged exponent of their faith. They flocked to meet him, sought his advice, and were able to clarify and deepen their understanding of the faith's teachings on theological, social, and moral issues. The public in the West gained a highly favorable view of the new religion, which was to prove of great importance to its followers in their subsequent efforts to promote its growth. 'Abdu'l-Bahá spoke not only to church congregations, but to peace societies, trade unions, university faculties, and a variety of societies for social reform. At the tour's end, Bahá'u'lláh's social message had been publicly proclaimed and a new generaton of Bahá'ís from every strata of Western society had been enlisted.[11]

'Abdu'l-Bahá spent the years during World War I in relative isolation at his home in Haifa in the Holy Land. His associations with the West and the interpretation put on them by his half-brother, Muḥammad-'Alí, had again succeeded in arousing the suspicion of the Ottoman authorities. Once more threats were made that he would be executed and the small Bahá'í colony in the Holy Land dispersed into exile. However, this danger was removed in 1918 when the war ended with the defeat of the Central Powers, followed by Turkey's loss of all her possessions in the Arab Near East.

'Abdu'l-Bahá again set in motion the highly significant processes

---

[11] The public addresses of 'Abdu'l-Bahá in North America are compiled under the title *The Promulgation of Universal Peace, Talks Delivered By 'Abdu'l-Bahá During His Visit to the United States and Canada in 1912.*

begun after his release from prison in Acre in 1908, for the building of an international community that would reflect the teachings of Bahá'u'lláh. A major feature of this work was the nurturing of Bahá'í administrative institutions. As called on to do under the terms of Bahá'u'lláh's Covenant, 'Abdu'l-Bahá encouraged the establishment of what he called "spiritual assemblies," in both North American and Persia. These elected bodies were authorized to supervise activities such as publishing literature, teaching programs, and devotional services at both the local and national levels. They were to serve as forerunners of what Bahá'u'lláh had termed "Houses of Justice."

In 1908 'Abdu'l-Bahá drafted a *Will and Testament* in which he outlined in considerable detail the nature and functions of the central institutions conceived by Bahá'u'lláh for the conduct of the affairs of his cause. The two principal institutions so named were the "Guardianship" and the "Universal House of Justice." The Guardianship conferred the sole authority for the interpretation of Bahá'í teachings on 'Abdu'l-Bahá's eldest grandson, Shoghi Effendi Rabbani. As was the case with the appointment of 'Abdu'l-Bahá in Bahá'u'lláh's Covenant as the Center and designated interpreter, the Guardian was designated the one to whom all the believers were to submit questions on any matter of Bahá'í belief. The other principal institution named in the *Will and Testament* was the Universal House of Justice, designated to be the primary legislative and administrative authority of the Bahá'í community. The Guardian of the Faith was to be assisted by a group of particularly qualified individuals selected by him and designated "Hands of the Cause of God," and the Universal House of Justice was to supervise the international administrative order of the Bahá'í community. As the supreme administrative body of the community, its elected membership would be chosen from among the adult Bahá'ís of the world at an international congress of all the national spiritual assemblies.

*The Will and Testament of 'Abdu'l-Bahá,* together with Bahá-'u'lláh's *Kitáb-i-'Ahd (Book of the Covenant)* were the instruments by which Bahá'u'lláh's Covenant gained practical expression, and the provisions therein shaped the steadily growing Bahá'í community after 'Abdu'l-Bahá's death.[12]

During the course of World War I, 'Abdu'l-Bahá dictated a series of messages to the North American believers. Four of these fourteen letters were addressed jointly to the Bahá'ís of the United States and Canada. Eight were written for the specific guidance of the believers in various regions of the United States, and two were specifically addressed to the Bahá'ís of Canada. The theme of all fourteen was what 'Abdu'l-Bahá termed "The Divine Plan" for the worldwide proclamation of Bahá'u'lláh's message to humankind. The American and Canadian Bahá'ís were called upon to take the lead in establishing the faith in every part of the globe. 'Abdu'l-Bahá assured them that a befitting response to this challenge would confer upon them, in the eyes of a grateful posterity, "spiritual primacy" among the Bahá'í communities of the world. The various international teaching plans through which the community has subsequently grown and by which the message and teachings of Bahá'u'lláh have spread to every corner of the world represent the response of the North American Bahá'ís to the summons contained in these letters.[13]

Early in the morning of November 28, 1921, after a brief illness, Abdu'l-Bahá died in his seventy-eighth year. The circumstances surrounding his funeral indicated that sweeping changes had occurred in the status of the Bahá'í Faith in the Holy Land in just a few short years. Only thirteen years before, as a helpless exile, 'Abdu'l-Bahá had faced the very real possibility that he would be publicly executed. By the time of his death, however, he had established an unequaled reputation as a sage and philanthropist, indeed as a kind of holy man revered by all the religious communities in Palestine. The removal of the restraints imposed by Turkish rule permitted this reputation to blossom. Honors were heaped on him from all segments of the population. A knighthood had been con-

---

[12] An English translation of this document is 'Abdu'l-Bahá, *Will and Testament of 'Abdu'l-Bahá.*

[13] 'Abdu'l-Bahá, *Tablets of the Divine Plan, Revealed By 'Abdu'l-Bahá to the North American Bahá'ís.*

ferred by the British Government in recognition of 'Abdu'l-Bahá's humanitarian services to the Palestinian people during the famine that followed World War I.

The funeral held on November 29 had probably seen no equal in the history of Palestine. A vast crowd, estimated to number over ten thousand people, including dignitaries of the Muslim, Roman Catholic, Greek Orthodox, Jewish, and Druze communities, as well as the British High Commissioner and the governors of Jerusalem and Phoenicia, made up the cortège. It was clear that whatever vicissitudes the new faith might still be obliged to suffer in various parts of the world, it had succeeded, during 'Abdu'l-Bahá's administration of its affairs, in establishing its international center on an impressive foundation of government recognition and public esteem.[14]

At this point in its history, the Bahá'í community included perhaps 100,000 believers living more or less on sufferance in Persia, together with small groups in a few other countries. Apart from Persia, the primary areas of the world in which communities of Bahá'ís were to be found were India and North America. Organization and literature were minimal, as were financial resources. Widespread publicity had been secured through the efforts of 'Abdu'l-Bahá and some of his immediate disciples, but this had yet to produce any significant growth in the size of the community as a whole. 'Abdu'l-Bahá himself had received considerable recognition from civil authorities, but this, too, had yet to be translated into any formal acknowledgment of the Bahá'í Faith as a viable religious system.

Today, a little more than half a century later, the situation has dramatically changed. The Bahá'í Faith has come to be widely recognized as one of the world's most rapidly growing religions,

---

[14] For a complete description, see the special commemorative issue of *World Order*, Vol. 6, no. 1. The outpouring of love from the Palestinian people is especially significant. The Shiah regime in present day Iran has sought to picture 'Abdu'l-Bahá's knighting by the British authorities as having a political meaning. In fact, it was a belated and formal recognition by the British authorities of a philanthropy that had already received its principal acknowledgment from the mass of the public who were its beneficiaries.

embracing adherents from almost every racial, social, cultural, and national origin, and carrying on a broad range of activities in some 200 sovereign states and major territories. An integrated administrative system has evolved at the local, national, and international levels, and in most instances has won formal recognition from the civil authorities.

The writings of Bahá'u'lláh, the Báb, and 'Abdu'l-Bahá, the central figures of the Bahá'í revelation, have been translated and published in over 660 languages. Houses of Worship, Bahá'í schools, administrative headquarters, and community centers have been erected throughout the world, and properties have been acquired for even more ambitious future developments. At the United Nations, the Bahá'í International Community is accredited as a member of the body of Non-Governmental Organizations, with consultative status in the Economic and Security Council. By any standard, the achievements have been extraordinary. The guiding spirit of this phenomenal expansion was Shoghi Effendi Rabbani, the grandson of 'Abdu'l-Bahá, appointed by him to be the Guardian of the Faith of Bahá'u'lláh.

The institution of the Guardianship was conceived by Bahá'u'lláh, but its specific functions and authority were first delineated in *The Will and Testament of 'Abdu'l-Bahá*. The two most important functions of the Guardianship were the interpretation of Bahá'í teachings and the guidance of the Bahá'í community. Mindful of the efforts Muḥammad-'Alí had made to seize control of the community's leadership, 'Abdu'l-Bahá used strong language to make certain that Shoghi Effendi was fully empowered to act as he saw best in all the affairs of the faith. Any opposition to him would constitute opposition to the founders of the faith:

O ye faithful loved ones of 'Abdu'l-Bahá! It is incumbent upon you to take the greatest care of Shoghi Effendi, the twig that hath branched from and the fruit given forth by the two hallowed and Divine Lote-Trees,[15] that no dust of despondency and sorrow may stain his radiant nature, that day

---

[15] Shoghi Effendi was a direct descendent of Bahá'u'lláh through his mother and of the family of the Báb through his father.

by day he may wax greater in happiness, in joy and spirituality, and may grow to become even as a fruitful tree.

For he is, after 'Abdu'l-Bahá, the guardian of the Cause of God. The Afnán, the Hands [pillars] of the Cause and the beloved of the Lord must obey him and turn unto him. He that obeyeth him not, hath not obeyed God; he that turneth away from him hath turned away from God and he that denieth him hath denied the True One. Beware lest anyone falsely interpret these words, and like unto them that have broken the Covenant after the Day of Ascension [of Bahá'u'lláh] advance a pretext, raise the standard of revolt, wax stubborn and open wide the door of false interpretation . . .[16]

From the beginning of his Guardianship, Shoghi Effendi made it clear that not only had the Bahá'í Faith entered a new stage in its growth, but that the authority conveyed by statements such as the above-quoted, involved a function quite different from the charismatic leadership of the community characterized by 'Abdu'l-Bahá. What he called the "apostolic era" had passed, and the 'formative age" had begun.[17]

In this new period, it was the institution of the Guardianship which should command the love and allegiance of the believers. The person of the appointed Guardian was entirely subordinate. The faithful were forbidden to commemorate any of the events associated with the Guardian's life; photographs were discouraged; appointed representatives carried out any public ceremonial functions that were required of the Guardian; and onerous administrative, interpretative, and writing tasks left Shoghi Effendi no time for speaking tours of the kind 'Abdu'l-Bahá had had been able to undertake during his lifetime.

The sole exception to the retirement from a public role was the Guardian's devotion of whatever degree of time he could spare to meeting with the steady flow of pilgrims visiting the Bahá'í World

---

[16] 'Abdu'l-Bahá, *Will and Testament of 'Abdu'l-Bahá,* pp. 25–26.

[17] For a detailed study of the work of Shoghi Effendi, see Rúhíyyih Rabbani, *The Priceless Pearl.* See also Ugo Giachery, *Shoghi Effendi, Recollections.* Giachery worked closely with Shoghi Effendi on the physical development of the Bahá'í World Centre in Haifa.

Centre from both East and West. Even these encounters were limited for the most part to mealtimes at the "Pilgrim House" in Haifa.

The period between 1921 and 1963 in Bahá'í history is most readily accessible through consideration of the major projects undertaken by Shoghi Effendi in the execution of his role as Guardian. Four areas of activity particularly stand out: the development of Bahá'í World Centre, the translation and interpretation of Bahá'í teachings, the expansion of the administrative order, and the implementation of the divine plan of 'Abdu'l-Bahá.

Immediately after assuming his responsibilities, and continuing throughout his life, Shoghi Effendi devoted a great deal of time to the physical development of the faith's international headquarters in the area surrounding the Bay of Haifa. During the lifetimes of Bahá'u'lláh and 'Abdu'l-Bahá, several parcels of land had been gradually acquired by the community of exiles. Of these, the two most important were the site of the shrine where the body of Bahá'u'lláh was interred (in the vicinity of the mansion of Bahjí just outside Acre), and the site of the shrine on the side of Mount Carmel above the city of Haifa which contained the remains of the Báb. Through the generosity of individual' Bahá'ís, bequests, and responses to special appeals by Shoghi Effendi, these properties were vastly increased during the Guardian's ministry. Magnificent gardens were laid out, the first of a number of monumental buildings were erected, and a master plan was created for the development of a spiritual center and administrative complex that would meet the needs of a rapidly growing international community and which would be able to expand with it, a complex designed to rank among the most beautiful in the world. A widely dispersed religious community was thus provided with a center of pilgrimage and guidance that would greatly contribute to creating a sense of common identity.

High on the list of priorities of any religious system must be the determination of the canon of its scripture and the application of these sacred writings to the circumstances of individual and community life. Empowered by 'Abdu'l-Bahá's *Will* as the sole authoritative interpreter of the Bahá'í writings, Shoghi Effendi interpreted world events in the light of the Bahá'í scriptures and shared with the Bahá'í community the results of these analyses in the form of lengthy letters to the Bahá'í world.[18]

At the same time, the nascent Bahá'í communities around the world were deluging Haifa with questions on an enormous range of subjects in the Bahá'í writings, and the Guardian's answers to these inquiries also formed a significant portion of the interpretation of the revelation of Bahá'u'lláh. In the early 1940s Shoghi Effendi focused his analytical attention on the events of Bahá'í history; and in 1944, in commemoration of the centenary of the declaration of the Báb, he produced a highly detailed study covering the entire century from the Báb's first announcement of his mission to Mullá Ḥusayn to the completion of the first "Seven Year Plan."[19]

Shoghi Effendi's program to interpret the Bahá'í writings was considerably aided by the fact that he was in a position to serve as the principal translator of the writings from Persian and Arabic into English.[20] He had studied English from early childhood and as a young man was able to continue his studies at the American University of Beirut and subsequently at Oxford University, where he remained until the time of 'Abdu'l-Bahá's death in 1921. Since the major administrative bodies of the Bahá'í Faith during the first critical decades of the Guardianship were located in English-speaking countries, Shoghi Effendi's ability to express and interpret Bahá'í concepts in the English language provided an invaluable source of guidance to the new faith in the Western world.

His role as an interpreter was also of long-range importance to the development of the Bahá'í community. It assured unity of doctrine during the early years of the faith's global expansion and thus greatly reduced the threat of schism.

Parallel with his translation activities and the development of the

---

[18] *Bahá'í Administration; The Advent of Divine Justice; The World Order of Bahá'u'lláh, Selected Letters; Messages to the Bahá'í World, 1950–1957; The Promised Day Is Come; Messages to Canada;* and *Citadel of Faith, Messages to America, 1947–1957.*

[19] Shoghi Effendi, *God Passes By.* For description of Plans, see below.

[20] *Gleanings from the Writings of Bahá'u'lláh; The Kitáb-i-Íqán, The Book of Certitude Revealed By Bahá'u'lláh; The Hidden Words of Bahá'u'lláh; The Seven Valleys and the Four Valleys; Epistle to the Son of the Wolf;* and *Prayers and Meditations by Bahá'u'lláh.*

World Centre of the faith, Shoghi Effendi devoted much of his energies to bringing into existence the system of administrative institutions as they had been conceived by Bahá'u'lláh and established in embryonic form by 'Abdu'l-Bahá. Each locality with nine or more adult believers was encouraged to elect a "Local Spiritual Assembly" to govern the affairs of the faith in that area. As soon as the number of local spiritual assemblies in any given country provided a sufficiently broad base, the Guardian urged the election of a national spiritual assembly, vested with full jurisdiction over the affairs of the faith in that particular country.

A steady stream of correspondence from Haifa provided these nascent institutions with guidance concerning the application of the Bahá'í writings to the conduct of community life. More general communications urged all believers to give their wholehearted support and obedience to the bodies they elected. Bahá'í principles of consultation were identified and assemblies were urged to conscientiously train themselves in group decision making.

In accordance with 'Abdu'l-Bahá's *Will,* between the years 1951 and 1957, the Guardian appointed a number of distinguished believers as Hands of the Cause of God and charged them with special responsibilities for teaching the faith and protecting its institutions. The crowning unit of this global administrative structure was the institution of the Universal House of Justice, conceived and named by Bahá'u'lláh. Shoghi Effendi indicated that, as soon as the expansion of the Bahá'í community permitted, a Universal House of Justice would be elected by the entire international Bahá'í community, acting through their national spiritual assemblies.

A word should be said about the role that the North American Bahá'í community, and particularly the Bahá'ís in the United States, played in this building process. 'Abdu'l-Bahá had been lavish in his praise of the spiritual capacities and the services of its members. He had been generous, too, in his recognition of many of the characteristics of the United States as a nation. More important, he had indicated that America would serve as the "cradle" of the administrative order which Bahá'u'lláh had conceived. Because of the importance of this turning point in human history, "the day is approaching when ye shall witness how . . . the West will have replaced the East, radiating the light of divine guidance."[21]

Accordingly, when Shoghi Effendi began building the administrative order, he turned to the American Bahá'ís as his chief collaborators. Already, several of them were involved in Bahá'í teaching projects beyond their own shores, and one of them, Martha Root, member of a distinguished American family, had been successful in bringing into the faith its first crowned head, Queen Marie of Rumania.[22] The American Bahá'ís were also the "Chief Executors" of 'Abdu'l-Bahá's *Will*. It was principally through this correspondence with the National Spiritual Assembly of the Bahá'ís of the United States and Canada[23] that Shoghi Effendi gradually molded local and national institutions which functioned in conformity with the principles in the writings of the faith. Communities in other lands were encouraged to follow this lead. While cultural differences would determine secondary matters, the administrative order should be uniform in essentials, and for this a model was needed.

The American community was to provide this model, but the members were cautioned by Shoghi Effendi that their mandate owed nothing to the political system with which they were familiar. On the contrary: Bahá'u'lláh had appeared in Persia not because of any cultural superiority that nation possessed, but because of its profound moral degradation. Similarly, his administrative order would be erected first in a social milieu characterized by materialism, lawlessness, and political corruption. There, as had already occurred in Persia, Bahá'u'lláh would demonstrate that it is only the power of God that can regenerate people and society.[24]

Shoghi Effendi's reasons for devoting so much time and energy

---

[21] Cited in Shoghi Effendi, *Citadel*, p. 30.

[22] For an account of the Queen's conversion see Rúḥíyyih Rabbani, *Priceless Pearl*, Chapter IV.

[23] The two communities separated in 1948 when Canada formed its own national spiritual assembly, incorporated the following year by special Act of Parliament.

[24] Shoghi Effendi, *Advent*, pp. 14–16.

to the development of the Bahá'í administrative order during the first years of his guardianship soon became apparent. The administrative institutions of the faith provided the necessary instruments for the implementation of 'Abdu'l-Bahá's "Divine Plan" to spread the Bahá'í message around the world. Before the widely scattered community could undertake so great a task, it was necessary to establish decision-making administrative bodies capable of mobilizing the necessary manpower and resources. Moreover, it was essential that adequate time be allowed for these institutions to learn the rudiments of Bahá'í administration and consultation.

Accordingly, it was not until 1937, sixteen years after the death of 'Abdu'l-Bahá, that Shoghi Effendi began systematically working on realizing the objectives laid out in the series of letters sent by 'Abdu'l-Bahá to the Bahá'ís of North America. In April 1937 the first seven-year plan was launched with three major goals: (1) to establish at least one local spiritual assembly in every state of the United States and every province of Canada; (2) to make certain that at least one Bahá'í teacher was residing in each Latin American republic; and (3) to complete the exterior design of the first Bahá'í house of worship in North America—a building whose cornerstone had been laid by 'Abdu'l-Bahá during his visit in 1912, and which, in many ways, symbolized the international Bahá'í community itself. Despite the obstacles created by the outbreak of World War II, this plan was successfully completed on the centenary of the declaration of the Báb, in May 1944.

Following a two-year interval, a second seven-year plan was launched in 1946. The focus of this effort was Europe, which at the time had only two national spiritual assemblies: those of Great Britain and Germany. The plan also called for the creation of local spiritual assemblies throughout Latin American and a great multiplication of those in North America. The successful conclusion of this plan likewise coincided with a major Bahá'í centenary, the one-hundredth anniversary of the inception of Bahá'u'lláh's mission in the Síyáh-Chál in 1853. One of the major goals of this seven-year plan was the establishment of an independent national spiritual assembly in Canada. This was achieved in 1948, and in 1949 was followed by its incorporation by a special Act of Parliament,[25] an achievement which Shoghi Effendi pointed out was "unique in the annals of the Faith, whether of East or West."

The two most impressive single achievements of this second plan had a special connection with the North American Bahá'í community. April 1953 marked the formal dedication of the house of worship at Wilmette, Illinois, which was to be the first of similar structures to be built on all five continents of the globe. The designer was a French-Canadian architect named Jean-Louis Bourgeois. His magnificent conception was hailed by the Italian architect Luigi Quaglino as "a new creation which will revolutionize architecture in the world. Without doubt," he added, "it will have a lasting page in history."[26] One other major triumph of these years was also a building, a magnificent shrine to crown the stone edifice built by 'Abdu'l-Bahá to serve as a mausoleum for the Báb. The architect of this shrine was another Canadian, William Sutherland Maxwell, with whom 'Abdu'l-Bahá had stayed during his visit to Montreal. The exquisite design, in which a golden dome crowns a white marble arcade and rose-colored granite pillars, has provided the Bahá'í World Centre on Mount Carmel with one of the most beautiful landmarks on the shores of the Mediterranean Sea.

In 1953, without any lapse of time, Shoghi Effendi launched the Bahá'í community on the most ambitious undertaking in its history —a global plan which he termed a "Ten Year World Crusade." This plan would conclude in 1963, the centenary of the declaration of Bahá'u'lláh in the Garden of Riḍván. One hundred and thirty-two new countries and major territories were to be opened to the faith and the existing communities in 120 countries and territories were to be expanded. National spiritual assemblies were to be established in most countries in Europe and Latin America, and vast increases were called for in the numbers of assemblies, believers, and property endowments. This plan, like those before, was achieved on schedule (indeed was far exceeded); but under circumstances very different from any the Bahá'í community might have anticipated.

---

[25] Shoghi Effendi, *Messages to Canada*, pp. 12–13.
[26] Louis J. Bourgeois, *The Bahá'í Temple: Press Comments, Symbolism*, p. 7.

In early November 1957, while on a visit to England to purchase furnishings for the Bahá'í archives building on Mount Carmel, Shoghi Effendi contracted Asian flu. On November 4, he died of a heart attack, leaving the Bahá'í world stunned and temporarily distracted, its ten-year plan only half completed.

The Guardianship was theoretically a continuous one. 'Abdu'l-Bahá's *Will and Testament* authorized the Guardian of the Bahá'í Faith to appoint a successor from among the direct descendants of Bahá'u'lláh but indicated certain qualities such a successor must possess. Shoghi Effendi died without designating a successor, as apparently no other members of the family met the demanding spiritual requirements laid down in the Covenant of Bahá'u'lláh and in *The Will and Testament of 'Abdu'l-Bahá*. There would, therefore, be no second Guardian; the only other institution endowed with the authority to assume the leadership of the Bahá'í community was the Universal House of Justice—a body which had yet to be elected.[27]

Three interrelated factors provided an answer to the dilemma facing the Bahá'í world: (1) from statements Shoghi Effendi had made, it was apparent that he considered that conditions would be ready for the election of the Universal House of Justice when the ten-year plan was successfully completed; (2) in the meantime, the Bahá'í community would receive the basic guidance it required from the detailed plan already laid down by Shoghi Effendi; and (3) finally, in one of his last messages to the Bahá'í world, he had named the Hands of the Cause as the "Chief Stewards" of the faith and called on them to collaborate closely with the national spiritual assemblies in assuring that the ten-year plan was carried out and that the unity of the faith was protected.[28]

Heartened by this last message, the Hands of the Cause organized their work around a series of annual "Conclaves." These

---

[27] See Universal House of Justice, *Wellspring of Guidance, Messages 1963–1968*, pp. 44–56 and pp. 81–91.

[28] A summary of the actions taken by the Hands of the Cause during the period of their stewardship, 1957–1963, together with the full text of statements made at their annual Conclaves, is provided in *The Bahá'í World: An International Record*. Vol. 13, 1954–1963, pp. 333–378.

consultations produced a number of major statements, including the formal declaration that Shoghi Effendi had left no will and had appointed no heir to the Guardianship (Conclave of 1957), and the announcement that the Universal House of Justice would be elected by the membership of all the national spiritual assemblies of the Bahá'ís of the world in 1963 (Conclave of 1959).

By April 1961 twenty-one new national spiritual assemblies were established in Latin America; and, a year later, an additional eleven were elected in Europe. The remaining goals of the ten-year plan were likewise either accomplished or surpassed. In the spring of 1963, precisely one hundred years after Bahá'u'lláh first declared his mission to a handful of followers in the Garden of Riḍván, the members of the fifty-six elected national spiritual assemblies around the world carried out an election of the first Universal House of Justice. In a remarkable gesture of renunciation, the Hands of the Cause disqualified themselves from serving as elected members of the supreme administrative institution of the Bahá'í community.

For Bahá'ís, the election of the first Universal House of Justice represented an event of transcendent importance. After more than a century of struggle, persecution, and recurrent internal crises, and through democratic electoral processes, the Bahá'í community had succeeded in bringing into existence a permanent institution for the guidance of all the affairs of the faith. Moreover, its establishment had been conceived by Bahá'u'lláh himself and was patterned on principles laid down in his writings and in those of 'Abdu'l-Bahá. The cosmopolitan membership of the first Universal House of Justice seemed particularly appropriate to the institution's nature and functions: the nine members from four continents represented three major religious backgrounds (Jewish, Christian, and Muslim) as well as several ethnic origins. [29]

Beyond its institutional importance, the establishment of the Universal House of Justice symbolized the element which Bahá'ís

---

[29] Subsequent elections of the Universal House of Justice have been held at five-year intervals since 1963: in 1968, 1973, 1978, and 1983. The election is held during the period of the Riḍván celebrations.

regard as the essence of their faith: unity. The emergence of the Universal House of Justice as the unchallenged authority in all the affairs of the community meant that the Bahá'í Faith had remained united through the most critical period of a religion's history, the vulnerable first century during which schism almost traditionally takes root.

As the stories of Mírzá Yaḥyá, Muḥammad-'Alí, and Ibrahim Kheiralla amply demonstrate, many abortive efforts were made to divide the Bahá'í community during this critical period. It is an impressive testimony to the successive leadership of Bahá'u'lláh, 'Abdu'l-Bahá, and Shoghi Effendi, that such efforts failed.[30] With the establishment of an accepted permanent authoritative body to which all individual believers and administrative bodies at the local and national levels within the Bahá'í community were subject, the unity of the community assumed an institutional form that directly involved every believer.[31]

The election of the Universal House of Justice opened the way to the resumption of two major activities initially undertaken by the Guardian: (1) the creation of new institutions and administrative agencies as the needs of a rapidly expanding faith dictated; and (2) the elaboration of new global teaching plans for continuing work on 'Abdu'l-Bahá's vision of a "spiritual conquest of the planet."

In 1964, the year following its first election, the Universal House of Justice launched a nine-year plan that was completed on schedule in 1973, the centennial anniversary of Bahá'u'lláh's reve-

---

[30] A further attempt to create a schism occurred in 1960, before the election of the first Universal House of Justice. One of the Hands, Charles Mason Remey, an American over eighty years of age, suddenly advanced the claim that he was, in some fashion not explained, "the hereditary successor" of Shoghi Effendi. Acting on the authority given them in 'Abdu'l-Bahá's *Will and Testament,* his fellow Hands expelled him from the Faith. Remey's claim aroused little interest and he died in 1974, ignored even by the small handful of people whom he had originally attracted.

[31] In 1973, at the same time as the publication of the initial *Synopsis and Codification of the Kitáb-i-Aqdas (Book of Laws),* The Universal House of Justice promulgated its constitution: *The Constitution of the Universal House of Justice.*

lation of the *Kitáb-i-Aqdas* or *Most Holy Book*. This was immediately followed by a five-year plan, achieved in 1979. The Universal House of Justice then assigned its third global teaching project: another seven-year plan, and the Bahá'í world undertook to complete its goals by 1986.

# 5. Basic Teachings

## THREE FUNDAMENTAL PRINCIPLES

In discussing the teachings of the Bahá'í Faith, we turn first to an examination of three basic principles: (1) the oneness of God; (2) the oneness of humankind; and (3) the fundamental unity of religion.

### THE ONENESS OF GOD

The Bahá'í belief in one God means that the universe and all creatures and forces within it have been created by one single super-human and supernatural Being. This Being, whom we call God, has absolute control over his creation (omnipotence) as well as perfect and complete knowledge of it (omniscience). Although we may have different concepts of God's nature, although we may pray to him in different languages and call him by different names—Allah or Yahweh, God or Brahma—nevertheless, we are speaking about the same unique Being.

Extolling God's act of creation, Bahá'u'lláh said:

All-praise to the unity of God, and all-honor to Him, the sovereign Lord, the incomparable and all-glorious Ruler of the universe, Who, out of utter nothingness, hath created the reality of all things, Who, from naught, hath brought into being the most refined and subtle elements of His creation, and Who, rescuing His creatures from the abasement of remoteness and the perils of ultimate extinction, hath received them into His kingdom of incorruptible glory. Nothing short of His all–encompassing grace, His all–pervading mercy, could have possibly achieved it.[1]

Bahá'u'lláh taught that God is too great and too subtle a being for the finite human mind ever to understand him adequately or to construct an accurate image of him:

---

[1] Bahá'u'lláh, *Gleanings*, pp. 64–65.

How wondrous is the unity of the Living, the Ever-Abiding God—a unity which is exalted above all limitations, that transcendeth the comprehension of all created things. . . . How lofty hath been His incorruptible Essence, how completely independent of the knowledge of all created things, and how immensely exalted will it remain above the praise of all the inhabitants of the heavens and the earth![2]

### THE ONENESS OF HUMANKIND

The second basic Bahá'í principle is the oneness of humankind. This means that the entire human race is one unified, distinct species, an organic unit. This one human race is the "apogee of creation," the highest form of life and consciousness which God has created; for among God's creatures, only human beings have the capacity to be aware of God's existence and to commune with his spirit:

Having created the world and all that liveth and moveth therein, He [God], through the direct operation of His unconstrained and sovereign Will, chose to confer upon man the unique distinction and capacity to know Him and to love Him—a capacity that must needs be regarded as the generating impulse and the primary purpose underlying the whole of creation. . . . Alone of all created things man hath been singled out for so great a favor, so enduring a bounty.[3]

The oneness of humankind also implies that all peoples have the same basic, God-given capacities. Physical differences such as skin color or hair texture are superficial and have nothing to do with any supposed superiority of one ethnic group over another. All theories of racial superiority are rejected by Bahá'í teachings as founded on false imagination and ignorance.[4]

Bahá'ís believe that humankind has always constituted one species, but that prejudice, ignorance, power-seeking, and egotism

---

[2] Bahá'u'lláh, *Gleanings,* pp. 261–62.
[3] Bahá'u'lláh, *Gleanings,* p. 65.
[4] According to Bahá'í precepts, apparent differences between ethnic groups in certain areas of cultural achievement are attributable to long-term differences in educational and cultural opportunities as well as to the cumulative effects of racial prejudice and oppression.

have prevented many people from recognizing and accepting this oneness. The essential mission of Bahá'u'lláh was to change this situation and to bring about the universal consciousness of the oneness of humankind. Bahá'ís believe that the organic unit which is humankind has undergone a collective growth process under the Fatherhood of God. Much as a single organism attains maturity in successive stages of development, so humankind has gradually evolved towards its collective maturity.

The basic expression of man's social evolution is his capacity to organize his society on ever higher levels of unity with greater specialization of the individual components, and with a consequent increase in the interdependence and the need for cooperation among the specialized parts. The family, the tribe, the city-state, the nation—these represent some of the signal stages in social evolution. The next stage in this collective growth process, representing the culmination of human evolution, is world unity: the organization of society as a planetary civilization.

Shoghi Effendi spoke of this Bahá'í teaching in the following way:

The principle of the Oneness of Mankind—the pivot round which all the teachings of Bahá'u'lláh revolve—is no mere outburst of ignorant emotionalism or an expression of vague and pious hope. . . . Its message is applicable not only to the individual, but concerns itself primarily with the nature of those essential relationships that must bind all the states and nations as members of one human family. . . . It implies an organic change in the structure of present-day society, a change such as the world has not yet experienced. . . . It calls for no less than the reconstruction and the demilitarization of the whole civilized world. . . . It represents the consummation of human evolution—an evolution that has had its earliest beginnings in the birth of family life, its subsequent development in the achievement of tribal solidarity, leading in turn to the constitution of the city-state, and expanding later into the institution of independent and sovereign nations.

The principle of the Oneness of Mankind, as proclaimed by Bahá'u'lláh, carries with it no more and no less than a solemn assertion that attainment to this final stage in this stupendous evolution is not only necessary but inevitable, that its realization is fast approaching and that nothing short of a power that is born of God can succeed in establishing it.[5]

Thus the principle of the oneness of humankind implies not only a new individual consciousness, but the establishment of the unity of nations, of world government, and ultimately of a planetary civilization. Accordingly, it is not sufficient that humankind simply acknowledge its oneness while continuing to live in a disunited world full of conflict, prejudice, and hatred. We must express unity by building a truly universal and unified social system based on spiritual principles. The achievement of such a system represents the God-directed goal of human social evolution:

. . . the object of life to a Bahá'í is to promote the oneness of mankind. The whole object of our lives is bound up with the lives of all human beings; not a personal salvation we are seeking, but a universal one. . . . Our aim is to produce a world civilization which will in turn react on the character of the individual. It is, in a way, the inverse of Christianity, which started with the individual unit and through it reached out to the conglomerate life of man.[6]

Thus, from the Bahá'í point of view, the fundamental, spiritual purpose of society is to create a milieu favorable to the healthy growth and development of all its members.

Bahá'u'lláh proposed a detailed system for the establishment of world unity, which is discussed in subsequent chapters of the present work. In a general way, what he proposed was the creation of new social structures based on participation and consultation. These new structures would serve the primary purpose of eliminating conflicts of interest and thus reducing the potential for disunity at all levels of society. The new structures envisaged include a number of potent international organs of world government: a world legislature with genuine representation and authority, an international court having final jurisdiction in all disputes between nations, and an international police force.

---

[5] Shoghi Effendi, *World Order of Bahá'u'lláh,* pp. 42–43.
[6] Shoghi Effendi, quoted in William Hatcher, *The Concept of Spirituality,* p. 29.

He taught that the creation of these new social structures must be accompanied by the indivdual and collective consciousness of the fundamental oneness of humankind:

Ye are the fruits of one tree, and the leaves of one branch. Deal ye one with another with the utmost love and harmony, with friendliness and fellowship. . . . So powerful is the light of unity that it can illuminate the whole earth.[7]

And in yet another passage:

It is not for him to pride himself who loveth his own country, but rather for him who loveth the whole world. The earth is but one country, and mankind its citizens.[8]

Unity, in the Bahá'í conception, is a unity in diversity rather than uniformity. It is not by the suppression of differences that we will arrive at unity, but rather by an increased awareness of and respect for the intrinsic value of each separate culture, and indeed, of each individual. It is not diversity itself which is deemed the cause of conflict, but rather our immature attitude towards it, our intolerance and prejudice. 'Abdu'l-Bahá expressed this viewpoint in the following passage:

Should any one contend that true and enduring unity can in no wise be realized in this world, inasmuch as its people widely differ in their manners and habits, their tastes, their temperament and character, their thoughts and their views, to this we make reply that differences are of two kinds; the one is the cause of destruction, as exemplified by the spirit of contention and strife which animates mutually conflicting and antagonistic peoples and nations, whilst the other is the sign of diversity, the symbol and the secret of perfection, and the revealer of the bounties of the All-glorious.

Consider the flowers of the garden; though differing in kind, color, form and shape, yet, inasmuch as they are refreshed by the waters of one spring, revived by the breath of one wind, invigorated by the rays of one sun, this diversity increaseth their charm and addeth unto their beauty.

---

[7] Bahá'u'lláh, *Gleanings,* p. 288.
[8] Bahá'u'lláh, *Gleanings,* p. 250.

How unpleasing to the eye if all the flowers and plants, the leaves and blossoms, the fruit, the branches, and the trees of the garden were all of the same shape and color! Diversity of color, form and shape encricheth and adorneth the garden, and heighteneth the effect thereof. In like manner, when divers shades of thought, temperament and character, are brought together under the power and influence of one central agency, the beauty and glory of human perfection will be revealed and made manifest. Naught but the celestial potency of the Word of God, which ruleth and transcendeth the realities of all things, is capable of harmonizing the divergent thoughts, sentiments, ideas and convictions of the children of men.[9]

Because the establishment of world unity and a planetary civilization represents the consummation of mankind's development on this planet, it represents the "coming of age" of humanity, the maturity of the human race. Shoghi Effendi expressed this idea as follows:

The Revelation of Bahá'u'lláh, whose supreme mission is none other but the achievement of this organic and spiritual unity of the whole body of nations, should, if we be faithful to its implications, be regarded as signalizing through its advent the *coming of age of the entire human race*. It should be viewed . . . as marking the last and highest stage in the stupendous evolution of man's collective life on this planet. The emergence of a world community, the consciousness of world citizenship, the founding of a world civilization and culture . . . should, by their very nature, be regarded, as far as this planetary life is concerned, as the furthermost limits in the organization of human society, though man, as an individual, will, nay must indeed as a result of such a consummation, continue indefinitely to progress and develop.[10]

The different stages in mankind's development are regarded as quite similar to the stages in the life of an individual. The current stage is described as that of adolescence, the stage immediately preceding full maturity:

---

[9] 'Abdu'l-Bahá, cited in Bahá'u'lláh and 'Abdu'l-Bahá, *The Divine Art of Living, Selections from Writings of Bahá'u'lláh and 'Abdu'l-Bahá*, pp. 109–110.
[10] Shoghi Effendi, *World Order of Bahá'u'lláh*, p. 163.

The long ages of infancy and childhood, through which the human race had to pass, have receded into the background. Humanity is now experiencing the commotions invariably associated with the most turbulent stage of its evolution, the stage of adolescence, when the impetuousity of youth and its vehemence reach their climax, and must gradually be superseded by the calmness, the wisdom, and the maturity that characterize the stage of manhood. Then will the human race reach that stature of ripeness which will enable it to acquire all the powers and capacities upon which its ultimate development must depend.[11]

Speaking of the age of mankind's full maturity, Shoghi Effendi said:

That mystic, all-pervasive, yet indefinable change, which we associate with the stage of maturity inevitable in the life of the individual . . . must . . . have its counterpart in the evolution of the organization of human society. A similar stage must sooner or later be attained in the collective life of mankind, producing an even more striking phenomenon in world relations, and endowing the whole human race with such potentialities of well-being as shall provide, throughout the succeeding ages, the chief incentive required for the eventual fulfillment of its high destiny.[12]

Of course, the history of mankind that we can observe is the history of man's infancy, childhood, and adolescence. Therefore, affirmed Bahá'u'lláh, we tend to underestimate the true capacities of the human race. But these latent capacities will become evident as humankind achieves its maturity:

Verily I say, in this most mighty Revelation, all the Dispensations of the past have attained their highest . . . consummation. . . . The potentialities inherent in the station of man, the full measure of his destiny on earth, the innate excellence of his reality, must all be manifested in this Promised Day of God.[13]

In summary, the Bahá'í principle of the oneness of humankind means that the human race represents an organic unit whose collective social life has gradually developed by being reorganized on

---

[11] Shoghi Effendi, *World Order of Bahá'u'lláh, p. 202.*
[12] Shoghi Effendi, *World Order of Bahá'u'lláh,* pp. 163–164.
[13] Bahá'u'lláh, *Gleanings, p. 340.*

ever-higher levels of unity (the family, the tribe, the city-state, the nation). The specific mission of Bahá'u'lláh was to provide the impetus for the next stage of this social evolution, namely the organization of human society as a planetary civilization. This is to be achieved through the development of new social structures which reduce and eliminate conflict of interest; and by the creation of a new level of human consciousness, that of the basic oneness of humanity. Moreover, the unification of humankind represents the attainment of the stage of maturity or adulthood in the collective life of humankind.

The Bahá'í community is seen as both the embryo and the prototype of the future world civilization. It also provides the individual with an opportunity to begin to live the experience of unity and to develop this new consciouosness. The subject will be treated in more detail in a later chapter.

THE ONENESS OF RELIGION

The third basic Bahá'í principle, the unity of religion, is closely related to the principle of the oneness of humankind. Our discussion of the concept of the organic unity of the human race has suggested that humanity is engaged in a collective growth process quite similar to the growth process of an individual: just as the individual begins life as a helpless infant and attains maturity in successive stages, so humankind began its collective social life in a primitive state, gradually attaining maturity. In the case of the individual, it is clear that his development takes place as a result of the education he receives from his parents, his teachers, and society in general. But what is the motive force in mankind's collective evolution?

The answer the Bahá'í Faith provides to this question is "revealed religion." In one of his major works, the *Kitáb-i-Íqán* (the *Book of Certitude*) Bahá'u'lláh explained that God, the Creator, has intervened and will continue to intervene in human history by means of chosen spokesmen or messengers. These messengers, whom Bahá'u'lláh called "Manifestations of God," are principally the founders of the major revealed religions, such as Abraham, Moses, Buddha, Jesus, Muhammad, and so forth. It is the spirit released by the coming of these Manifestations, together with the influence of their teachings and the social systems established by their laws and precepts, that enable humankind to progress in its collective evolution. Simply put: the Manifestations of God are the chief educators of humanity.

With regard to the various religious systems that have appeared in human history, Bahá'u'lláh has said:

These principles and laws, these firmly-established and mighty systems, have proceeded from one Source and are the rays of one Light. That they differ one from another is to be attributed to the varying requirements of the ages in which they were promulgated.[14]

Thus the principle of the unity of religion means that all of the great religious founders—the Manifestations—have come from God, and that all of the religious systems established by them are part of a single divine plan directed by God.

In reality, there is only one religion, the religion of God. This one religion is continually evolving, and each particular religious system represents a stage in the evolution of the whole. The Bahá'í Faith represents the current stage in the evolution of religion.

To emphasize the idea that all of the teachings and actions of the Manifestation are directed by God and do not originate from natural, human sources, Bahá'u'lláh used the term "revelation" to describe the phenomenon that occurs each time a Manifestation appears. In particular, the writings of the Manifestation represent the infallible Word of God. Because these writings remain long after the earthly life of the Manifestation is finished, they constitute an especially important part of the phenomenon of revelation. So much is this so, that the term "revelation" is sometimes used in a restricted sense to refer to the writings and words of the Manifestation.

Religious history is seen as a succession of revelations from God and the term "progressive revelation" is used to describe this process. Thus, according to Bahá'ís, progressive revelation is the mo-

---

[14] Bahá'u'lláh, *Gleanings*, pp. 287–288.

tive force of human progress, and the Manifestation Bahá'u'lláh is the most recent instance of revelation.[15]

To put the Bahá'í concept of religion more clearly in focus, let us compare it with some other ways in which religion has been regarded. On one hand is the view that the various religious systems result from human striving after truth. In this conception, the founders of the great religions do not reveal God to us, but are rather philosophers or thinkers, human beings who may have progressed farther than others in the discovery of truth. This notion excludes the idea of a basic unity of religion since the various religious systems are seen as representing different opinions and beliefs arrived at by fallible human beings rather than infallible revelations of truth from a single source.

Many orthodox adherents of various religious traditions, on the other hand, argue that the prophet or founder of their particular tradition represents a true revelation of God to humanity, but that the other religious founders are false prophets, or at least essentially inferior to the founder of the tradition in question. For example, many Jews believe that Moses was a true messenger of God, but that Jesus was not. Similarly, many Christians believe in Jesus' revelation, but consider that Muhammad was a false prophet, and hold that Moses was inferior in status to Christ.

The Bahá'í principle of the oneness of religion differs fundamentally from both of these traditional concepts. Bahá'u'lláh attributed the differences in some teachings of the great religions not to any human fallibility of the founders, but rather to the different requirements of the ages in which the revelations occurred. In addition, he maintained that there has been a great deal of human error introduced into religion through the corruption of texts and the addition of extraneous ideas. Moreover, Bahá'ís consider that no one of the

---

[15] Bahá'u'lláh taught that the time interval between two Manifestations may be about one thousand years. He also taught that the process of revelation will not stop with his revelation and that another Manifestation will come after him, though not before the expiration of one thousand years from Bahá'u'lláh's coming. According to the Bahá'í writings, the process of revelation will continue indefinitely into the future and humankind will see the coming of a great many more Manifestations.

founders is superior to another. Shoghi Effendi has summarized this view in the following words:

The fundamental principle enunciated by Bahá'u'lláh, the followers of His Faith firmly believe, is that religious truth is not absolute but relative, that Divine Revelation is a continuous and progressive process, that all the great religions of the world are divine in origin, that their basic principles are in complete harmony, that their aims and purposes are one and the same, that their teachings are but facets of one truth, that their functions are complementary, that they differ only in the nonessential aspects of their doctrines, and that their missions represent successive stages in the spiritual evolution of human society.[16]

## THE BAHÁ'Í REVELATION—THE SACRED WRITINGS

Bahá'u'lláh's writings include over one hundred books and tablets, most of which were written under the difficult conditions of imprisonment described earlier. This vast body of literature comprises the Bahá'í revelation. The writings of 'Abdu'l-Bahá and the interpretations of Shoghi Effendi have, for Bahá'ís, a derived but equally binding authority.

The subject matter of the writings of Bahá'u'lláh falls into several categories: (1) In one category are basic concepts, typified by the *Kitáb-i-Íqán* with its explanation of the theme of progressive revelation. (2) In another category are principles of human life and conduct, as outlined in exhortations by Bahá'u'lláh speaking as God's representative on earth. In these he explained the nature and purpose of life, described its processes, counseled men to act in accordance with the Divine Will, and gave both warnings and promises related to human response. (3) A third category consists of laws and ordinances which are similar to the counsels except that, for Bahá'ís, they are binding and obligatory. (4) Further, Bahá'u'lláh established social and administrative institutions, carefully setting the limitations of their authority as well as their prerogatives and powers.

---

[16] Shoghi Effendi, "The Faith of Bahá'u'lláh" in *World Order,* vol. 7, no. 2, 1972–1973, p. 7.

The last two categories, the laws and the institutions, together constitute a system called the "Administrative Order of Bahá-'u'lláh." The purpose of the Administrative Order is to safeguard the unity of the Bahá'í community as well as to serve as an instrument for the establishment of world unity. Later chapters of this book deal with the Administrative Order in greater depth.

Other categories of Bahá'u'lláh's writings that can be readily distinguished are the devotional, the mystical, the philosophical, and the historiographical. The variety is great and attests to the extraordinary range of Bahá'u'lláh's concern with the needs of man and society.

Most of the major principles to be found in these writings may be regarded as auxiliary to the realization of the fundamental Bahá'í goal of achieving a unified world order. Their application would serve to reduce conflict between groups and between individuals and thus create a social climate favorable to the development of unity. Shoghi Effendi provided a summary statement of some of the major Bahá'í principles. It is quoted in full to serve as a basis for further discussion:

The Bahá'í Faith recognizes the unity of God and of His Prophets, upholds the principle of an unfettered search after truth, condemns all forms of superstition and prejudice, teaches that the fundamental purpose of religion is to promote concord and harmony, that it must go hand-in-hand with science, and that it constitutes the sole and ultimate basis of a peaceful, an ordered and progressive society. It inculcates the principle of equal opportunity, rights and privileges for both sexes, advocates compulsory education, abolishes extremes of poverty and wealth, exalts work performed in the spirit of service to the rank of worship, recommends the adoption of an auxiliary international language, and provides the necessary agencies for the establishment and safeguarding of a permanent and universal peace.[17]

It is in this context that certain of these principles will now be considered in greater detail.

---

[17] Shoghi Effendi, *World Order of Bahá'u'lláh* (1938 ed.), pp. xi–xii.

### THE INDEPENDENT INVESTIGATION OF TRUTH

One of the main sources of conflict in the world today is the fact that many people blindly and uncritically follow various traditions, movements, and opinions. God has given each human being a mind and the capacity to differentiate truth from falsehood. If one fails to use his reasoning capacity and chooses instead to accept without question certain opinions and ideas, either out of admiration for or fear of those who hold them, then he is neglecting his basic moral responsibility as a human being.

Moreover, when people act in this way, they often become fanatically attached to some particular opinion or tradition and thus intolerant of those who do not share it. Such attachments can, in turn, lead to conflict. History has witnessed conflict and even bloodshed over slight alterations in religious practice, or a minor change in the interpretation of doctrine.

Personal search for truth enables the individual to know why he adheres to a given ideology or doctrine. Bahá'ís believe that, as there is only one reality, all people will gradually discover its different facets and will ultimately come to mutual understanding and unity, provided they sincerely seek after truth. In this connection, 'Abdu'l-Bahá said:

Being one, truth cannot be divided, and the differences that appear to exist among the many nations only result from their attachment to prejudice. If only men would search out truth, they would find themselves united.[18]

And again:

The fact that we imagine ourselves to be right and everybody else wrong is the greatest of all obstacles in the path towards unity, and unity is necessary if we would reach truth, for truth is *one*.[19]

### ABANDONING PREJUDICE AND SUPERSTITION

Bahá'u'lláh gave special attention to the problem of prejudice. A prejudice is a strong emotional attachment to an idea, regardless of

[18] 'Abdu'l-Bahá, *Paris Talks*, p. 129.
[19] 'Abdu'l-Bahá, *Paris Talks*, p. 136.

whether or not the idea is reasonable. A common form of prejudice occurs when a person strongly identifies with some group to which he belongs and which he regards as superior to other groups. Consequently, he maintains a negative image of all people outside of his group, with no regard for their individual qualities. Group prejudices can be based on racial, economic, social, linguistic, or other such criteria. They cause conflict because they create disunity between groups. The hatred created by prejudice can, and often has, led to social unrest, war, and even genocide. Bahá'u'lláh specifically counseled his followers to make an active effort to rid themselves of all prejudices and superstitions about human nature which breed such aversions.

In his primary ethical work, *The Hidden Words*, Bahá'u'lláh incited man to reflect on this question:

O CHILDREN OF MEN!

Know ye not why We created you all from the same dust? That no one should exalt himself over the other. Ponder at all times in your hearts how ye were created. Since we have created you all from one same substance it is incumbent on you to be even as one soul, to walk with the same feet, eat with the same mouth and dwell in the same land, that from your inmost being, by your deeds and actions, the signs of oneness and the essence of detachment may be made manifest.[20]

THE UNITY OF RELIGION AND SCIENCE

A major source of conflict and disunity in the world today is the widespread opinion that there is some basic opposition between science and religion, that scientific truth contradicts religion on some points, and that one must choose between being a religious person, a believer in God, or a scientist, a follower of reason.

The Bahá'í teachings stress the fundamental oneness of science and religion. Such a view is implicit in 'Abdu'l-Bahá's statement, quoted above, that truth (or reality) is one. For if truth is indeed one, it is not possible for something to be scientifically false and reli-

---

[20] Bahá'u'lláh, *Hidden Words*, p. 20.

giously true. 'Abdu'l-Bahá expressed forcefully this idea in the following passage:

If religious beliefs and opinions are found contrary to the standards of science, they are mere superstitions and imaginations; for the antithesis of knowledge is ignorance, and the child of ignorance is superstition. Unquestionably there must be agreement between true religion and science. If a question be found contrary to reason, faith and belief in it are impossible, and there is no outcome but wavering and vacillation.[21]

Bahá'u'lláh affirmed that man's intelligence and reasoning powers are a gift from God. Science results from our systematic use of these God-given powers. The truths of science are thus *discovered* truths. The truths of prophetic religion are *revealed* truths, i.e., truths which God has shown to us without our having to discover them for ourselves. Bahá'ís consider that it is the same unique God who is both the Author of revelation and the Creator of the reality which science investigates, and hence there can be no contradiction between the two.

Contradictions between science and traditional religious beliefs are attributed to human fallibility and arrogance. Over the centuries, distortions have gradually infiltrated the doctrines of many religious systems and diluted the pure teachings originally given by the Manifestation who was their founder. With time these distortions become increasingly difficult to distinguish from the original message. Similarly, unsupported speculations of various schools of scientific thought have at times become more popular and influential than the results of rigorous scientific research, and have further blurred the picture.

'Abdu'l-Bahá affirmed that religion and science are, in fact, complementary:

Religion and science are the two wings upon which man's intelligence can soar into the heights, with which the human soul can progress. It is not possible to fly with one wing alone! Should a man try to fly with the wing of religion alone he would quickly fall into the quagmire of superstition, whilst on the other hand, with the wing of science alone he would also

---

[21] 'Abdu'l-Bahá, *The Promulgation of Universal Peace,* p. 181.

make no progress, but fall into the despairing slough of materialism. All religions of the present day have fallen into superstitious practices, out of harmony alike with the true principles of the teaching they represent and with the scientific discoveries of the time.[22]

In another passage from the same work, he affirmed that the result of the practice of the unity of science and religion will be a strengthening of religion rather than its weakening as is feared by many religious apologists:

When religion, shorn of its superstitions, traditions, and unintelligent dogmas, shows its conformity with science, then will there be a great unifying, cleansing force in the world which will sweep before it all wars, disagreements, discords and struggles—and then will mankind be united in the power of the Love of God.[23]

### THE EQUALITY OF MEN AND WOMEN

Whereas many religious and philosophical traditions teach that women should be subordinate to men in certain aspects of social life, or even that women are naturally inferior to men, the Bahá'í Faith teaches the equality of men and women. Both Bahá'u'lláh and 'Abdu'l-Bahá stressed that women have all the intellectual abilities of men and will in the future more clearly demonstrate their capacity for intellectual and scientific achievement in all aspects of human endeavor. The only reason why women have not yet reached this level of achievement is because they have not received adequate educational and social opportunities. Furthermore, men, because of greater physical strength, have physically dominated women through the ages and thus have prevented them from developing their true potential:

The world in the past has been ruled by force and man has dominated over woman by reason of his more forceful and aggressive qualities both of body and mind. But the scales are already shifting, force is losing its weight, and mental alertness, intuition, and the spiritual qualities of love and service, in which woman is strong, are gaining ascendancy. Hence the new age will be an age less masculine and more permeated with the femi-

---

[22] 'Abdu'l-Bahá, *Paris Talks*, p. 143.
[23] 'Abdu'l-Bahá, *Paris Talks*, p. 146.

nine ideals, or, to speak more exactly, will be an age in which the masculine and feminine elements of civilization will be more properly balanced.[24]

An important aspect of world unity will be the attainment of a greater balance between feminine and masculine influences on society. In fact, it will be largely as a result of this greater feminine influence that war will be eliminated and permanent peace attained:

> In past ages humanity has been defective and inefficient because it has been incomplete. War and its ravages have blighted the world; the education of woman will be a mighty step toward its abolition and ending, for she will use her whole influence against war. . . . In truth, she will be the greatest factor in establishing universal peace and international arbitration. Assuredly, woman will abolish warfare among mankind.[25]

## UNIVERSAL EDUCATION

As with many other themes in his teachings, Bahá'u'lláh provided practical guidelines to his call for equality of opportunity between the sexes. People are urged to assure the education of all children. If, however, financial or other family difficulties prevent this in some instances, and if the community cannot meet the need, preference must unhesitatingly be given to the education of female children. This accomplishes two objectives. It assists women to overcome the handicap of past inequalities. It also assures that, since mothers are the first teachers in society, the next generation will derive the greatest possible benefit from whatever education a family or community can provide.

## ECONOMIC JUSTICE: ABOLISHING THE EXTREMES OF POVERTY AND WEALTH

The unity of humankind foreseen by Bahá'u'lláh is unity based on justice. One of the most striking examples of injustice in the world today is the grave imbalance in economic and material condi-

---

[24] 'Abdu'l-Bahá, cited in *Star of the West,* vol. 9, no. 7, p. 87.
[25] 'Abdu'l-Bahá, *The Promulgation of Universal Peace,* p. 108.

tions. A relatively small percentage of humankind has immense wealth. This minority maintains essential control over the means of production and distribution, while the majority of the world's population lives in dire poverty and misery. This imbalance exists both within nations and between nations; some highly industrialized nations hold immense wealth, while others remain deprived and undeveloped. Moreover, the gap that separates rich and poor continues to widen each year, which indicates that existing economic systems are incapable of restoring a just balance. Bahá'u'lláh asserted that economic injustice is a moral evil and as such is condemned by God. 'Abdu'l-Bahá wrote, "When we see poverty allowed to reach a condition of starvation, it is a sure sign that somewhere we shall find tyranny."[26]

In *The Hidden Words,* Bahá'u'lláh addressed the perpetrators of tyranny in these terms:

O OPPRESSORS ON EARTH!
Withdraw your hands from tyranny, for I have pledged Myself not to forgive any man's injustice.[27]

Speaking specifically of economic injustice, he said:

O CHILDREN OF DUST!
Tell the rich of the midnight sighing of the poor, lest heedlessness lead them into the path of destruction, and deprive them of the Tree of Wealth.[28]

One of the basic causes of economic injustice is excessive and wasteful competition. Although limited competition no doubt served as a useful stimulus to production during the period of history when means of production were less developed, cooperation must now replace it. The human and material resources at our disposal must be used for the long-term good of all, not for the short-term profit of a few. This can be done only if cooperation replaces competition as the basis of organized economic activity.

Cooperation must occur at all levels of the economy. 'Abdu'l-

26 'Abdu'l-Bahá, *Paris Talks,* p. 153.
27 Bahá'u'lláh, *Hidden Words,* p. 44.
28 Bahá'u'lláh, *Hidden Words,* p. 39.

Bahá explained that even a single enterprise should reflect the essential partnership of workers and owners. Specifically, the workers in an enterprise should all share in the profits of the enterprise: each worker should receive his salary plus a fixed percentage of the profits. In this way, both the workers and the owners are engaged in a cooperative venture in which conflict of interest is eliminated. The present system in which all profit goes to the owners creates conflict between owners and workers, leading to economic imbalance, injustice, and often exploitation.

Concerning competition and power-seeking, Bahá'u'lláh wrote that:

Ever since the seeking of preference and distinction came into play, the world hath been laid waste. It hath become desolate. . . . Indeed, man is noble, inasmuch as each one is a repository of the signs of God. Nevertheless to regard oneself as superior in knowledge, learning or virtue, or to exalt oneself or seek preference, is a grievous transgression.[29]

'Abdu'l-Bahá said that cooperation gives life to society just as the life of an organism is maintained by the cooperation of the various elements of which it is composed:

the base of life is this mutual aid and helpfulness, and the cause of destruction and non-existence would be the interruption of this mutual assistance. The more the world aspires to civilization the more this important matter of cooperation becomes manifest.[30]

Within the framework of an economic system based on cooperation, the Bahá'í teachings accept the idea of private ownership of property and the need for private economic initiative. Moreover, the economic principles taught by Bahá'u'lláh do not imply that all individuals should receive the same income. There are natural differences in human needs and capacities, and some categories of service to society (education, for example) merit greater recompense than others.

However, all degrees of income should be established within

---

[29] Bahá'u'lláh, cited in a letter from the Universal House of Justice dated March 27, 1978, *The Continental Boards of Counselors*, p. 60.

[30] Bahá'u'lláh and 'Abdu'l-Bahá, *Divine Art of Living*, p. 108.

absolute limits. There must be, on the one hand, a minimum income level that meets the basic needs for human well-being and of which all are assured. If, for whatever reason (incapacity or other misfortune), the revenue of a given individual is inadequate to meet his recognized needs, he would be compensated from the public treasury. On the other hand, there should be an absolute maximum income level. Through progressive taxation and other measures, an individual would be prevented from accumulating wealth beyond this level. According to explicit statements of 'Abdu'l-Bahá, "millionaires" would not exist in a society based on Bahá'í principles because it would be impossible to accumulate vast and unnecessary wealth.

Certain differences in salaries would continue to exist in order to enable society to encourage the efforts of those (such as doctors or farmers) whose services are especially vital to the welfare of the community; but these differences would be established within well-defined absolute limits in order to guarantee that no one would suffer deprivation and that no one would accumulate excessive wealth. Thus Bahá'í economic teachings contain some elements in common with the various existing systems, but they envision a new and unique economic order based on a just distribution of goods and services and which, in its global scope, has no known equivalent.[31]

## THE SPIRITUAL FOUNDATION OF SOCIETY

In discussing economic and social questions, Bahá'u'lláh and 'Abdu'l-Bahá stressed that the reorganization of economic activity to reduce conflict of interest is only part of the solution. The ultimate root of economic injustice is human greed. Thus attitudes

---

[31] A detailed discussion of the Bahá'í position on economic questions is beyond the scope of the present work. The interested reader is referred to 'Abdu'l-Bahá's statements on the subject. See 'Abdu'l-Bahá, *Promulgation of Universal Peace*, pp. 107, 216–217, 238–239; *Paris Talks*, pp. 151–154; *'Abdu'l-Bahá in Canada*, pp. 31–36; Bahá'u'lláh & 'Abdu'l-Bahá, *Bahá'í World Faith*, p. 288; Gregory C. Dahl, "Economics & the Bahá'í Teachings" in *World Order*, Vol. 10, no. 1, 1975, p. 19; W. S. Hatcher, "Economics and Moral Values" in *World Order*, Vol. 9, no. 2, 1974, pp. 14–27.

must also change in a fundamental way. If individuals remain self-ish, immature, greedy, and unspiritual, even the most perfect economic scheme will not work. A satisfactory solution to the world's present economic calamity lies in a profound change of heart and mind which only religion can produce: "The fundamentals of the whole economic condition are divine in nature and are associated with the world of the heart and spirit."[32]

This principle is seen as valid not only for economics, but for the whole range of human activities and problems. The Bahá'í teachings insist that man's fundamental nature is spiritual, and that there can be no lasting solution to any human problem that does not take this fact into account. Everything is ultimately related to the spiritual purpose of human existence, which is the knowledge and love of God, and the development of spiritual qualities and virtues.

This is why Bahá'u'lláh and 'Abdu'l-Bahá provided guidance covering such a broad scope of human activities. There can be no sharp division drawn between the secular and the religious aspects of life. All of life must be lived from the spiritual perspective if it is to be lived successfully.

Since religion, represented by the progressive revelation of God to man, has the spiritual dimension of man as its special focus, it follows that only true religion can form the basis of society, and all purely human attempts to solve the world's problems without reference to religion and the will of God for man are doomed to failure. In this conection, Shoghi Effendi wrote:

Humanity . . . has, alas, strayed too far and suffered too great a decline to be redeemed through the unaided efforts of the best among its recognized rulers and statesmen—however disinterested their motives, however concerted their action. . . . No scheme which the calculations of the highest statesmanship may yet devise; no doctrine which the most distinguished exponents of economic theory may hope to advance; no principle which the most ardent of moralists may strive to inculcate, can provide, in the last resort, adequate foundations upon which the future of a distracted world can be built.[33]

---

[32] 'Abdu'l-Bahá, *The Promulgation of Universal Peace,* p. 238.
[33] Shoghi Effendi, *World Order of Bahá'u'lláh,* pp. 33–34.

### AN AUXILIARY INTERNATIONAL LANGUAGE

The multiplicity of languages that characterizes the modern world is a major impediment to world unity. On the level of practical communication, the existence of so many different language groups cuts the free flow of information and makes it difficult for the average unilingual individual to obtain a universal perspective on world events. There is also the tendency on the part of a given group or nation to be attached to its language and literature and subsequently to consider its own as superior to that of other peoples. This linguistic chauvinism frequently leads to conflict.

It is therefore not surprising that Bahá'u'lláh's prescription for the unification of humankind included the adoption of a universal auxiliary language. He urged that one single language be taught as a second language in all the school systems of the world. Thus, in one generation, everyone would learn his or her mother tongue plus the universal language. This world language could either be an invented one, such as Esperanto, or an existing natural language. The advantage of a natural language is that a certain portion of the world's people may already have learned to speak it. However, an invented language would have the advantage of being emotionally neutral and of allowing for a more simplified and regular grammar.[34]

Bahá'ís are committed to the principle of establishing such a universal auxiliary language, but not to one specific language over any other, whether natural or invented. The choice of the language to be used would be made by an international committee of experts and ratified by the nations of the world.

---

[34] There is an interesting historical connection between the Bahá'í Faith and Esperanto, the language invented by Dr. Zamenhof. Dr. Zamenhof's daughter, Lydia, was an active member of the Bahá'í Faith, and 'Abdu'l-Bahá praised her father for his accomplishment. While never stating that Esperanto would become the universal language, 'Abdu'l-Bahá did say that it would significantly aid the cause of world unity. At the very least, the successful invention of a viable language like Esperanto shows that such a thing is possible, and thus that humankind is not limited to making a choice from among the existing natural languages alone. This fact may serve to decrease resistance to the idea of a universal language, regardless of what language, natural or constructed, may ultimately be chosen by the nations of the world.

Bahá'u'lláh stressed that the universal language would be an auxiliary one, i.e., that it would not suppress existing natural languages. The concept of unity in diversity must be applied to differences of language in the same way as it is applied to other differences. Since the pressures for the assimilation of minority linguistic groups come from the natural aggrandizement of majority language groups, the existence of a universal auxiliary language would help to preserve minority languages and thus minority cultural patterns.[35]

## THE TWO ASPECTS OF REVELATION

Fundamental to an understanding of all Bahá'í teachings is a grasp of the role that revelation plays in human history. In their discussion of the concept of progressive revelation, Bahá'u'lláh and 'Abdu'l-Bahá explained that each revelation has two fundamental purposes. First, each serves in a general way to increase our knowledge of God and of God's Will for us, our knowledge of others, and our knowledge of ourselves. But each revelation comes at a particular time and place in social evolution, a time when humanity is confronted with particular problems and has specific needs. Thus each revelation has the secondary purpose of providing humankind with practical guidance and the knowledge necessary to meet current challenges.

The only real difference between the two purposes is that one is general and the other specific. In the first instance, the Manifestation addresses mankind on such universal themes and perennial aspects of life as suffering, birth, death, fear, and love. Experiences in these areas are the elements of every human life, in whatever time or place it is lived. In the second instance, the Manifestation addresses humankind within the dimensions of a given time and place.

---

[35] In this way, Bahá'ís feel that a universal auxiliary language will foster unity by facilitating communication, while, at the same time, it will give universal access to the cultural wealth of minority cultures—and, in fact, will preserve and protect them. This is a typical example of Bahá'u'lláh's way of promoting unity in diversity rather than mere uniformity for the sake of convenience.

Therefore, in order to fill the requirements of each new age, the guiding ordinances of each revelation have two aspects: (1) the universal (or eternal); and (2) the social (or temporary). 'Abdu'l-Bahá described these two aspects of religion as follows:

> The divine religions embody two kinds of ordinances. First there are those which constitute essential, or spiritual, teachings of the Word of God. These are faith in God, the acquirement of the virtues which characterize perfect manhood, praiseworthy moralities, the acquisition of the bestowals and bounties emanating from the divine effulgences—in brief, the ordinances which conern the realm of morals and ethics. This is the fundamental aspect of the religion of God, and this is of the highest importance because knowledge of God is the fundamental requirement of man. . . . This is the essential foundation of all the divine religions, the reality itself, common to all. . . .
>
> Second, there are laws and ordinances which are temporary and nonessential. These concern human transactions and relations. They are accidental and subject to change according to the exigencies of time and place. These ordinances are neither permanent nor fundamental. . . . The accidental or nonessential laws which regulate the transactions of the social body and everyday affairs of life are changeable and subject to abrogation.[36]

One of the major sources of conflict between different religious systems is the failure of their followers to distinguish between the two aspects of revelation. Since social laws are subject to change as humanity evolves, believers are bound to become upset if they regard these laws as unchanging absolutes. Jesus, for example, changed a number of Jewish social laws, to the great distress of the orthodox followers of the Mosaic dispensation.

Some of the Bahá'í principles discussed in the preceding sections of this chapter fall into the category of social teachings. According to Bahá'í belief, the single most important social problem of our age is disunity. Principles such as the establishment of a universal auxiliary language are clearly intended as practical aids to the establishment of world unity.

However, unity is an expression of love, while disunity is a

---

[36] 'Abdu'l-Bahá, *The Promulgation of Universal Peace*, pp. 403–405.

form of hatred. 'Abdu'l-Bahá has said that love is the fundamental teaching given by God to humanity and is a universal principle common to all religions. Thus the many social problems related to disunity derive, in the final analysis, from a lack of spirituality. Bahá'ís therefore regard many of the principles taught by Bahá-'u'lláh (e.g., the equality of men and women) both as expressions of universal spiritual truths and also as essential factors in the solution of current social problems.

# 6. God, His Manifestations, and Man

On the basis of the discussion of the Bahá'í teachings in the previous chapter, the present chapter will look more deeply at what Bahá'u'lláh taught about the great concerns that lie at the heart of all religions: What does the Bahá'í Faith see as the purpose of human existence? What is the true nature of man and what role does religion play in his spiritual development? What is "good" and what is "evil"? What are man's responsibilities to God and what is the spiritual meaning of life? Finally, what is really meant by the term "Manifestation of God" and how does this Bahá'í concept relate to ideas of divine revelation with which one may be familiar from the teachings of other major faiths?

## THE BAHÁ'Í CONCEPTION OF HUMAN NATURE

Many people live their lives without ever reflecting on life itself or its meaning for them. Their lives may be full of activities. They may marry, have children, run a business, or become scientists or musicians, without ever obtaining any degree of understanding of why they do these things. Their lives have no overall purpose to give meaning to separate events, and they may have no clear idea of their own nature or identity, of who they really are.

Bahá'u'lláh taught that only true religion can give purpose to human existence. If there were no Creator, if man were simply the chance produce of a thermodynamic system, as many in the world today assert, there would be no purpose in life. Each individual human being would represent the temporary material existence of a conscious animal who tries to move through his or her brief life with as much pleasure and as little pain and suffering as possible.

It is only in relation to the Creator, and the purpose which that Creator has fixed for his creatures, that human existence has any meaning. Bahá'u'lláh described God's purpose for man in the following way:

> The purpose of God in creating man hath been, and will ever be, to enable him to know his Creator and to attain His Presence. To this most excellent aim, this supreme objective, all the heavenly Books and the divinely-revealed and weighty Scriptures unequivocally bear witness.[1]

Life should be seen as an eternal process of joyous spiritual discovery and growth: in the beginning stages of earthly life, the individual undergoes a period of training and education which, if it is successful, gives him the basic intellectual and spiritual tools necessary for continued growth. When one attains physical maturity in adulthood, he becomes responsible for his further progress, which now depends entirely on the efforts he himself makes. Through the daily struggles of material existence, one gradually deepens his understanding of the spiritual principles underlying reality, and this understanding enables him to relate more effectively to himself, to others, and to God. After physical death, the individual continues to grow and develop in the spiritual world, which is greater than the physical world, just as the physical world is greater than the world we inhabit while in our mother's womb.

This last statement is based on the Bahá'í concept of the soul and of life after physical death. According to the Bahá'í teachings, man's true nature is spiritual. Beyond the physical body, each human being has a rational soul, created by God. This soul is a nonmaterial entity, which does not depend on the body. Rather, the body serves as its vehicle in the physical world. The soul of an individual comes into being at the moment the physical body is conceived and continues to exist after the death of the physical body. The soul (also called the spirit) of the individual is the seat or locus of his personality, self, and consciousness.

The evolution or development of the soul and its capacities is

---

[1] Bahá'u'lláh, *Gleanings,* p. 70.

the basic purpose of human existence. This evolution is towards God and its motive force is knowledge of God and love for him. As we learn about God, our love for him increases; and this, in turn, enables us to attain a closer communion with our Creator. Also, as we draw closer to God, our character becomes more refined and our actions reflect more and more the attributes and qualities of God.

Bahá'u'lláh taught that this potential to reflect the attributes of God is the soul's essential reality. It is the meaning of man being created "in the image of God." The divine qualities are not external to the soul. They are latent within it, just as the color, the fragrance, and the vitality of a flower are latent within the seed. They need only to be developed. In the words of Bahá'u'lláh:

Upon the inmost reality of each and every created thing He [God] hath shed the light of one of His names, and made it a recipient of the glory of one of His attributes. Upon the reality of man, however, He hath focused the radiance of all His names and attributes, and made it a mirror of His own self. Alone of all created things man hath been singled out for so great a favour, so enduring a bounty.[2]

The Bahá'í writings refer to the gradual evolution or development of the individual soul as "spiritual progress." Spiritual progress means acquiring the capacity to act in conformity with the Will of God and to express the attributes and spirit of God in one's dealings with one's self and with other human beings. Bahá'u'lláh teaches that the only true and enduring happiness for man lies in the pursuit of spiritual development.

A person who has become aware of his spiritual nature and who consciously strives to progress spiritually is called a "seeker" by Bahá'u'lláh. Bahá'u'lláh described some of the qualities of the true seeker:

That seeker must, at all times, put his trust in God, must renounce the peoples of the earth, must detach himself from the world of dust, and cleave unto Him Who is the Lord of Lords. He must never seek to exalt himself above any one, must wash away from the tablet of his heart every

---

[2] Bahá'u'lláh, Gleanings, p. 65.

trace of pride and vain-glory, must cling unto patience and resignation, observe silence and refrain from idle talk. For the tongue is a smoldering fire, and excess of speech a deadly poison. Material fire consumeth the body, whereas the fire of the tongue devoureth both heart and soul. The force of the former lasteth but for a time, whilst the effects of the latter endureth a century.

That seeker should, also, regard backbiting as grievous error, and keep himself aloof from its dominion, inasmuch as backbiting quencheth the light of the heart, and extinguisheth the life of the soul. He should be content with little, and be freed from all inordinate desire. He should treasure the companionship of them that have renounced the world, and regard avoidance of boastful and worldly people a precious benefit. At the dawn of every day he should commune with God, and with all his soul, persevere in the quest of his Beloved. . . . He should not wish for others that which he doth not wish for himself, nor promise that which he doth not fulfill. . . . He should forgive the sinful, and never despise his low estate, for none knoweth what his own end shall be. How often hath a sinner attained, at the hour of death, to the essence of faith, and quaffing the immortal draught, hath taken his flight unto the Concourse of high! And how often hath a devout believer, at the hour of his soul's ascension, been so changed as to fall into the nethermost fire!

Our purpose in revealing these convincing and weighty utterances is to impress upon the seeker that he should regard all else beside God as transient, and count all things save Him, Who is the Object of all adoration, as utter nothingness.

These are among the attributes of the exalted, and constitute the hallmark of the spiritually-minded. . . . When the detached wayfarer and sincere seeker hath fulfilled these essential conditions, then and only then can he be called a true seeker.[3]

Bahá'u'lláh explained that the fundamental, spiritual role of religion is to enable man to achieve a true understanding of his own nature and of God's Will and purpose for him. The spiritual teachings sent down to man by God through the Manifestations serve to guide us to a proper comprehension of the spiritual dynamics of life. These principles enable us to understand the laws of existence. Moreover, the very efforts we must make to conform to the teach-

---

[3] Bahá'u'lláh, *Gleanings,* pp. 264–266.

ings of the Manifestations serve to develop our spiritual capacities. For example, when one makes an effort to rid oneself of prejudice and superstition in response to the teachings of Bahá'u'lláh, the result is an increased knowledge of and love for other human beings, and this, in turn, helps the individual to live life more effectively.

Bahá'u'lláh stressed that, without the coming of the Manifestations and their revelation of God's laws and teachings, we would not be able to grow and develop spiritually. The spiritual meaning of life would remain hidden from us, even if we made great efforts to discover it. This is why revealed religion is seen by Bahá'ís as the necessary key to successful spiritual living.

Speaking of the Manifestations, and their influence on human spiritual development, Bahá'u'lláh said:

Through the Teachings of the Day Star of Truth [i.e. the Manifestation] every man will advance and develop until he attaineth the station at which he can manifest all the potential forces with which his inmost true self hath been endowed. It is for this very purpose that in every age and dispensation, the Prophets of God and His chosen Ones have appeared amongst men, and have evinced such power as is born of God and such might, as only the Eternal can reveal.[4]

Since religion has a social dimension, Bahá'ís feel that prolonged withdrawal from the world and from contact with society and one's fellow human beings is usually not necessary or helpful to spiritual growth (although a temporary withdrawal from time to time may be legitimate and healthy). Because we are social beings, our greatest progress is made through living in association with others. Indeed, close association with others in the spirit of loving service and cooperation is essential to the process of spiritual growth.

Bahá'u'lláh related God's purpose for man to the two aspects of religion, the spiritual and the social:

God's purpose in sending His Prophets unto men is twofold. The first is to liberate the children of men from the darkness of ignorance, and guide them to the light of true understanding. The second is to ensure the peace

---

[4] Bahá'u'lláh, *Gleanings,* p. 68.

and tranquillity of mankind, and provide all the means by which they can be established.[5]

In other words, mankind's social development, if properly carried out, should be a collective expression of his spiritual development:

All men have been created to carry forward an ever-advancing civilization. The Almighty beareth Me witness: To act like the beasts of the field is unworthy of man. Those virtues that befit his dignity are forbearance, mercy, compassion and loving-kindness towards all the peoples and kindreds of the earth.[6]

Concerning the soul or spirit of man and its relationship to the physical body, Bahá'u'lláh explained:

Know thou that the soul of man is exalted above, and is independent of all infirmities of body or mind. That a sick person showeth signs of weakness is due to the hindrances that interpose themselves between his soul and his body, for the soul itself remaineth unaffected by any bodily ailments. . . . When it leaveth the body, however, it will evince such ascendancy, and reveal such influence as no force on earth can equal . . . consider the sun which hath been obscured by the clouds. Observe how its splendor appeareth to have diminished, when in reality the source of that light hath remained unchanged. The soul of man should be likened unto this sun, and all things on earth should be regarded as his body. So long as no external impediment interveneth between them, the body will, in its entirety, continue to reflect the light of the soul, and to be sustained by its power. As soon as, however, a veil interposeth itself between them, the brightness of the light seemeth to lessen. . . . The soul of man is the sun by which his body is illumined, and from which it draweth its sustenance, and should be so regarded.[7]

The soul not only continues to live after the physical death of the human body, but is, in fact, immortal. Bahá'u'lláh wrote:

Know thou of a truth that the soul, after its separation from the body, will continue to progress until it attaineth the presence of God, in a state

---

[5] Bahá'u'lláh, *Gleanings,* pp. 79–80.
[6] Bahá'u'lláh, *Gleanings,* p. 215.
[7] Bahá'u'lláh, *Gleanings,* pp. 153–155.

and condition which neither the revolution of ages and centuries, nor the changes and chances of this world, can alter. It will endure as long as the Kingdom of God, His sovereignty, His dominion and power will endure.[8]

In commenting on the immortality of the rational soul, 'Abdu'l-Bahá explained that everything in creation which is composed of elements is subject to decomposition:

The soul is not a combination of elements, it is not composed of many atoms, it is of one indivisible substance and therefore eternal. It is entirely out of the order of the physical creation; it is immortal![9]

Bahá'u'lláh taught that man has no existence previous to his life here on earth. Neither is the soul reborn several times in different bodies. He explained, rather, that the soul's evolution is always towards God and away from the material world. A human being spends nine months in the womb in preparation for entry into this physical life. During that nine-month period, the fetus acquires the physical tools (e.g., eyes, limbs, and so forth) necessary for existence in this world. Similarly, this physical world is like a womb for entry into the spiritual world. Our time here is thus a period of preparation during which we are to acquire the spiritual and intellectual tools necessary for life in the next world.

The crucial difference is that, whereas physical development in the mother's womb is involuntary, spiritual and intellectual development in this world depend strictly on conscious individual effort:

The incomparable Creator hath created all men from one same substance, and hath exalted their reality above the rest of His creatures. Success or failure, gain or loss, must, therefore, depend upon man's own exertions. The more he striveth, the greater will be his progress.[10]

The Bahá'í writings often speak of the bounty or grace of God towards humanity, but explain that an appropriate human response is always necessary for God's grace and mercy to penetrate the

[8] Bahá'u'lláh, *Gleanings*, pp. 155–156.
[9] 'Abdu'l-Bahá, *Paris Talks*, p. 91.
[10] Bahá'u'lláh, *Gleanings*, pp. 81–82.

human soul and bring about any genuine change within us: "No matter how strong the measure of Divine grace, unless supplemented by personal, sustained and intelligent effort, it cannot become fully effective and be of any real and abiding advantage."[11] Thus, in the Bahá'í conception, salvation is not simply a unidirectional gift from God to us, but is rather a dialogue, a collaborative venture initiated by God but requiring vigorous and intelligent human participation.

Since man's basic nature is spiritual, his essential capacities are the capacities of his soul. In other words, one's personality, one's basic intellectual and spiritual faculties, reside in the soul, even though they are expressed through the instrumentality of the body for the short duration of earthly life. Some of the faculties that Bahá'u'lláh mentioned as capacities of the soul are (1) the mind, which represents the capacity for rational thought and intellectual investigation; (2) the will, which represents the capacity for self-initiated action; and (3) the "heart," or the capacity for conscious, deliberate, self-sacrificing love (sometimes called altruism).

These faculties are unique to the human species. Animal and other forms of life do not have a rational soul. Animal life expresses a form of intelligence and affectivity, but it does not express the consciousness or the self-awareness of man. Animals are bound to act in certain ways because of the instincts that form part of their physical make-up, but they do not have the capacities of conscious thought, of rational investigation, or of will that characterize a human being. An animal does not have a conscious sense of the purpose of its existence.

The Bahá'í Faith explicitly teaches, however, that the physical race of man has indeed gradually evolved, passing from lower to higher forms until it attained the present, mature human form. The earth has been the matrix for the formation of the human race, just as the mother's womb is the matrix for the formation of the individual human being. In the words of 'Abdu'l-Bahá:

. . . man, in the beginning of his existence and in the womb of the earth,

---

[11] Shoghi Effendi, quoted in William Hatcher, *The Concept of Spirituality*, p. 9.

like the embryo in the womb of the mother, gradually grew and developed, and passed from one form to another, from one shape to another, until he appeared with this beauty and perfection, this force and this power. It is certain that in the beginning he had not this loveliness and grace and elegance, and that he only by degrees attained this shape, this form, this beauty, and this grace.[12]

'Abdu'l-Bahá nevertheless stressed that, throughout its long process of physical evolution, the human race has always been a species distinct from animal species:

. . . the embryo passes through different states and traverses numerous degrees . . . until the signs of reason and maturity appear. And in the same way, man's existence on this earth, from the beginning until it reaches this state, form and condition, necessarily lasts a long time, and goes through many degrees. . . . But from the beginning of man's existence he is a distinct species. In the same way, the embryo of man in the womb of the mother was at first in a strange form; then this body passes from shape to shape, from state to state, from form to form, until it appears in utmost beauty and perfection. But even when in the womb of the mother and in this strange form, entirely different from his present form and figure, he is the embryo of the superior species, and not of the animal; his species and essence undergo no change.[13]

Thus, even in his lower forms of physical existence when he resembled some animals in superficial ways, man was a distinct and superior physical species, as well as being distinguished by the existence of the nonmaterial rational soul which, as has been explained, is unique to man.

However, man's physical body is composed of elements, and functions according to the same physiological principals as does that of an animal. During our earthly life we are subject to much the same physical desires and sufferings as an animal: hunger, sexual drive, fear, pain, anger, physical and mental illness, and so forth. This produces a creative tension within us: our physical needs and desires push us at times to act like animals, while our spiritual nature draws us towards very different goals. Bahá'u'lláh

[12] 'Abdu'l-Bahá, *Some Answered Questions,* p. 183 (1981 ed.).
[13] 'Abdu'l-Bahá, *Some Answered Questions,* pp. 183–184 (1981 ed.).

explained that the struggle to gain control of physical desires and to channel them creatively is a necessary part of man's growth process. It is by harmonizing our spiritual and physical natures that we achieve completeness.

If we do not make the effort to adapt our physical resources to our spiritual nature, we can be taken over and dominated by physical passions. We can become slaves to one or another of our appetites and thereby lose much of our capacity to act in accordance with our spiritual nature. For example, a man who is addicted to morphine or alcohol is not really able to develop his spiritual capacities until he frees himself from his addiction. Similarly, intense devotion to purely materialistic pursuits can rob a human being of the energy and time needed to cultivate his essential, spiritual nature.

In contrast to a number of other religious doctrines and philosophies, the Bahá'í Faith does not teach that man's physical desires are "evil" or "bad." Everything in God's creation is regarded as essentially and fundamentally good. In fact, the very purpose of the human body and its physical faculties is to serve as a proper vehicle for the development of the soul. As the energies of the body are gradually brought under the conscious control of the soul, they become instruments for the expression of spiritual qualities. It is only undisciplined physical passions that become causes of harm, and hinder spiritual progress.

For example, the human sexual urge is considered to be a gift from God. Its disciplined expression within the legitimate bonds of marriage can be a powerful expression of the spiritual quality of love. However, the same sexual urge, if misused, can lead one into perverse, wasteful, and even destructive actions.

Since the body is the vehicle of the rational soul in this life on earth, it is important to maintain and care for it. Bahá'u'lláh strongly discouraged any form of asceticism or extreme self-denial. His emphasis was on healthy discipline. Therefore the Bahá'í writings contain a number of practical laws relating to the care of the human body: proper nutrition, regular bathing, and so forth. Underlying these, as with many other aspects of Bahá'í belief, is the principle of moderation: things that are beneficial when kept within the limits of moderation become harmful when taken to extremes.

The Bahá'í writings acknowledge explicitly that certain physical factors beyond the control of the individual, such as genetic weaknesses, or inadequate childhood nutrition, can have a significant effect on one's development during his earthly life. But such material influences are not permanent, and they have no power in themselves to harm or damage the soul. At most, they can only retard temporarily the spiritual growth process, and even this effect can be counterbalanced by a subsequent burst of more rapid development. Indeed, the Bahá'í writings explain that it is often in the individual's determined and courageous struggle against physical, emotional, and mental handicaps that the greatest spiritual growth occurs, and the individual may come to view his handicaps as blessings in disguise that have, ultimately, helped him grow spiritually. Thus, admitting that physical conditions can affect, temporarily but significantly, the spiritual growth process is far from believing, as many philosophical materialists do, that we are totally determined by some combination of genetic and environmental physical factors:

. . . movement is essential to all existence. All material things progress to a certain point, then begin to decline. This is the law which governs the whole physical creation. . . . But with the human soul, there is no decline. Its only movement is toward perfection; growth and progress alone constitute the motion of the soul. . . .

The world of mortality is a world of contradictions, of opposites; motion being compulsory everything must either go forward or retreat. In the realm of spirit there is no retreat possible, all movement is bound to be towards a perfect state.[14]

The theme of growth through struggle and suffering occurs at several places in the Bahá'í writings. Although many of our sufferings result from careless living and are therefore potentially avoid-

---

[14] 'Abdúl-Bahá, *Paris Talks,* pp. 89–90. However, there are inherent limits to human spiritual development, whether in this world or the next. The Bahá'í writings affirm that man can approach but never attain a state of absolute perfection. See our discussion below, in particular the passage from the Bahá'í writings cited in note 32 of this chapter.

able, a certain amount of suffering is necessary in any growth process. Indeed, we understand and accept that suffering and self-sacrifice are essential components of achieving material or intellectual success. Thus, we should not be surprised that the even more important endeavor of achieving spiritual growth might also involve those same elements:

Everything of importance in this world demands the close attention of its seeker. The one in pursuit of anything must undergo difficulties and hardships until the object in view is attained and the great success is obtained. This is the case of things pertaining to the world. How much higher is that which concerns the Supreme Concourse![15]

This brings us to the Bahá'í concept of the relationship between good and evil in man. 'Abdul'l-Bahá describes it thus:

In creation there is no evil, all is good. Certain qualities and natures innate in some men and apparently blameworthy are not so in reality. For example, from the beginning of his life you can see in a nursing child the signs of greed, of anger, and of temper. Then, it may be said, good and evil are innate in the reality of man, and this is contrary to the pure goodness of nature and creation. The answer to this is that greed, which is to ask for something more, is a praiseworthy quality provided that it is used suitably. So, if a man is greedy to acquire science and knowledge, or to become compassionate, generous, and just, it is most praiseworthy. If he exercises his anger and wrath against the bloodthirsty tyrants who are like ferocious beasts, it is very praiseworthy; but if he does not use these qualities in a right way, they are blameworthy. . . . It is the same with all the natural qualities of man, which constitute the capital of life; if they be used and displayed in an unlawful way, they become blameworthy. Therefore, it is clear that creation is purely good.[16]

The Bahá'í Faith does not therefore accept the concept of "original sin" or any related doctrine which considers that people are basically evil or have intrinsically evil elements in their nature. All the forces and faculties within us are God-given and thus potentially beneficial to our spiritual development. In the same way, the Bahá'í

---

[15] 'Abdul-Bahá, *Divine Art of Living,* p. 92.
[16] 'Abdu'l-Bahá, *Some Answered Questions,* p. 215 (1981 ed.).

teachings deny the existence of Satan, a devil, or an "evil force." Evil, it is explained, is the absence of good; darkness is the absence of light; cold is the absence of heat.[17] Just as the sun is the unique source of all life in a solar system, so ultimately is there only one force or power in the universe, the force we call God.

However, if a person, through his own God-given free will, turns away from this force or fails to make the necessary effort to develop his spiritual capacities, the result is imperfection. Both within the individual and in society, there will be what one might term "dark spots." These dark spots are imperfections, and 'Abdu'l-Bahá has said that "evil is imperfection."

If a tiger kills and eats another animal, this is not evil, because it is an expression of the tiger's natural instinct for survival. But if a person kills and eats a fellow human being, this same act may be considered evil because man is capable of doing otherwise. Such an act is not an expression of his true nature.

As relatively undeveloped creatures, we have certain intrinsic needs that demand satisfaction. These needs are partly physical and tangible and partly spiritual and intangible. It is God who has created us in this manner and placed us in this situation. Because God truly loves us, he has provided for the legitimate satisfaction of all our needs. But if, whether through simple ignorance or willful rebellion, we try to satisfy some of our needs in an illegitimate or unhealthy way, then we may distort our true nature and generate within ourselves new appetites incapable of genuine satisfaction:

. . . capacity is of two kinds: natural capacity and acquired capacity. The

---

[17] Bahá'u'lláh explained that references to Satan in the Scriptures of earlier religions are symbolic and should not be taken literally. Satan is the personification of man's lower nature which can destroy him if it is not brought into harmony with his spiritual nature. There is, in fact, a well-known philosophical problem concerning God's goodness and omnipotence and the possible existence of a Satan. This problem is discussed in some detail in both the writings of Bahá'u'lláh and 'Abdu'l-Bahá.

In the same way, heaven and hell are, Bahá'u'lláh taught, not literal places. Rather, they symbolize the psychological and spiritual states of being close to God or far from him. Heaven is the natural consequence of spiritual progress while hell represents the results of failure to progress spiritually.

first, which is the creation of God, is purely good—in the creation of God there is no evil; but the acquired capacity has become the cause of the appearance of evil. For example, God has created all men in such a manner and has given them such a constitution and such capacities that they are benefited by sugar and honey and harmed and destroyed by poison. This nature and constitution is innate, and God has given it equally to all mankind. But man begins little by little to accustom himself to poison by taking a small quantity each day, and gradually increasing it, until he reaches such a point that he cannot live without a gram of opium every day. The natural capacities are thus completely perverted. Observe how much the natural capacity and constitution can be changed, until by different habits and training they become entirely perverted. One does not criticize vicious people because of their innate capacities and nature, but rather for their acquired capacities and nature.[18]

Bahá'u'lláh said that pride, or self-centeredness, is one of the greatest hindrances to spiritual progress. Pride represents an exaggerated sense of one's own importance in the universe and leads to an attitude of superiority over others. The prideful person feels as though he is or ought to be in absolute control of his life and the circumstances surrounding it, and he seeks power and dominance over others because such power helps him maintain this illusion of superiority. Thus, pride is such a hindrance to spiritual growth because it impels the prideful individual on an endless quest to fulfill the expectations of his vainly-conceived and illusory self-concept.

In other words, the key to understanding Bahá'í morality and ethics is to be found in the Bahá'í notion of spiritual progress: that which is conducive to spiritual progress is good, and whatever tends to hinder spiritual progress is bad. Thus, from the Bahá'í viewpoint, learning "good" from "bad" (or "right" from "wrong") means attaining a degree of self-knowledge that permits us to know when something is helpful to our spiritual growth and when it is not.[19] And this knowledge can only be obtained through the teachings of the Manifestations.

---

[18] 'Abdu'l-Bahá, *Some Answered Questions,* pp. 214–215 (1981 ed.).

[19] In this connection, Bahá'u'lláh has said: " . . . man should know his own self and know those things which lead to loftiness or to baseness, to shame or to honor." (Bahá'u'lláh and 'Abdu'l-Bahá, *Bahá'í World Faith,* p. 167.)

Bahá'u'lláh repeatedly stressed that only revealed religion can save us from our imperfections. It is because God has sent his Manifestations to show us the path to spiritual development and to touch our hearts with the spirit of God's love that we are able to realize our true potential and make the effort to be united with God. This is the "salvation" that religion brings. It does not save us from the stain of some "original sin," nor does it protect us from some external evil force or devil. Rather, it delivers us from captivity to our own lower nature, a captivity that breeds private despair and threatens social destruction, and it shows us the path to a deep and satisfying happiness.

Indeed, the essential reason for such widespread unhappiness and terrible social conflict and crises in the world today is that mankind has turned away from true religion and spiritual principles. The only salvation in any age, Bahá'ís believe, is to turn again towards God, to accept his Manifestation for that day, and to follow his teachings. Bahá'u'lláh pointed out that, if we reflect deeply on the conditions of our existence, we must eventually realize and admit to ourselves that, in absolute terms, we possess nothing. Everything we are or have—our physical body and our rational soul—all comes from our Creator. Since God has freely given us so much, we have, in turn, an obligation to God. Bahá'u'lláh stated that man has two basic duties towards God:

> The first duty prescribed by God for His servants is the recognition of Him Who is the Day Spring of His Revelation and the Fountain of His laws, Who representeth the Godhead in both the Kingdom of His Cause and the world of creation [i.e. the Manifestation]. . . . It behoveth every one who reacheth this most sublime station, this summit of transcendent glory, to observe every ordinance of Him Who is the Desire of the world. These twin duties are inseparable. Neither is acceptable without the other.[20]

In another passage, Bahá'u'lláh reminded his followers that the duties which God has given to us are only for our benefit: God himself has no need of our worship or allegiance, for God is entirely

---

[20] Bahá'u'lláh, *Gleanings*, pp. 330–331.

self-sufficient and independent of all his creation. We can therefore be certain that everything God does is motivated uniquely by his pure love for us. There is no "self-interest" on the part of God:

Whatever duty Thou [God] hast prescribed unto Thy servants of extolling to the utmost Thy majesty and glory is but a token of Thy grace unto them, that they may be enabled to ascend unto the station conferred upon their own inmost being, the station of the knowledge of their own selves.[21]

In summary, the spiritual reason for our life on earth is to provide us with a training ground; our life is a period of growth during which we focus on the development of our innate spiritual and intellectual capacities. Because these capacities are faculties of our immortal soul, they are eternal, and we must make great efforts to develop them. But such efforts are worthwhile, since the soul is the only part of us which endures. Whatever promotes our spiritual development is good, and whatever hinders it is bad.

God has sent the Manifestations to teach us the true principles that govern our spiritual nature. In order to grow successfullly, we must turn to revealed religion and accept the teachings of the Manifestations. The result of this growth process is that the individual is able to reflect more completely the attributes of God and draw close to him. At the same time, the social principles taught by the Manifestations, if truly applied, help create a social milieu favorable to the spiritual growth process. Creating such a milieu is, from the spiritual viewpoint, the very purpose of society.

Bahá'u'lláh set before man the highest standard of morality and urged him to strive with all his might to attain it. Since God has given us a free will, we are, in the last analysis, responsible to God for our actions. God is just and does not require of any of us that of which we are not capable. At the same time, God is merciful and will always forgive any soul who is sincerely sorry for past misdeeds or errors.

In a poetic passage, Bahá'u'lláh described the actions of the moral individual and urged his followers to live accordingly:

---

[21] Bahá'u'lláh, *Gleanings,* pp. 4–5.

Be generous in prosperity, and thankful in adversity. Be worthy of the trust of thy neighbor, and look upon him with a bright and friendly face. Be a treasure to the poor, an admonisher to the rich, an answerer of the cry of the needy, a preserver of the sanctity of thy pledge. Be fair in thy judgment, and guarded in thy speech. Be unjust to no man, and show all meekness to all men. Be as a lamp unto them that walk in darkness, a joy to the sorrowful, a sea for the thirsty, a haven for the distressed, an upholder and defender of the victim of oppression. Let integrity and uprightness distinguish all thine acts. Be a home for the stranger, a balm to the suffering, a tower of strength for the fugitive. Be eyes to the blind, and a guiding light unto the feet of the erring. Be an ornament to the countenance of truth, a crown to the brow of fidelity, a pillar of the temple of righteousness, a breath of life to the body of mankind, an ensign of the hosts of justice, a luminary above the horizon of virtue, a dew to the soil of the human heart, an ark on the ocean of knowledge, a sun in the heaven of bounty, a gem on the diadem of wisdom, a shining light in the firmament of thy generation, a fruit upon the tree of humility.[22]

## THE MANIFESTATIONS

As we have already noted, the Bahá'í teachings hold that the motive force in all human development is the coming of the Manifestations or Prophets of God. There can be little disagreement that human history is strongly influenced by the founders of the world's great religions. The powerful impact on civilization of Jesus Christ, the Buddha, Moses, or Muhammad is seen not only in the cultural forms and value systems which arise from their works and teachings, but is also reflected in the effects that the example of their lives has on humankind. Even those who have not been believers or followers have neverthelsss acknowledged the profound influence of these figures on man's individual and collective life.

The realization of the extraordinary impact on human history of the founders of the major religions naturally leads to the philosophical question of their exact nature. This is one of the most controversial of all questions in the philosophy of religion, and many different answers have been given. On the one hand, the

---

[22] Bahá'u'lláh, *Gleanings,* p. 285.

religious founders have been viewed as human philosophers or great thinkers who have perhaps gone further or studied more profoundly than other philosophers of their age. On the other hand, they have been declared to be God or the incarnation of God. There have also been a multitude of theories that fall somewhere between these two extremes.[23]

It is thus not surprising that the Bahá'í writings deal extensively with this subject, which lies so close to the heart of religion. One of Bahá'u'lláh's major works, the *Kitáb-i-Íqán, (Book of Certitude),* sets out in some detail the Bahá'í concept of the nature of the Manifestations of God.

According to Bahá'u'lláh, all of the Manifestations of God have the same metaphysical nature and the same spiritual stature. There is absolute equality among them. No one of them is superior to another. Speaking of the Manifestations, he wrote:

These sanctified Mirrors, these Day Springs of ancient glory, are, one and all, the Exponents on earth of Him Who is the central Orb of the universe, its Essence and ultimate Purpose. From Him proceed their knowledge and power; from Him is derived their sovereignty. . . . By the revelation of these Gems of Divine virtue all the names and attributes of God, such as knowledge and power, sovereignty and dominion, mercy and wisdom, glory, bounty, and grace, are made manifest.

These attributes of God are not, and have never been, vouchsafed specially unto certain Prophets, and withheld from others. . . . That a certain attribute of God hath not been outwardly manifested by these Essences of Detachment doth in no wise imply that they who are the Day Springs of

---

[23] An objective discussion of this fundamental question of the nature of what Bahá'ís refer to as the Manifestation of God is made more difficult by traditional loyalties. Orthodox followers of each Manifestation have tended to claim some kind of uniqueness or superiority for the founder of their faith. For example, many Christians view Jesus Christ as God incarnate, consider Moses to be inferior to him in some way, and regard Muhammad as an imposter. A majority of orthodox Jews see Moses as the revelation of God to man and consider Jesus Christ to be a false prophet. Muslims consider both Moses and Jesus Christ to be valid prophets, but the majority reject the Buddha and the founders of other major faiths. For them, Muhammad was the last prophet whom God will send to man, and revelation of the Divine Will ended with the Qur'án.

God's attributes and the Treasuries of His holy names did not actually possess it.[24]

As mentioned in the discussion on the principle of the oneness of religions in chapter 5, Bahá'u'lláh explained that the differences which exist between the teachings of the various Manifestations of God are not due to any differences in stature or level of importance, but only to the varying needs and capacities of the civilizations to which they appeared:

These . . . mighty systems, have proceeded from one Source, and are the rays of one Light. That they differ one from another is to be attributed to the varying requirements of the ages in which they were promulgated.[25]

In the strongest terms, he warned people not to take the variations in the teachings and personalities of the Manifestations to imply a difference in their statures:

Beware, O believers in the Unity of God, lest ye be tempted to make any distinction between any of the Manifestations of His Cause, or to discriminate against the signs that have accompanied and proclaimed their Revelation. This indeed is the true meaning of Divine unity. . . . Be ye assured, moreover, that the works and acts of each and every one of these Manifestations of God . . . are all ordained by God, and are a reflection of His will and Purpose. Whoso maketh the slightest possible difference between their persons, their words, their messages, their acts and manners, hath indeed disbelieved in God, hath repudiated His signs and betrayed the Cause of His Messengers.[26]

However, the Bahá'í doctrine of the oneness of the Manifestations does not mean that the same individual soul is born again in different physical bodies. Moses, Jesus Christ, Muhammad, and Bahá'u'lláh were all different personalities, separate individual realities. Their oneness lies in the fact that each manifested and revealed the qualities and attributes of God to the same degree: the spirit of God which dwelled within any one of them was identical to that which dwelled in the others.

---

[24] Bahá'u'lláh, *Gleanings*, pp. 47–48. For a detailed discussion of this subject, see Juan R. Cole, *The Concept of Manifestation in the Bahá'í Writings*.
[25] Bahá'u'lláh, *Gleanings*, pp. 287–288.
[26] *Bahá'í World Faith*, pp. 27–28.

Bahá'u'lláh offered an analogy to explain the relationship between the different Manifestations, and the relationship between each Manifestation and God. In this analogy, God is likened to the sun because he is the unique source of life in the universe in the same way that the physical sun is the unique source of all physical life on earth. The spirit and attributes of God are the rays of this sun and the individual Manifestation is like a perfect mirror. If there are several mirrors all turned toward the same sun, that unique sun is reflected in each mirror. Yet the individual mirrors are different, each having been made in its own form and distinct from any other.

In the same way, each Manifestation is a distinct individual being, but the spirit and attributes of God reflected in each are the same.[27]

The Manifestations represent a level of existence intermediate between God and man. Just as man is superior to the animal because he possesses capacities that the animal does not (i.e., the capacities of his nonmaterial soul), so the Manifestations possess capacities which ordinary humans lack. It is not a difference in degree, but rather a difference in kind which distinguishes them from other men. The Manifestations are not simply great human

---

[27] The analogy of the sun and the mirrors enables us to understand the Bahá'í interpretation of the traditional notion of the "return" or "reappearance" of former Manifestations. The theme of return is found in the sacred scriptures of all the major religions, often couched in highly symbolic language. Western readers will be most familiar with the Christian expectation of the return or "Second Coming" of Christ, based on certain passages of the Old and New Testaments of the Bible. Bahá'u'lláh explains that the return alluded to in former scriptures is the return of the attributes and spirit of God in the mirror of another Manifestation, not the return of the same human personality: "It is clear and evident . . . that all the Prophets are the Temples of the Cause of God, Who have appeared clothed in divers attire. If thou wilt observe with discriminating eyes, thou wilt behold Them all abiding in the same tabernacle, soaring in the same heaven, seated upon the same throne, uttering the same speech, and proclaiming the same Faith. . . . Wherefore, should one of these Manifestations of Holiness proclaim saying: 'I am the return of all the Prophets,' He, verily, speaketh the truth. In like manner, in every subsequent Revelation, the return of the former Revelation is a fact, the truth of which is firmly established. . . ." (Bahá'u'lláh, *Gleanings,* p. 52). In this way, Bahá'ís consider that the Manifestation Bahá'u'lláh fulfills the promise of the return of Christ, even though Bahá'u'lláh and Jesus have distinct individual souls and therefore distinct human personalities.

thinkers, or philosophers, with a greater understanding or knowledge than others. They are, by their very nature, superior to those who do not possess a similar capacity.

It has been noted that human beings have a dual nature: the physical body, which is composed of elements and which functions according to the same principles as an animal's body; and the nonmaterial rational and immortal human soul. The Manifestations, Bahá'u'lláh taught, also have these two natures, but in addition they possess a third nature unique to their station: the capacity to receive divine revelation and to transmit it infallibly to humanity.

Know that the Holy manifestations, though they have the degrees of endless perfections, yet, speaking generally, have only three stations. The first station is the physical; the second station is the human, which is that of the rational soul; the third is that of the divine appearance and the heavenly splendor.

The physical station is phenomenal; it is composed of elements, and necessarily everything that is composed is subject to decomposition. . . . The second is the station of the rational soul, which is the human reality. This also is phenomenal, and the Holy Manifestations share it with all mankind. . . . The spirit of man has a beginning, but it has no end; it continues eternally. . . . The third station is that of the divine appearance and heavenly splendor: it is the Word of God, the Eternal Bounty, the Holy Spirit. It has neither beginning nor end. . . . the reality of prophethood, which is the Word of God and the perfect state of manifestation, did not have any beginning and will not have any end; its rising is different from all others and is like that of the sun.[28]

'Abdu'l-Bahá explained that even the individual soul of the Manifestation is different from that of ordinary people:

But the individual reality of the Manifestations of God is a holy reality, and for that reason, it is sanctified, and in that which concerns its nature and quality, is distinguished from all other things. It is like the sun, which by its essential nature produces light and cannot be compared to the

---

[28] 'Abdu'l-Bahá, *Some Answered Questions,* pp. 151–152 (1981 ed.).

moon. . . . So other human realities are those souls who, like the moon, take light from the sun; but that holy reality is luminous in Himself.[29]

The Manifestation then, is not simply an ordinary person whom God chooses at some point in his natural lifetime to be his messenger. Rather, the Manifestation is a special being, having a unique relationship to God and sent by him from the spiritual world as an instrument of divine revelation. Even though the individual soul of the Manifestation had a phenomenal beginning, it nevertheless existed in the spiritual world prior to physical birth in this life. The immortal souls of ordinary men, on the other hand, have no such preexistence, but come into existence at the moment of human conception. Of the preexistence of the souls of the Manifestations, Shoghi Effendi said:

The Prophets, unlike us, are pre-existent. The soul of Christ existed in the spiritual world before His birth in this world. We cannot imagine what that world is like, so words are inadequate to picture His state of being.[30]

The Manifestation has the awareness of his reality and identity even from childhood, though he may not begin his mission of openly teaching and instructing others until later in life. Because they are the direct recipients of revelation from God, the Manifestations possess absolute knowledge of the realities of life. This innate, divinely revealed knowledge alone enables them to formulate teachings and laws that correspond to human needs and conditions at a given time in history:

Since the Sanctified Realities, the supreme Manifestations of God, surround the essence and qualities of the creatures, transcend and contain existing realities and understand all things, therefore Their knowledge is divine knowledge, and not acquired—that is to say, it is a holy bounty, it is a divine revelation. . . . the supreme Manifestations of God are aware of the reality of the mysteries of beings. Therefore They establish laws which are suitable and adapted to the state of the world of man, for religion is the essential connection which proceeds from the realities of

---

[29] 'Abdu'l-Bahá, *Some Answered Questions,* p. 154 (1981 ed.).
[30] Shoghi Effendi, *High Endeavours, Messages to Alaska,* p. 71.

things. . . . the supreme Manifestations of God . . . understand this essential connection, and by this knowledge establish the Law of God.[31]

No man can "become" a Manifestation of God. Each individual soul is capable of being touched by the spirit of God and may therefore make spiritual progress, as has been explained in the above. But the Manifestation remains on an ideal level beyond that which even the most perfect man is capable of attaining.

Extending the mirror analogy, the souls of ordinary men may also be likened to mirrors—but, unlike the Manifestations, they are imperfect. In other words, each human being can reflect something of God's attributes, but only in an imperfect and limited way. For ordinary men, spiritual progress implies perfecting, cleansing, and polishing the mirror of the soul so that it may reflect ever more clearly the attributes of God. In several passages, Bahá'u'lláh explicitly used this example of "cleansing the mirror" as an analogy for spiritual progress. The analogy emphasizes the belief that man is created imperfect, but with an endless potential for perfection; whereas the Manifestation is already in a perfected state of being.

Bahá'u'lláh and 'Abdu'l-Bahá taught that there are no levels of being other than the three discussed above: human beings, the Manifestations, and God. There is no hierarchy of demons, angels, and archangels. Insofar as these terms have any significant meaning, they are seen as symbolic of varying stages of human development, imperfection being demonic and spirituality being angelic. The Manifestations are already in a state of perfection, while other men are potentially perfect in that each human soul has the potential to reflect the attributes of its Creator. The ultimate state of perfection for man, as explained below by 'Abdu'l-Bahá, is one of absolute servitude to God:

Know that the conditions of existence are limited to the conditions of servitude, of prophethood, and of Deity, but the divine and the contin-

---

[31] 'Abdu'l-Bahá, *Some Answered Questions,* pp. 157–159 (1981 ed.). This passage makes clear that God's laws are inherent in the structure of reality: the Manifestation understands these laws, but did not create them. Man can therefore discover some of these laws for himself, but other statements in the Bahá'í writings indicate that man would destroy himself if left unaided (i.e., without Divine Revelation) to discover all of them.

gent perfections are unlimited. . . . As the divine bounties are endless, so human perfections are endless. If it were possible to reach a limit of perfection, then one of the realities of the beings might reach the condition of being independent of God, and the contingent might attain to the condition of the absolute. But for every being there is a point which it cannot overpass . . . he who is in the condition of servitude, however far he may progress in gaining limitless perfections, will never reach the condition of Deity. . . . Peter cannot become Christ. All that he can do is, in the condition of servitude, to attain endless perfections. . . .[32]

However, because man is capable of entering into communion with God and thereby becoming aware of the spirit of God, he is also capable of "inspiration." The Bahá'í writings distinguish between inspiration and revelation. Revelation is that infallible and direct perception of God's creative Word that is accessible only to the Manifestations, who transmit it to mankind. Inspiration is the indirect and relative perception of spiritual truth which is available to every human soul. It arises out of the context of the spiritual life of a culture influenced by a Manifestation of God. Any human is capable of being inspired by the spirit of God. But the experience of inspiration is available to us because the spirit of God is mediated to us through the Manifestations. In short: inspiration depends upon revelation.

Bahá'u'lláh explained that the Divine Will of God does sometimes choose ordinary people as "prophets" and inspires them to play certain roles in human affairs. Examples include the Hebrew prophets Isaiah and Jeremiah. Still others have been inspired as "seers" or "saints." Not even the prophets, however, are anywhere close to the station of the Manifestations, who provide humankind with God's infallible revelation. The prophets are still ordinary men and women whose powers of inspiration have been developed and used by God. They are referred to as "minor prophets" or "dependent prophets" in the Bahá'í writings. When this terminology is used, the Manifestations are called "universal" or "independent" Prophets:

Universally, the Prophets are of two kinds. One are the independent Prophets who are followed; the other kind are not independent, and are themselves followers.

---

[32] 'Abdu'l-Bahá, *Some Answered Questions,* pp. 230–231. (1981 ed.).

The independent Prophets are the lawgivers and the founders of a new cycle. . . . Without an intermediary They receive bounty from the Reality of the Divinity, and Their illumination is an essential illumination. They are like the sun which is luminous in itself. . . . The other Prophets are followers and promoters, for they are branches and not independent; they receive the Bounty of the independent Prophets, and they profit by the light of the Guidance of the universal Prophets. They are like the moon which is not luminous and radiant in itself, but receives its light from the sun.[33]

Consequently, Bahá'ís consider philosophers, reformers, saints, mystics, and founders of humanitarian movements as ordinary people. In many cases they may have been inspired by God. Revelation, however, is the endowment of the Manifestations alone, and it is the ultimate generating force of all human progress.

## THE BAHÁ'Í CONCEPT OF GOD

Who is the God thus revealed by the succession of Manifestations? According to Bahá'í teachings, God is so far beyond his creation that, throughout all eternity, man will never be able to formulate any clear image of him or attain to anything but the most remote appreciation of his superior nature. Even if we say that God is the All-Powerful, the All-Loving, the Infinitely Just, such terms are derived from a very limited human experience of power, love, or justice. Indeed, our knowledge of anything is limited to our knowledge of those attributes or qualities perceptible to us:

Know that there are two kinds of knowledge: the knowledge of the essence of a thing and the knowledge of its qualities. The essence of a thing is known through its qualities; otherwise, it is unknown and hidden.

As our knowledge of things, even of created and limited things, is knowledge of their qualities and not of their essence, how is it possible to comprehend in its essence the Divine Reality, which is unlimited? . . . Knowing God, therefore, means the comprehension and the knowledge of His attributes, and not of His Reality. This knowledge of the attributes is also proportioned to the capacity and power of man; it is not absolute.[34]

---

[33] 'Abdu'l-Bahá, *Some Answered Questions,* p. 164 (1981 ed.).
[34] 'Abdu'l-Bahá, *Some Answered Questions,* pp. 220–221 (1981 ed.).

Thus for human beings the knowledge of God means the knowledge of the attributes and qualities of God, not a direct knowledge of his essence. But how are we to attain the knowledge of the attributes of God? Bahá'u'lláh wrote that everything in creation is God's handiwork and therefore reflects something of his attributes. For example, even in the intimate structure of a rock or a crystal can be seen the order of God's creation. However, the more refined the object, the more completely is it capable of reflecting God's attributes. Since the Manifestation is the highest form of creation known to us, the Manifestation affords the most complete knowledge of God available to us:

Whatever is in the heavens and whatever is on the earth is a direct evidence of the revelation within it of the attributes and names of God, inasmuch as within every atom are enshrined the signs that bear eloquent testimony to the revelation of that Most Great Light. . . . To a supreme degree is this true of man. . . . For in him are potentially revealed all the attributes and names of God to a degree that no other created being hath excelled or surpasssed. . . . And of all men, the most accomplished, the most distinguished, and the most excellent are the Manifestations of the Sun of Truth. Nay, all else besides these Manifestations, live by the operation of their Will, and move and have their being through the outpourings of their grace.[35].

Although a rock or a tree reveals something of the subtlety of its Creator, only a conscious being such as man can dramatize God's attributes in his life and actions. Since the Manifestations are already in a perfected state, it is in their lives that the deeper meaning of God's attributes can be most perfectly understood. God is not limited by a physical body, and so we cannot see him directly or observe his personality. Hence our knowledge of the Manifestation is, in fact, the closest we can come to the knowledge of God.

Know thou of a certainty that the Unseen can in no wise incarnate His essence and reveal it unto men. He is, and hath ever been, immensely exalted beyond all that can either be recounted or perceived. . . . He Who

---

[35] Bahá'u'lláh, *Gleanings,* pp. 177–179.

is everlastingly hidden from the eyes of men can never be known except through His Manifestation, and His Manifestation can adduce no greater proof of the truth of His mission than the proof of His Own Person.[36]

And in another similar passage:

The door of the knowledge of the Ancient Being hath ever been, and will continue to be, closed in the face of men. No man's understanding shall ever gain access unto His holy court. As a token of His mercy, however, and as a proof of His loving-kindness, He hath manifested unto men the Day Stars of His divine guidance, the Symbols of His divine unity, and hath ordained the knowledge of these sanctified Beings to be identical with the knowledge of His own Self.[37]

Of course, only those who live during the time of a Manifestation have the opportunity of observing him directly. It is for this reason, Bahá'u'lláh explained, that the essential connection between the individual and God is maintained through the writings and words of each Manifestation. For Bahá'ís, the word of the Manifestation is the Word of God, and it is to this Word that the individual can turn in his daily life in order to grow closer to God and to acquire a deeper knowledge of him. The written Word of God is the instrument that creates a consciousness of God's presence in one's daily life:

Say: The first and foremost testimony establishing His truth is His own Self. Next to this testimony is His Revelation. For whoso faileth to recognize either the one or the other He hath established the words He hath revealed as proof of His reality and truth. . . . He hath endowed every soul with the capacity to recognize the signs of God.[38]

It is for this reason that the discipline of daily prayer, meditation, and study of the holy writings constitutes an important part of the individual spiritual practice of Bahá'ís. They feel that this discipline is one of the most important ways of growing closer to their Creator.

Let us sum up: the Bahá'í view of God is that his essence is

---

[36] Bahá'u'lláh, *Gleanings*, p. 49.
[37] Bahá'u'lláh, *Gleanings*, pp. 49–50.
[38] Bahá'u'lláh, *Gleanings*, pp. 105–106.

eternally transcendent, but that his attributes and qualities are completely immanent in the Manifestations.[39] Since our knowledge of anything is limited to our knowledge of the perceptible attributes of that thing, knowledge of the Manifestations is (for ordinary humans) equivalent to knowledge of God.[40] In practical terms, this knowledge is gained through study, prayer, meditation, and practical application based on the revealed Word of God (i.e., the sacred scriptures of the Manifestations).

---

[39] In this connection, Shoghi Effendi spoke of the Manifestation of Bahá'u'lláh as the "complete incarnation of the names and attributes of God." (See *World Order of Bahá'u'lláh*, p. 112.)

[40] In this regard, 'Abdu'l-Bahá said, "The knowledge of the Reality of the Divinity is impossible and unattainable, but the knowledge of the Manifestations of God is the knowledge of God, for the bounties, splendors and divine attributes are apparent in Them. Therefore, if man attains to the knowledge of the Manifestations of God, he will attain to the knowledge of God; and if he be neglectful of the knowledge of the Holy Manifestations, he will be bereft of the knowledge of God." (See *Some Answered Questions*, p. 222 (1981 ed.).)

# 7. The World Order of Bahá'u'lláh

Many people have doubts about the existence of God because they are unable to discover anything that proves to them that he does exist. How we can know about God and be sure of his existence is certainly one of the greatest philosophical and religious questions. In chapter 6, the Bahá'í response to this question was discussed in some depth. The Bahá'í Faith teaches that God has given us a clear sign of his existence and his love for us: the Manifestations whom he sends from time to time to make his Will known to humankind.

According to Bahá'u'lláh, God has promised that he will send a succession of Manifestations to guide and instruct man. In the Bahá'í writings, this promise is called "the Great Covenant." The succession of Manifestations or Messengers of God extends back to the dawn of time: Moses succeeded Abraham; Jesus followed Moses; and Muhammad appeared after Jesus. In this age, the promised succession has been fulfilled by the advent of Bahá'u'lláh. Each of the other divine messengers, both those known to recorded history and those the memory of whom has been lost, has had an important role to play in the divine scheme of things.[1]

---

[1] The subject of the sucession of the Manifestations is the principal theme of the *Kitáb-i-Íqán (Book of Certitude)*. The concept of a covenant can be found in the scriptures of many religions. For example, in the Bible, Genesis 17 describes God's covenant with Abraham, saying that the latter would become "the father of a multitude of nations." The passage continues: "I will make you exceedingly fruitful; and I will make nations of you and kings shall come forth from you. And I will establish my covenant between me and you and your descendants after you throughout their generations for an everlasting covenant, to be God to you and to your descendants after you" (Genesis 17:6–7).

It is now evident that the covenant in question was not for the Jews and Christians alone (i.e., the descendants of Abraham through his son, Isaac, by his first wife, Sarah), but was also for the descendants of Abraham's marriages to Hagar

A covenant is an agreement or contract involving obligations by both parties. God's part in the Great Covenant is his promise of a succession of Manifestations. Bahá'u'lláh taught that people, in response to this divine undertaking, have a two-fold obligation towards God: they must recognize and accept the Manifestation when he comes, and obey and strive to put into practice the teachings which the Manifestation gives. Bahá'u'lláh said, "These twin duties are inseparable. Neither is acceptable without the other."[2]

It is for this reason that Bahá'ís of Jewish, Christian, or other religious backgrounds do not consider that they have abandoned their former faiths in becoming Bahá'ís. They believe they are responding to their obligations as believers in and followers of whichever Manifestation of God founded their own religious tradition. They have, so to speak, "kept the Covenant" in recognizing the succession of God's Manifestations instead of following only one and holding onto his teachings as superior to all others. They regard themselves as fulfilling the spiritual obligations they inherited from their parent faith.

One other point about the Bahá'í concept of the Great Covenant should be stressed. As the succession of the Manifestations had no beginning, neither will it have an end. The Bahá'í revelation does not claim to be the final stage in God's direction of the course of human spiritual evolution. In the words of Bahá'u'lláh: "God hath sent down His Messengers to succeed Moses and Jesus, and He will continue to do so till the 'end that hath no end'. . . ."[3] The Bahá'í writings contain the assurance that, after "the expiration of a full

---

(see Genesis 16:15–16) and Keturah (See Genesis 25:1–2). As the Prophet Muhammad was descended from Ishmael, the son of Abraham and Hagar (see Genesis 25:5–6), Muslims regard themselves co-heirs of the covenant of Abraham. Bahá'u'lláh was descended from Abraham by the patriarch's third wife, Keturah (see Shoghi Effendi, *God Passes By*, p. 94). Thus Bahá'ís regard the covenant of Abraham as the motive force in the appearance of at least four major Messengers of God: Moses and Jesus Christ (through Sarah, by Isaac), Muhammad (through Hagar, by Ishmael), and Bahá'u'lláh (through Keturah).

[2] Bahá'u'lláh, *Gleanings*, p. 331.

[3] Bahá'u'lláh, cited by Shoghi Effendi in *World Order of Bahá'u'lláh*, p. 116.

thousand years," another Messenger or Manifestation of God will appear to carry forward the never-ending evolutionary process.[4]

Within this all-embracing covenant there are other ties between man and God which relate to specific stages in the evolution of mankind and in the unfoldment of civilization. Both have gone through many stages, and Bahá'ís believe that each one of the revealed religions has served to attain a particular goal in the total process. Much as a growing child gradually and progressively learns different skills (eating, walking, reading, working with others, and so forth) in order to mature, so has humankind grown slowly towards spiritual maturity by successively focusing attention on the development of different spiritual capacities.

For example, through the revelation of Abraham, the Hebrews became aware of the oneness of God and were able to explore the potentialities of human development which this great truth revealed. In time the concept came to influence profoundly the whole of the Western and Islamic civilizations. Similarly, Moses revealed the "Law of God" to humankind, the Buddha showed the way to achieve detachment from self, and Jesus Christ taught the love of God and the love of one's fellow man. Bahá'u'lláh explained that this gradual development of man's spiritual consciousness is both natural and necessary. The child must learn to walk before he can learn to run and jump.

To accomplish a particular task, one needs to learn the appropriate means to do so. According to Bahá'í belief, each Manifestation has provided those who recognized his station with these essential means by making a covenant between his followers and himself. In the Bahá'í teachings, this covenant is referred to as the "Lesser Covenant." It is reformulated by each Messenger of God according to the changing needs of an evolving human race. It is "lesser" not because it is unimportant, but because it functions within the framework of the goals and purposes of the Great Covenant. The Lesser Covenant might be called an "auxiliary covenant" or a "subsidiary

---

[4] Bahá'u'lláh, *Bahá'í World Faith*, p. 211.

covenant," since it serves as an aid to the larger, eternal purposes of God.[5]

As has been noted, Bahá'ís consider the specific mission of the Bahá'í revelation to be the establishment of world unity. The Covenant of Bahá'u'lláh, therefore, is directed toward this end. For Bahá'ís, world unity must involve not only the emergence of a strong sentiment of fraternity and love among all peoples, but it must also involve the creation of global institutions necessary for the establishment of a harmonious and unified social life for the planet. War must be permanently eliminated and universal peace firmly established among all the nations and communities of the earth.

In the Bahá'í writings, this vision of the future of humankind is called the "World Order" of Bahá'u'lláh. Such a vision is breathtaking in its scope. While most people would probably agree that this Bahá'í goal is a worthy one, many would regard it as utopian to believe that such an ideal society could ever be actually achieved. Moreover, many people feel that religion should be concerned exclusively with the inner development of the individual, and they are surprised to find a faith that places so great an emphasis on mankind's collective life, on forms of social organization, and on the achievement of social goals.

The reason for the Bahá'ís' confidence that the time for the unification of humanity has come lies in their belief that world unity is the Will of God: it is God who wants humankind to be united; he has created man with the potential for unity and has provided him with the means to develop this potential. The Covenant of Bahá'u'lláh is regarded as the primary God-given instrument for releasing this spiritual potential in man and for the subsequent achieve-

---

5 Bahá'í scholars note that there are also references to the "Lesser Covenant" in the scriptures of other faiths. In Deuteronomy 29:10–13, Moses made a "sworn covenant" with his followers, the people of Israel, that God would be their protector and defender if they in turn would be "his people" and obey his laws. An analogous pattern exists in the New Testament, evidenced in the promises which Jesus gave to his followers that, if they obeyed his teachings, they would receive certain powers and blessings. Christians were commanded, for example, to "go forth and teach all nations," "to observe all that I have commanded you." In return, they were promised: "Ask, and it will be given to you; seek and you shall find; knock, and it will be opened to you" (see Matthew 7:7–8; and 28:19–20).

ment of world unity. This Covenant provides man with a spiritual power which creates hope, changes hearts, and dissolves prejudices. It also provides a system of social laws and institutions which operates on the basis of spiritual principles and which relates them to the practical affairs of human life. Through this system, Bahá'ís feel, mankind can create a global society based on justice:

The world's equilibrum hath been upset through the vibrating influence of this most great, this new World Order. Mankind's ordered life hath been revolutionized through the agency of this unique, this wondrous System—the like of which mortal eyes have never witnessed.[6]

The principal role in laying the foundations of Bahá'u'lláh's system was played by his son, 'Abdu'l-Bahá. The part which 'Abdu'l-Bahá played in Bahá'í history was discussed earlier; the importance of his role in the mission of Bahá'u'lláh is reflected in the fact that Bahá'u'lláh designated him the "Center of My Covenant." 'Abdu'l-Bahá was given the authority to interpret the Bahá'í revelation and was assured that his interpretation would be infallibly guided by God.[7] Bahá'u'lláh also left the direction of the application of his teachings to his son, together with the responsibility of making all decisions related to the founding of the institutions of Bahá'u'lláh's World Order. It was acting on this designated authority that 'Abdu'l-Bahá produced the vast range of writings that are now included in the basic literature of the Bahá'í Faith.

'Abdu'l-Bahá in turn appointed Shoghi Effendi Rabbani as the Guardian of the Bahá'í community and the interpreter of the sacred writings after him, and 'Abdu'l-Bahá supervised the creation of the first local spiritual assemblies, destined to evolve into the fundamental institutions of the World Order. The work of Shoghi Effendi made possible the establishment of the Universal House of Justice.

---

[6] Bahá'u'lláh, Gleanings, p. 136.

[7] Bahá'u'lláh said that: "When the ocean of My presence hath ebbed and the Book of My Revelation is ended, turn your faces toward Him ['Abdu'l-Bahá] Whom God hath purposed, Who hath branched from this Ancient Root. . . . refer ye whatsoever ye understand not in the Book to Him. . . . The object of this sacred verse is none other except the Most Mighty Branch ('Abdu'l-Bahá)." (Cited by Shoghi Effendi in World Order of Bahá'u'lláh, p. 134).

The example of 'Abdu'l-Bahá's life demonstrated the practicality and validity of Bahá'u'lláh's teachings on individual spiritual life and development. However, he is not regarded as another Manifestation or Messenger of the station of the Báb and Bahá'u'lláh. While the authority of a Manifestation comes directly from God and is part of his very spiritual nature, the authority of 'Abdu'l-Bahá was conferred on him by Bahá'u'lláh. However, Bahá'ís consider 'Abdu'l-Bahá to have been uniquely qualified to serve as the perfect exemplar of the Bahá'í teachings, and Shoghi Effendi described him in these terms:

He is, and should for all time be regarded, first and foremost, as the Center and Pivot of Bahá'u'lláh's peerless and all-enfolding Covenant, His most exalted handiwork, the stainless Mirror of His light, the perfect Exemplar of His Teachings, the unerring Interpreter of His Word, the embodiment of every Bahá'í ideal. . . . in the person of 'Abdu'l-Bahá the incompatible characteristics of a human nature and superhuman knowledge and perfection have been blended and are completely harmonized.[8]

The conviction of the practicability of world unity, coupled with a dedication and willingness to work toward this goal, is probably the single most distinguishing characteristic of the Bahá'í community. It is the most obvious difference between the Bahá'í Faith and earlier revealed religions. With regard to its spiritual teachings and basic doctrines, the Bahá'í Faith has many points of contact with traditional religions, especially those of the Semitic group (Judaism, Christianity, and Islam). But the Bahá'í focus on achieving world unity and a world civilization, arising out of a faith in Bahá'u'lláh's Covenant with them, is both contemporary and unique. In a widely read survey on the possibilities for world unity and global civilization, American social scientist Professor Warren Wagar said: ". . . of all the positive religions on the contemporary scene claiming divine authority, the only one unambiguously and almost single-mindedly consecrated to the job of unifying mankind is the Bahá'í Faith."[9]

---

[8] Shoghi Effendi, *World Order of Bahá'u'lláh*, p. 134.
[9] Warren Wagar, *The City of Man, Prophecies of a World Civilization in Twentieth Century Thought*, p. 117.

The special Covenant Bahá'u'lláh has made with humankind operates through a system called the Administrative Order. We have already seen that the teachings and writings of Bahá'u'lláh fall into a number of different categories. Among the themes with which Bahá'u'lláh dealt are certain basic concepts and doctrines; principles and exhortations for the guidance of humankind; laws and ordinances regarded as essential to personal development and social organization; and specific institutions that form an integral part of the Bahá'í revelation and that cannot be dissociated from the spiritual teachings.

The laws and ordinances on one hand, and the institutions of the Bahá'í community on the other, together constitute the system called the "Administrative Order" of the Bahá'í Faith. It is this Administrative Order which provides the essential expression of Bahá'u'lláh's Lesser Covenant with humankind.[10] The distinctive feature of the Lesser Covenant is the fact that the founder specified the laws and institutions that are to govern the community of his followers through history. Moreover, he explained in his own writings, over his personal seal and signature, the exact nature of each of these institutions: its limitations, its prerogatives, its function and its role. The foundations of the system were laid by 'Abdu'l-Bahá and by the Guardian of the Bahá'í Faith, Shoghi Effendi, both acting on the authority explicitly conferred upon them by Bahá'u'lláh and in accordance with Bahá'u'lláh's written directives.

The two principal institutions of the Administrative Order, described by Shoghi Effendi as its "pillars," are the Guardianship and the Universal House of Justice. The role that the Guardian performed and the nature of the authority conferred upon him in the Covenant were considered earlier. Although he is no longer living, his interpretations of the Bahá'í teachings continue to hold the same degree of authority for the Bahá'í community as they did during his Guardianship. The Universal House of Justice was instituted by Bahá'u'lláh himself as the supreme legislative organ of

---

[10] Shoghi Effendi summarized the principal features of the Administrative Order in *World Order of Bahá'u'lláh*, pp. 143–157.

the Bahá'í Administrative Order. Regarding the relationship between the Universal House of Justice and the Guardianship, the former has written:

It should be understood . . . that before legislating upon any matter the Universal House of Justice studies carefully and exhaustively both the Sacred Texts and the writings of Shoghi Effendi on the subject. The interpretations written by the beloved Guardian cover a vast range of subjects and are equally as binding as the Text itself.[11]

Bahá'u'lláh gave the name "Houses of Justice" to the central legislative institutions of his faith. A House of Justice is comprised of nine adults elected periodically by all adult believers in the community. Houses of Justice will eventually be established on three levels: (1) local (a municipality or distinct settlement); (2) secondary (usually national); and (3) international. To date, this institution has emerged only at the international level, through the election of the first Universal House of Justice at an international convention held in 1963. It is this body which today governs the Bahá'ís around the world. It is the sole legislative agency of the faith and, according to explicit texts of Bahá'u'lláh and 'Abdu'l-Bahá, its enactments have the same authority for Bahá'ís as do the texts themselves. The difference is that the House of Justice has the right to repeal and alter any of its enactments as the Bahá'í community evolves and new conditions emerge, whereas the laws enshrined in the Bahá'í texts will remain unchanged.

The administration of the Bahá'í Faith on the national and local levels is presently handled through national and local "spiritual assemblies." These institutions are elected and function in a manner similar to the House of Justice and will eventually be called secondary and local "Houses of Justice."

Bahá'ís believe that, while local and secondary Houses of Justice will be under the guidance of God, the decisions of the Universal House of Justice are uniquely inspired and authoritative. For them this institution represents humankind's supreme effort to reach up to God in a spirit of unity and harmony. Bahá'u'lláh stated that God

---

[11] The Universal House of Justice, *Wellspring of Guidance,* p. 52.

himself has made this possible and will preserve the enactments of the Universal House of Justice from error.[12]

There are also Bahá'í institutions at the continental, national, regional, and local levels, some of them elective and functioning through corporate consultation and decision making, others appointive and operating principally through services performed by their individual members. This system will be examined in greater detail in the chapter which follows.

The system of institutions forms an integral part of the Bahá'í Faith which cannot be separated from the purely spiritual principles and teachings. Bahá'ís believe that their Administrative Order represents the "nucleus" and "pattern" of a new social order destined to bring about the unification of mankind. Shoghi Effendi said of it:

> ... this Administrative Order is fundamentally different from anything that any Prophet has previously established, inasmuch as Bahá'u'lláh Himself revealed its principles, established its institutions, appointed the person to interpret His Word, and conferred the necessary authority on the body [the Universal House of Justice] designed to supplement and apply His legislative ordinances.[13]

It is important to make a clear distinction between the Administrative Order of the Bahá'í Faith and the future World Order conceived by Bahá'u'lláh. In speaking of the World Order, Bahá'ís refer to the full effect which they believe the teachings of the founder of their faith will eventually have on the establishment of a world government, a lasting peace and a united planetary civilization. This World Order obviously does not yet exist; rather, it is the goal

---

[12] In his *Will and Testament,* 'Abdu'l-Bahá said: "Unto the Most Holy Book every one must turn and all that is not expressly recorded therein must be referred to the Universal House of Justice. That which this body, whether unanimously or by majority doth carry, that is verily the Truth and the Purpose of God Himself. . . . Whatsoever they decide has the same effect as the Text itself. And inasmuch as this House of Justice hath power to enact laws that are not expressly recorded in the Book and bear upon daily transactions, so also it hath the power to repeal the same" (see Bahá'u'lláh and 'Abdu'l-Bahá, *Bahá'í World Faith,* pp. 447–448).

[13] Shoghi Effendi, *World Order of Bahá'u'lláh,* p. 145.

towards which the Bahá'í community is striving. But the principal institutions of the Administrative Order already exist and function as an integral part of the international community of Bahá'ís.

Shoghi Effendi gave a summary of Bahá'u'lláh's vision of the future World Order which we quote here in part:

The unity of the human race, as envisaged by Bahá'u'lláh, implies the establishment of a world commonwealth in which all nations, races, creeds and classes are closely and permanently united, and in which the autonomy of its state members and the personal freedom and initiative of the individuals that compose them are definitely and completely safeguarded. This commonwealth must, as far as we can visualize it, consist of a world legislature, whose members will, as the trustees of the whole of mankind, ultimately control the entire resources of all the component nations, and will enact such laws as shall be required to regulate the life, satisfy the needs and adjust the relationships of all races and peoples. A world executive, backed by an international Force, will carry out the decisions arrived at, and apply the laws enacted by this world legislature, and will safeguard the organic unity of the whole commonwealth. A world tribunal will adjudicate and deliver its compulsory and final verdict in all and any disputes that may arise between the various elements constituting this universal system. . . . A world script, a world literature, a uniform and universal system of currency, of weights and measures, will simplify and facilitate intercourse and understanding among the nations and races of mankind. . . .

National rivalries, hatred, and intrigues will cease, and racial animosity and prejudice will be replaced by racial amity, understanding and cooperation. The causes of religious strife will be permanently removed, economic barriers and restrictions will be completely abolished, and the inordinate distinction between classes will be obliterated. . . .[14]

Bahá'ís do not believe that the World Order will be brought into being solely through their efforts or through their faith. They believe that the Will of God operates in many different ways and at various levels, in all corners of the world and through all peoples, to bring about this great consummation. The League of Nations and the United Nations are seen as particularly important steps along the road to unification. Therefore many Bahá'ís are active participants

---

[14] Shoghi Effendi, *World Order of Bahá'u'lláh*, pp. 203–204.

in United Nations activities and agencies as well as in many other nonpolitical international movements. They do maintain, however, that their faith and its Administrative Order have a central and vital role to play in the process of the creation of a united world.

To understand how Bahá'ís view the relationship between their faith and its Administrative Order on the one hand, and the goal of attaining world peace and establishing a World Order on the other, it is helpful to remember that they associate the future world civilization with the millenium or the coming of the "Kingdom of God" mentioned in the sacred scriptures of other religions. They believe that the establishment of world peace and unity represents the establishment of God's Kingdom on earth, the ultimate triumph of good over evil as anticipated in symbolic terms in past religions. They believe that it is God's Will to bring about this World Order and that such has been his intention throughout human history.

In some religious traditions, the establishment of the Kingdom of God is associated solely with an act of God. It is assumed that man's role in the process will be essentially passive and that the advent of the Kingdom will occur instantly, magically, and supernaturally.[15]

Bahá'ís believe that God is all-powerful and that he could certainly impose his Kingdom on earth instantly if this was in fact his

---

[15] This traditional view has created some difficulty for modern exponents of what is termed "social Christianity." Beginning early in the twentieth century, a number of prominent Christian thinkers developed the outlines of what they referred to as a "social Gospel," in which the coming of the Kingdom of God was interpreted as the creation of a just and peaceful society on earth. The effort foundered on the opposing argument of traditional Christian thinkers that the Kingdom could be established only through the return of Christ Himself. Efforts toward social reform, in their view, however beneficial, could not claim to represent anything more than mankind's imperfect striving after improvement. The controversy has been reawakened in our time through the controversy between orthodox circles in the Christian Church and liberal elements influenced by the Marxist diagnosis of the contemporary social condition.

Bahá'ís feel that the conflict is the result of a misunderstanding—on both sides. Since, according to Bahá'í belief, Christ has returned in the Manifestation of Bahá'u'lláh, the worldwide movement toward the building of a new society founded on humanitarian pursuits of improving the social condition for mankind as a whole does represent the gradual establishment of the Kingdom of God on earth through the active participation of its inhabitants.

will. But, Bahá'u'lláh explained that God seeks to teach us certain lessons by the manner in which the Kingdom is brought into being. Bahá'ís consider that present-day societies fail to meet our real needs because they are founded on attitudes and practices that are contrary to Divine Law. Thus, at the same time that God is establishing his promised Kingdom on earth, he is also allowing us to learn through experience—the experience of living with the consequences of our own acts—the true nature of our capacities and limitations. Bahá'u'lláh warned that it is only through our profound realization and acceptance of past errors that we will be protected from repeating the same tragic mistakes that have led to the present world situation, with its perpetual menace of war and its suffering, exploitation, and despair.[16]

Bahá'u'lláh envisioned the establishment of a World Order as occurring in three successive stages. The first stage is a period of social breakdown and widespread suffering, suffering greater in scope and intensity than any previously known. Bahá'ís believe that this first stage is already well advanced and that the turmoil presently afflicting the world will, in time, test every human life and all existing social institutions. In his work *The Promised Day is Come,* Shoghi Effendi described this human suffering as both "a retributory calamity" and "an act of holy and supreme discipline" on the part of God:

It is at once a visitation from God and a cleansing process for all mankind. Its fires punish the perversity of the human race, and weld its component parts into one organic, indivisible, world-embracing community. Mankind, in these fateful years . . . is . . . being simultaneously called upon to give account of its past actions, and is being purged and prepared for its future mission. It can neither escape the responsibilities of the past, nor shirk those of the future.[17]

According to Bahá'í belief, the present period of suffering and difficulties will culminate in a worldwide spiritual, physical, and social convulsion. That crisis will mark the end of the first stage and

---

16 See Shoghi Effendi, *The Promised Day Is Come,* p. 53.
17 Shoghi Effendi, *The Promised Day Is Come,* pp. 2–3.

the transition into the second stage of God's plan. Bahá'u'lláh referred to this crisis as follows:

We have a fixed time for you, O people! If ye fail, at the appointed hour, to turn towards God, He, verily, will lay violent hold on you, and will cause grievous afflictions to assail you from every direction. How severe indeed is the chastisement with which your Lord will then chastise you.![18]

The second stage in mankind's progress towards the World Order will see the accomplishment of the "Lesser Peace." In the light of various statements in the Bahá'í writings, it would probably be accurate to say that this second stage is seen as the permanent cessation of war rather than as a positive and complete global peace. The Lesser Peace is a term used to describe a political peace, which would be concluded by the nations of the world through international agreement. The fundamental feature of the Lesser Peace is the establishment of international security safeguards to prevent the recurrence of war among nations. These safeguards would be explicitly outlined in a formal agreement supported by all the nations of the earth, and based on the principle of "collective security" according to which all the nations should arise collectively to suppress any aggressor nation. Bahá'u'lláh has said: "Should any one among you take up arms against another, rise ye all against him, for this is naught but manifest justice."[19]

'Abdu'l-Bahá elaborated on this theme in the following passage:

They [the sovereigns of the world] must conclude a binding treaty and establish a covenant, the provisions of which shall be sound, inviolable and definite. They must proclaim it to all the world and obtain for it the sanction of all the human race. . . . All the forces of humanity must be mobilized to ensure the stability and permanence of this Most Great Covenant. In this all-embracing Pact the limits and frontiers of each and every nation should be clearly fixed, the principles underlying the relations of governments towards one another definitely laid down, and all international agreements and obligations ascertained. . . . The fundamental principle underlying this solemn Pact should be so fixed that if any govern-

---

[18] Quoted in Shoghi, Effendi, *The Promised Day Is Come*, p. 3.
[19] Bahá'u'lláh, *Gleanings*, p. 254.

ment later violate any one of its provisions, all the governments on earth should arise to reduce it to utter submission, nay the human race as a whole should resolve, with every power at its disposal, to destroy that government. Should this greatest of all remedies be applied to the sick body of the world, it will assuredly recover from its ills and will remain eternally safe and secure.[20]

Bahá'ís believe that the Lesser Peace will follow very soon after the end of the present period of suffering and social upheaval. Indeed, they maintain that these latter tragedies will be the chief influence in driving men and nations to put an end to war at whatever cost. 'Abdu'l-Bahá predicted that the Lesser Peace will be inaugurated in this century.[21]

The Lesser Peace is seen as the necessary prelude to a third stage in the emergence of a World Order, a stage which will come about far more gradually. Bahá'u'lláh called this final stage the "Most Great Peace." Its advent, he said, will coincide with the emergence of the Bahá'í World Order. Shoghi Effendi's description of this future World Order has already been quoted in part earlier in this chapter. In another passage, he spoke of it as the "ultimate fusion of all races, creeds, classes and nations." Whereas the Lesser Peace will be achieved by the "nations of the earth, as yet unconscious of [Bahá'u'lláh's] Revelation and yet unwittingly enforcing [its] general principles"; the Most Great Peace can come only "consequent to the recognition of the character, and the acknowledgment of the claims, of the Faith of Bahá'u'lláh."[22] Bahá'ís believe that it is during the evolution from the Lesser Peace to the Most Great Peace that Bahá'u'lláh's mission will be fully recognized by the peoples of the earth and its principles consciously accepted and applied by the generality of humankind.

The Administrative Order of the Bahá'í Faith is seen as the "embryonic form" of the future World Order. According to Shoghi Effendi, the institutions and laws of the Bahá'í Administrative Order "are destined to be a pattern for future society, a supreme

---

[20] 'Abdu'l-Bahá, *The Secret of Divine Civilization*, pp. 64–65.
[21] "Abdu'l-Bahá, *Selections from the Writings of 'Abdu'l-Bahá*, p. 32.
[22] Shoghi Effendi, *The Promised Day Is Come*, p. 128.

instrument for the establishment of the Most Great Peace, and the one agency for the unification of the world, and the proclamation of the reign of righteousness and justice upon the earth."[23]

The vision of the Most Great Peace corresponds to a similar vision of Habakkuk of the time when "the earth shall be filled with the knowledge of the glory of the Lord, as the waters cover the sea" (Habakkuk, 2:14). It will mark the "healing of the nations" promised in the Christian apocalypse (Revelation 22:2). It will bring not only a world civilization, but also the "spiritualization of the masses." It represents the "coming of age of the entire human race."[24]

Speaking of the Most Great Peace, Shoghi Effendi said:

Then will a world civilization be born, flourish, and perpetuate itself, a civilization with a fullness of life such as the world has never seen nor can as yet conceive. Then will the Everlasting Covenant be fulfilled in its completeness. Then will the promise enshrined in all the Books of God be redeemed, and all the prophecies uttered by the Prophets of old come to pass, and the vision of seers and poets be realized. Then will the planet, galvanized through the universal belief of its dwellers in one God, and their allegiance to one common Revelation, mirror, within the limitations imposed upon it, the effulgent glories of the sovereignty of Bahá'u'lláh . . . and [be] acclaimed as the earthly heaven, capable of fulfilling that ineffable destiny fixed for it, from time immemorial, by the love and wisdom of its Creator.[25]

Bahá'ís perceive the Will of God to be working in two ways or on two levels. On the one hand, there is the general Will of God which pervades everything and which moves at the heart of every event in human history, however apparently insignificant. All things, in the long run, serve God's goal of unifying humankind. For this reason, Bahá'ís warmly support many universal and humanitarian causes and try to appreciate the positive elements in other causes with whose philosophies they may not be in complete accord.

---

[23] Shoghi Effendi, *World Order of Bahá'u'lláh*, p. 19.
[24] Shoghi Effendi, *The Promised Day Is Come*, p. 128.
[25] Shoghi Effendi, *The Promised Day Is Come*, pp. 128–129.

On the other hand, Bahá'ís believe that their faith and its Administrative Order represent a specific articulation of God's Will for this age. Through it, the spirit and pattern of unity have entered human affairs. Bahá'ís see their primary task as the perfection of this God-given instrument. As the influences of the new revelation begin to penetrate society as a whole, the process of the evolution from the Lesser Peace to the Most Great Peace will take place. People will come to recognize the Will of God for humankind and will witness the establishment of God's Kingdom on earth.

# 8.  Administration and Laws

Bahá'ís consider one of the distinguishing features of their religion to be the special Covenant of Bahá'u'lláh, through which a future world order and world civilization will come into being. They believe that the nucleus and pattern of this future global system already exist in the laws and Administrative Order conceived by the founder of their faith, and implemented and developed by 'Abdu'l-Bahá and Shoghi Effendi. For this reason, Bahá'ís devote a great deal of time and energy to developing the institutions of their community. These agencies of the Bahá'í administrative order are not used only to solve problems and make collective decisions within the community of believers; they are also steadily exercised and refined so that their divinely endowed administrative potentials will slowly emerge, just as human capacities emerge with instruction and continuous effort.

This accounts for the great concern with administrative processes on which many observers of the Bahá'í community have remarked. Bahá'ís believe that God has redeemed one of the most humanly corrupted and abused activities of modern-day civilization for divine purposes. They consider that God intends that administrative service should become a spiritual pursuit, blessing not only those who contribute directly to it, but the entire society which depends upon it.[1]

---

[1] For example, 'Abdu'l-Bahá said that: "These Spiritual Assemblies are shining lamps and heavenly gardens from which the fragrances of holiness are diffused over all regions. . . . From them the spirit of light streameth in every direction. They, indeed, are the potent sources of the progress of man. . . ." Cited by Shoghi Effendi in *God Passes By*, p. 332.

## INSTITUTIONS OF THE BAHÁ'Í FAITH

Under the direction of the writings of the Guardian of the Bahá'í Faith, and the authority of the legislative and executive role of the Universal House of Justice, the organization of the Bahá'í community is structured around two basic types of institutions: (1) those designed to make decisions with respect to the life and goals of the community; and (2) those which function to protect the community and to contribute in special ways to the propagation of the faith. The decision-making institutions are, essentially, the Universal House of Justice, operating on the international level, and the spiritual assemblies, which exist at both national and local levels. The protection/propagation institutions are derived from the powers conferred by the Covenant of Bahá'u'lláh on the Hands of the Cause of God, and expanded by the Guardian and then by the Universal House of Justice to include boards of counsellors and auxiliary boards. They advise, counsel, encourage, and stimulate both the spiritual assemblies and individual believers. These two branches of the Bahá'í administrative order are hereafter discussed.

## THE UNIVERSAL HOUSE OF JUSTICE AND THE SPIRITUAL ASSEMBLIES

In preparation for the eventual establishment in every city of a House of Justice, as called for in the writings of Bahá'u'lláh, 'Abdu'l-Bahá stated that as soon as the number of adult Bahá'ís in any locality reaches nine or more, an election should be held for the creation of a "Local Spiritual Assembly" to serve as the governing body of the faith in that locality. Each spiritual assembly consists of nine persons elected from among the full adult membership in that local community. The tasks of the spiritual assemblies include the supervision of all local Bahá'í activities, such as propagation (teaching) of the faith, the conduct of educational programs, the handling of local publicity and publishing, the conduct of devotional services, the use of Bahá'í funds, the counseling of believers on the specific requirements of the Bahá'í laws and teachings, and a range of other related responsibilities.[2]

'Abdu'l-Bahá supervised the establishment of the first spiritual assemblies in Persia and in the West, and he guided them in their initial efforts. A great deal of Shoghi Effendi's time as Guardian of the Bahá'í community was devoted to this same task. The body of administrative principles outlined in the voluminous correspondence of these two designated interpreters has been published in a series of books and manuals used throughout the Bahá'í world. The guidance provided therein covers an extraordinary range of subjects, and guarantees that the development of the Bahá'í community over the coming centuries will be molded in the precise pattern conceived by Bahá'u'lláh and those appointed by his Covenant to be its interpreters.[3]

Spiritual assemblies have also been created on the national (or occasionally on the regional) level. Their responsibilities are analogous to those of the local spiritual assemblies, though far greater in scope and complexity. In addition, they have the responsibility of supervising the work of the local spiritual assemblies and of determining what concerns are the responsibility of the local bodies and which ones must be handled at the national or regional level.

While the membership of each local spiritual assembly is directly elected by the members of its own local community, the national spiritual assembly membership is chosen by means of a two-stage balloting system. All the adult members of the Bahá'í community in a given district elect a specified number of delegates. The number is dependent on the size and scope of the Bahá'í community in that particular part of the country. Then the delegates from the entire country meet at an annual national convention and elect the nine-person membership of the national spiritual assembly from among

---

[2] For an introduction to the subject of the nature and functions of Bahá'í Spiritual Assemblies, see Adib Taherzadeh, *Trustees of the Merciful.*

[3] For a more detailed examination, see the various compilations of the writings of Shoghi Effendi on the subject of Bahá'í administration, including *Principles of Bahá'í Administration, A Compilation;* Shoghi Effendi, *Bahá'í Administration, Selected Messages, 1922–32; The Local Spiritual Assembly;* and *The National Spiritual Assembly.*

all the adults of the national Bahá'í community, regardless of whether or not they are delegates to the national convention.

The electoral process by which Bahá'í spiritual assemblies come into being contains a number of interesting and perhaps unique features. All voting is done by secret ballot. Moreover, the Bahá'í teachings forbid any form of electioneering, including the nomination of candidates. Each voter lists nine different names on the ballot. After the votes are counted, those nine individuals having the greatest number of votes are declared to be elected. Any tie vote for the ninth member is broken by a subsequent ballot between the tied individuals. This system removes the necessity for the nomination and presentation of candidates, thereby giving maximum freedom of choice to each elector and avoiding the power-seeking behavior inherent in many other forms of election. It is assumed that all adult believers, once chosen by the electorate, will be able and prepared to take up their duties as members of the national or local spiritual assembly.

Elections occur each year in late April and coincide with the Bahá'í festival of Riḍván. Then the elected spiritual assembly serves for one full year, beginning immediately following its election or as soon thereafter as is feasible.

The spirit and form this process takes is perhaps best illustrated by the following words of Shoghi Effendi:

If we but turn our gaze to the high qualifications of the members of Bahá'í Assemblies, as enumerated in 'Abdu'l-Bahá's Tablets, we are filled with feelings of unworthiness and dismay, and would feel truly disheartened but for the comforting thought that if we rise to play nobly our part every deficiency in our lives will be more than compensated by the all-conquering spirit of His grace and power. Hence it is incumbent upon the chosen delegates to consider without the least trace of passion and prejudice, and irrespective of any material consideration, the names of only those who can best combine the necessary qualities of unquestioned loyalty, of selfless devotion, of a well-trained mind, of recognized ability and mature experience.[4]

One other important aspect of Bahá'í elections should be noted:

---

[4] Shoghi Effendi, *Principles of Bahá'í Administration,* p. 62.

As in many other areas of his teachings (see, for example, the discussion on the equality of the sexes in chapter 5), Bahá'u'lláh gave practical expression to a spiritual command. He pointed out that minority races and ethnic groups have been greatly disadvantaged by discrimination in many parts of the world. Members of these minorities have never had the opportunity to develop the qualities of mind which they nevertheless possess in equal measure with more fortunate peoples. The Bahá'í community must deliberately arrange its affairs so that, to the extent possible, these injustices and handicaps are eliminated. In the electoral process, therefore, wherever the qualifications for a particular office are balanced between a person representing a minority group and some other individual, the elector is bound by his or her conscience to vote for the person representing the minority group. Similarly, if a tie vote occurs in a Bahá'í election and one of the persons involved represents a minority, preference should be given to him or her in the vote which breaks the tie.

The same basic electoral principles apply to the election of the membership of the Universal House of Justice. In this case, the electors are the members of the national spiritual assemblies of the Bahá'í world. Unlike the local and national spiritual assemblies, however, the Universal House of Justice is elected only once in five years, at an international convention held at the World Centre of the Bahá'í Faith in Haifa, Israel.[5]

## THE HANDS OF THE CAUSE, THE BOARDS OF COUNSELORS, AND THEIR DEPUTIES

This system of group decision-making is supplemented by a number of advisory bodies. During their lifetimes both Bahá'u'lláh and 'Abdu'l-Bahá appointed distinguished believers to serve as Hands of the Cause in propagating and protecting the Bahá'í Faith. The *Will and Testament of 'Abdu'l-Bahá* provided that these functions should continue throughout the Bahá'í dispensation; and

---

[5] The most recent election of the Universal House of Justice was held in April 1983.

therefore Shoghi Effendi also appointed Hands of the Cause, twenty-seven of whom were still living at the time of his death in November 1957. The *Will and Testament* reads in part:

O friends! The Hands of the Cause of God must be nominated and appointed by the guardian of the Cause of God. All must be under his shadow and obey his command. . . .

The obligations of the Hands of the Cause of God are to diffuse the Divine Fragrances, to edify the souls of men, to promote learning, to improve the character of men and to be, at all times, and under all conditions, sanctified and detached from earthly things. They must manifest the fear of God by their conduct, their manners, their deeds and their words.[6]

In the absence of a Guardian of the faith, there was no way in which other Hands of the Cause could be appointed following the death of Shoghi Effendi. The Universal House of Justice, however, is fully empowered by the explicit terms of the Covenant of Bahá'u'lláh to create whatever institutions it feels the evolution of the Bahá'í community requires. Since the *Will and Testament* called for the functions performed by the Hands of the Cause to be carried on as an integral part of the Administrative Order, the Universal House of Justice created a specialized institution for this purpose, an institution entirely separate from the elective system of spiritual assemblies. This institution is known as the "Boards of Counselors"[7] and its members serve on a continental level. The counselors are distinguished believers who are appointed to terms of five years, and each continental board has from seven to sixteen members.

The Hands of the Cause, encouraged by Shoghi Effendi, had already appointed groups of deputies on each continent, designated as auxiliary boards by the Guardian. These subsidiary boards have been attached to the boards of counselors by the Universal House of Justice, and they serve them in the same way as they did

---

[6] 'Abdu'l-Bahá, *Will and Testament of Abdu'l-Bahá*, pp. 12–13; also cited in *Bahá'í World Faith*, p. 444.

[7] See a general statement by the Universal House of Justice dated June 24, 1968, and published in *Wellspring of Guidance*, pp. 140–144.

the Hands of the Cause previously. Further, as the Bahá'í Faith has grown very rapidly in recent years, the Universal House of Justice has authorized each auxiliary board member to appoint "assistants" to help him or her in carrying on the work at the local level. Thus, parallel with the system of national and local spiritual assemblies, a separate branch of the administrative order now exists to carry out specialized functions at the continental, regional, and local levels.

## THE RELATIONSHIP OF THE COUNSELORS TO THE SPIRITUAL ASSEMBLIES

There are two principal differences between the institutions that make up the two branches of the Bahá'í administrative order. These differences relate to their modes of operation and to the powers conferred upon them. The spiritual assemblies are corporate bodies which come into being through election by the Bahá'í community as a whole, and they function through the normal process of majority decision. The counselors and their deputies are individually appointed by the Universal House of Justice and the boards of counselors, respectively, and they continue to function primarily as individual servants of the Cause of Bahá'u'lláh. Although spiritual assembly members may occasionally perform individual duties, as elected officers for example, and though there is consultation between the counselors and the auxiliary boards, the assemblies remain essentially corporate agencies, while the other institutions represent teams of individual coworkers.

The second difference lies in the nature of the authority conferred upon each one of the branches of the Bahá'í administration. The power to make decisions concerning the life of the community resides solely with the spiritual assemblies, and ultimately with the Universal House of Justice. The counselors and auxiliary board members advise the spiritual assemblies, comment on their plans and do whatever is deemed necessary to stimulate them, but their role is limited to these activities. The ultimate responsibility and decision-making authority rest with the spiritual assemblies, as they are the elected representatives of the Bahá'í community. It is this, perhaps more than any other factor, which distinguishes the role of the Hands, the counselors, and the auxiliary board members in the Bahá'í Faith from that of a "clergy" (as it is commonly defined by other faiths). The Hands and their successors, the counselors and auxiliary boards, have neither decision-making authority nor sacerdotal functions; nor do they have a right to interpret the sacred writings.[9] Moreover, the counselors serve only for the specified period of their appointment rather than for life.

Their role is, nevertheless, very significant. As individuals, they are chosen because each has demonstrated a high degree of spiritual maturity and the capacity to make valuable contributions to the life of the community. The Bahá'í writings accord them a high rank in the membership of the community, and both spiritual assemblies and individual believers are expected to take advantage of the assistance which their experience can provide.

## THE INTERNATIONAL TEACHING CENTRE

In 1973 the counselors and auxiliary boards were brought together under the direction of a single international institution functioning at the World Centre of the Bahá'í Faith in Haifa, Israel.[10] This institution is known as the International Teaching Centre. Its membership consists of the surviving Hands and a number of counselors appointed for this purpose by the Universal House of Justice. In time, when all the Hands will have passed away, the full membership of the Centre will consist of appointees of the Universal House of Justice, and the institution of the Teaching Centre will continue to function under the supervison of the House of Justice.

The principal duties of the International Teaching Centre are to coordinate the activities of the various boards of counselors; and to assist the Universal House of Justice in developing the global plans

---

[9] "Authority and direction flow from the Assemblies, whereas the power to acomplish the tasks resides primarily in the entire body of the believers. It is the principal task of the Auxiliary Boards to assist in arousing and releasing this power." Quoted from a letter of the Universal House of Justice dated October 1, 1969, *The Continental Boards of Counselors,* p. 37.

[10] *The Continental Boards of Counselors,* pp. 45–48.

through which the faith expands. It may be helpful to note the distinction the Bahá'í writings make between the spiritual station of individual believers and the rank which they may hold or the function which they may perform in the Bahá'í community. The Universal House of Justice has said:

Courtesy, reverence, dignity, respect for the rank and achievements of others are virtues which contribute to the harmony and well-being of every community, but pride and self-aggrandizement are among the most deadly of sins. . . . the ultimate aim in the life of every soul should be to attain spiritual excellence—to win the good pleasure of God. The true spiritual station of any soul is known only to God. It is quite a different thing from the ranks and stations that men and women occupy in the various sectors of society.[11]

## COMMUNITY LIFE AND THE "NINETEEN-DAY FEAST"

At the local level the activities of the Bahá'í community are centered on a periodic all-community meeting called a "feast." The dates for these gatherings are the same for the entire Bahá'í world and they are based on the Bahá'í solar calendar, which originated with the Báb. This calendar consists of nineteen months each having nineteen days, making a total of 361 days.[12] The four extra days of the solar year (five in leap years) are designated as "Intercalary Days" and they constitute a period of gift-giving, hospitality, and festivity.[13] The feast is held on the first day of each Bahá'í month and thus there are nineteen feasts in the Bahá'í year.

The feast has three basic parts. The first is devotional and consists of the reading of prayers and meditations, which may be taken not only from the Bahá'í holy writings, but also from the scriptures of other revealed religions. The second portion is

---

[11] *The Continental Boards of Counselors,* p. 60.

[12] *Bahá'í World,* vol. 13, p. 751.

[13] The four or five Intercalary Days are inserted into the Bahá'í calendar just prior to the final month of the year, the month of the Fast, which begins on March 2 of each Gregorian-calendar year. Besides the Feast days and the Intercalary Days, there are special Bahá'í holy days throughout the year, on some of which work is suspended. Many of these holy days comemmorate cardinal events in the Faith's early history, such as the birthdays of the Báb and Bahá'u'lluh.

administrative: the business of the community is consulted upon by all those present, including youth and children. The local spiritual assembly reports on those decisions it has made that are relevant to the general life of the community; a treasurer's report is given; and the members of the community are encouraged to offer suggestions, raise questions, or express their concerns in consultation with the representatives of the local spiritual assembly. The spiritual assembly is not bound to accept the recommendations put forward at the feast, but it must consider them and report back to the community on the action taken in each instance. The third portion of the feast is a social gathering. Together with refreshments and informal fellowship, this portion may include musical or other artistic presentations, games, and entertainment. All three parts are necessary to the feast, and Bahá'ís are encouraged to see the spiritual possibilities not only of the devotional, but also of the consultative and social portions.

In most Bahá'í communities the feast takes place in private homes or in small community centers. This is because these communities are not yet large enough to warrant the investment in more elaborate facilities. The pattern of community development envisaged by Bahá'u'lláh is capable of accommodating communities of much larger size. It is intended that, in time, each village or other locality will have its own "House of Worship" (Mashriqu'l-Adhkár or "Dawning place of the praises of God"). This house of worship will become the center of Bahá'í community life, and around it will be built a variety of supportive service agencies.[14]

## BAHÁ'Í LAW: SPIRITUAL LIBERTY THROUGH DISCIPLINE

All of the Bahá'í institutions we have been discussing operate in conjunction with a pattern of revealed law. Law, Bahá'u'lláh asserted, is the foundation of all human society.[15] Without it order is impossible, and without order, there is no framework within which

---

14 See also chapter 9.
15 Bahá'u'lláh, *Gleanings*, pp. 330–333; and pp. 335–336.

the spiritual, cultural, technological, and intellectual activities that depend on human interactions can develop. Even personal freedom depends upon law. By surrendering a degree of personal freedom to a commonly accepted system of laws, the individual assists in the creation of an environment that returns far greater benefits in terms of freedom than the personal investment it requires.

It is primarily the animal aspects of human nature that sound laws seek to discipline. Earlier this subject was examined in some depth. It is necessary here merely to note again the Bahá'í belief that man's spiritual, intellectual, and moral attributes become liberated only when his physical nature has been disciplined and refined as a reliable instrument. Whenever the demands of the physical body prevail, man's true nature remains hobbled and imprisoned by his physical, animal nature.

The ultimate source of all law beneficial to spiritual development is the successive revelations of the Manifestations of God.[16] The laws revealed by Moses, Jesus, or Muhammad are not merely regulations or moral precepts. Because the Manifestation's love for us touches our hearts, the laws he gives are capable of remolding the human conscience. The standards of right and wrong change in ways dictated by each successive revelation, and upon this foundation society itself constructs new systems of laws. "Think not," Bahá'u'lláh stated, "that We have revealed unto you a mere code of laws. Nay, rather, We have unsealed the choice Wine with the fingers of might and power."[17]

## THE KITÁB-I-AQDAS, THE BOOK OF LAWS

In the light of this view of the importance of Divine Law, it is not surprising to find Shoghi Effendi referring to Bahá'u'lláh's book of laws, the Kitáb-i-Aqdas (literally, the Most Holy Book) as "the most signal act" of Bahá'u'lláh's life, "the brightest emanation of the mind of Bahá'u'lláh" and "the Charter of His new World

---

[16] 'Abdu'l-Bahá, Secret of Divine Civilization, pp. 94–99.
[17] Bahá'u'lláh, Gleanings, p. 332.

Order."[18] The *Kitáb-i-Aqdas* lays down the basic laws for the spiritual life of the individual and the membership of the Bahá'í community. By any standards, it is an extraordinary document. A thorough discussion on the subject is beyond the scope of the present work, but three features in particular stand out: its comprehensiveness, its progressive application, and the manner of its publication.

The laws of Bahá'u'lláh deal with a very wide range of individual and community concerns. Among the subjects considered are prayer, fasting, marriage, divorce, inheritance, education, burial, wills and testaments, hunting, tithing, sexual relationships, care of the body, work, and eating habits.

Both Bahá'u'lláh and 'Abdu'l-Bahá emphasized that the application of the laws of the *Kitáb-i-Aqdas* was to occur gradually, as people develop the capacity to respond to the requisite responsibilities. Training in certain of the laws accelerates the process of spiritual maturity and makes possible the application of still other provisions. Bahá'u'lláh explained this progressive principle:

Know of a certainty that in every Dispensation the light of divine Revelation hath been vouchsafed to men in direct proportion to their spiritual capacity. Consider the sun. How feeble its rays the moment it appeareth above the horizon. How gradually its warmth and potency increase as it approacheth its zenith, enabling meanwhile all created things to adapt themselves to the growing intensity of its light. . . . Were it all of a sudden to manifest the energies latent within it, it would no doubt cause injury to all created things. . . . In like manner, if the Sun of Truth were suddenly to reveal, at the earliest stages of its manifestation, the full measure of the potencies which the providence of the Almighty hath bestowed upon it, the earth of human understanding would waste away and be consumed; for men's hearts would neither sustain the intensity of its revelation, nor be able to mirror forth the radiance of its light.[19]

Guided by this, both the Guardian and the Universal House of Justice have gradually introduced provisions of the *Kitáb-i-Aqdas* as

---

[18] Shoghi Effendi, *God Passes By*, p. 213.
[19] Bahá'u'lláh, *Synopsis and Codification of the Laws and Ordinances of the Kitáb-i-Aqdas*, p. 5.

the Bahá'í community grows and matures. Clearly, the process will be a lengthy one. Certain laws, Shoghi Effendi pointed out, have been "formulated in anticipation of a state of society destined to emerge from the chaotic conditions that prevail today."[20]

The *Kitáb-i-Aqdas* is only nominally a "book." More precisely, it is the core of a vast body of literature in which the laws of the Bahá'í Faith are stated and explained. The original volume in Arabic is a very small work. Bahá'u'lláh supplemented it with a large number of writings which elaborated the statements it contained, and he wrote commentaries on certain questions advanced by nineteenth-century Persian Bahá'í scholars who had read the work. 'Abdu'l-Bahá added to these secondary materials and provided further extensive interpretations and commentaries on the provisions of the *Kitáb-i-Aqdas,* just as Bahá'u'lláh had indicated would be necessary. The entire corpus was then greatly increased by the detailed interpretations of Shoghi Effendi, functioning in his role as the Guardian of the Bahá'í community.

Therefore the specific provisions of the *Kitáb-i-Aqdas* can only be determined by tracing their individual development through the entire process of codification. Shoghi Effendi indicated that, ultimately, a codification of the laws and ordinances of the *Kitáb-i-Aqdas* would be completed and published. He himself worked extensively on it, translating several passages of the original work, and leaving an outline of the *Synopsis and Codification* with supplementary notes. In 1973, on the one-hundredth anniversary of the completion of the *Kitáb-i-Aqdas* by Bahá'u'lláh, the Universal House of Justice published the collected passages, as they had been translated by the Guardian, together with a complete summary of the topics dealt with in the original work, under the title *Synopsis and Codification of the Laws and Ordinances of the Kitáb-i-Aqdas.*[21]

---

[20] Cited in Bahá'u'lláh, *Synopsis and Codification,* p. 7.

[21] Opponents of the Bahá'í Faith, particularly those among Muslim and Christian clergy, have attempted to suggest that by failing simply to translate and publish the text of the *Kitáb-i-Aqdas,* the leadership of the Bahá'í community had denied to the members of the community the opportunity to follow Bahá'u'lláh's injunctions to "turn unto the Most Holy Book." However, as has been noted, Bahá'u'lláh was explicit in insisting that the only way in which his followers could turn

## SPECIFIC LAWS OF THE *KITÁB-I-AQDAS*

A survey of some of the specific areas of human conduct to which the provisions of the *Kitáb-i-Aqdas* have already been applied by the Bahá'í community will indicate the general outline of Bahá'u'lláh's instructions and will illustrate the three features just mentioned.

### PRAYER AND MEDITATION

One of the most important of the laws Bahá'u'lláh prescribed for individual discipline is daily prayer and meditation. Compilations of the prayers of Bahá'u'lláh and 'Abdu'l-Bahá have been published in a great many languages, and there exists in English a three-hundred-page volume consisting entirely of Bahá'u'lláh's meditations. These books serve as resources for Bahá'ís in their devotional life.

Beyond the general injunction to pray and meditate, Bahá'u'lláh also ordained an obligatory prayer to be said each day by every believer who has attained the "age of maturity."[22] This obligatory prayer has three different forms, and the individual is free to choose whichever form he prefers on any given day. The so-called "Short Obligatory Prayer," for example, is to be said sometime between noon and sunset each day:

I bear witness, O my God, that Thou hast created me to know Thee and to worship Thee. I testify, at this moment, to my powerlessness and to

---

to and follow his teachings was through the interpretations of his authorized successor, 'Abdu'l-Bahá. 'Abdu'l-Bahá was equally explicit in conferring the sole interpretative authority after him upon Shoghi Effendi. Throughout their respective ministries, for a period totalling sixty-five years, 'Abdu'l-Bahá and Shoghi Effendi provided exhaustive interpretation of Bahá'u'lláh's teachings for the guidance of the Bahá'í community. Indeed, without this interpretation, it is impossible to imagine how the principles and laws outlined in the *Kitáb-i-Aqdas* could have had so pervasive and widespread an effect as has been achieved in only a few decades.

[22] The *Kitáb-i-Aqdas* fixes the age of maturity at fifteen. It is upon reaching fifteen that the individual believer assumes the full responsibility for his own spiritual life and development.

Thy might, to my poverty and to Thy wealth. There is none other God but Thee, the Help in Peril, the Self-Subsisting.[23]

## ABSTENTION FROM ALCOHOL AND NARCOTIC DRUGS

Bahá'u'lláh taught that the use of alcohol and narcotic or hallucinogenic drugs does harm to the higher physical and mental faculties, thereby hampering spiritual development. Bahá'ís are forbidden to use them in any form. The only exception to this is the right of a physician to prescribe alcohol or drugs for conditions for which there is no known alternative mode of treatment. There are no other prohibitions concerning food or drink in the Bahá'í teachings. Smoking tobacco, for example, is not forbidden, though it is strongly condemned as harmful to physical health and often socially repellent.[24]

## FASTING

As has been the case with other revealed religions, the Bahá'í Faith sees great value in the practice of fasting as a discipline for the soul. Bahá'u'lláh designated a nineteen-day period each year when adult Bahá'ís fast from sunrise to sunset each day. This period coincides with the Bahá'í month of 'Alá (meaning Loftiness), from March 2 to 21, inclusive. This is the month immediately preceding the Bahá'í Naw–Rúz, or New Year, which occurs the day of the vernal equinox; and the period of fasting is therefore viewed as a time of spiritual preparation and regeneration for a new year's activities. However, according to the *Kitáb-i-Aqdas,* women who are nursing or pregnant, the aged, the sick, the traveler, those engaged in heavy labor, as well as children under the age of fifteen, are exempt from observance of the Fast.[25]

---

[23] *Bahá'í Prayers, A Selection of Prayers revealed by Bahá'u'lláh, the Báb and 'Abdu'l-Bahá,* p. 4.

[24] See also Bahá'u'lláh and 'Abdu'l-Bahá, *Bahá'í World Faith,* pp. 333–336, for a statement of 'Abdu'l-Bahá on this subject.

[25] During the Fast, Bahá'ís rise and eat breakfast before dawn. They then refrain from food or drink until sunset of each day. The day often begins with family prayers, and the times which would normally be spent preparing and eating meals during the daylight hours are frequently used for prayer and meditation.

## ABSTENTION FROM BACKBITING

Besides the laws for the individual believer, Bahá'u'lláh laid down a number of other social laws and principles. For example, backbiting and criticism of others are condemned by him as extremely injurious to spiritual health: "backbiting quencheth the light of the heart, and extinguisheth the life of the soul."[26] Backbiting is considered to be criticism of others to third parties, whether or not the criticism is maliciously intended. Members of the Bahá'í community may take a concern about another's actions, in confidence, to their local spiritual assembly, but they must then leave the matter in the hands of the spiritual assembly and refrain from further discussion of it.

## MARRIAGE

Marriage is regarded in Bahá'í law as both a spiritual and a social institution. It affects not only the couple and their children, but also the parents, grandparents, grandchildren, and other collateral relations. Indeed, it affects (or in a healthy society should affect) all other community associations that surround it. Consequently, Bahá'u'lláh placed great emphasis on the education of the couple to learn to recognize the capacities and limitations of one another, thereby providing them with a reasonable amount of protection from making frivolous mistakes in their relations with each other. A Bahá'í who wishes to marry must obtain the consent of his or her living natural parents as well as those of the prospective spouse (whether or not the latter is a Bahá'í). Unlike the tradition which long prevailed in the East, parents do not have the right to choose a mate for their sons or daughters. But unlike the conditions which presently exist in the West, the couple is not free, by themselves and without the consideration of their parents (who may be directly affected by the consequences of their decision to marry), to make a decision which will intimately concern many others.[27]

The Bahá'í teachings enjoin chastity before marriage, as the sex-

---

[26] Bahá'u'lláh, *Gleanings,* p. 265.

[27] See *A Fortress for Well-Being, Bahá'í Teachings on Marriage* for a complete study of the Bahá'í teachings related to marriage.

ual instinct is an endowment related to the procreation of children and the strengthening of the marriage bond. For this reason, absolute faithfulness between the partners within a marriage is another law to which the Bahá'í writings attach great importance. While marriage is by no means compulsory for Bahá'ís, it is strongly recommended as "a fortress for well-being." Far from being regarded as a special virtue, celibacy is viewed by the Bahá'í writings as an undesirable limitation.[28]

The Bahá'í marriage service has no set form and may be extremely simple. All that is strictly required is an exchange of the vow: "We will all, verily, abide by the will of God." The service must be authorized by a spiritual assembly which has verified the parental consent and appointed witnesses. Prayers and devotions chosen by the bride and groom, as well as music, often complete the event.

PROVISIONS FOR DIVORCE

Divorce is permitted in the Bahá'í Faith, but it is strongly discouraged. The normal difficulties of married life are designed to "purify the characters" of the married couple and strengthen their union as the elementary building-block of society itself. Nevertheless, the Bahá'í teachings recognize that insoluble problems can develop in marital relationships where the couple may be entirely unsuited to one another. Therefore, if an estrangement between the Bahá'í husband and wife grows to the point where they are seriously considering divorce, Bahá'í law provides an institution called the "year of waiting": the parties live separately for one year's time, which provides them the opportunity to obtain counseling and

---

[28] In his summons to the Christian clergy, Bahá'u'lláh said: "Say: O concourse of monks! Seclude not yourselves in churches and cloisters. Come forth by My leave, and occupy yourselves with that which will profit your souls and the souls of men. . . . Enter ye into wedlock, that after you someone may fill your place. We have forbidden you perfidious acts, and not that which will demonstrate fidelity. Have ye clung to the standards fixed by your own selves, and cast the standards of God behind your backs? Fear God, and be not of the foolish. But for man, who would make mention of Me on My earth, and how could My attributes and My name have been revealed?" Cited by Shoghi Effendi in *Promised Day is Come*, p. 106.

undertake efforts to overcome the difficulties that have led to the marriage breakdown. Either of the parties may take the problem to the local spiritual assembly, which then meets with each of them and determines whether or not there is a willingness to attempt a reconciliation. Should that possibility not be apparent, the spiritual assembly will set the date of the beginning of the year of waiting as the date on which the couple establishes separate residences.

During the course of the year of waiting, the spiritual assembly will, often with professional assistance, attempt to help the couple to overcome their dificulties. A Bahá'í divorce can be obtained only after the full year of waiting is ended.

In a sense, one might consider this institution as a kind of "marriage hospital" where ailing marital relations are treated and by means of which the immediate pressures are temporarily removed and healing processes introduced, until such time as the healthy forces in the union are able to reassert themselves.

### ABSTENTION FROM POLITICAL INVOLVEMENT

Yet another law upon which Bahá'u'lláh placed great emphasis is the requirement that his followers strictly abstain from political involvement of any kind. At a first glance, one might expect to find the members of the Bahá'í community actively engaged in a wide range of political pursuits in furtherance of its universal ideals. The opposite is in fact the case. Bahá'ís are permitted to vote for any candidate who, in the privacy of their own conscience, they believe would make the most valuable contribution to the society in which they live. Bahá'ís may also accept nonpolitical government appointments. But they may not identify themselves with or campaign for any political party or partisan movement.[29]

The reason for this is the basic Bahá'í belief that the fundamental challenge to all people and nations today is the attainment of the

---

[29] There are a number of statements in the Bahá'í writings on the subject of obedience to government and of avoiding politics. See, for example, The Universal House of Justice, *Wellspring of Guidance*, pp. 131–136. "Relationship of Bahá'ís to Politics"; and The Universal House of Justice, *Messages from the Universal House of Justice, 1968–1973*.

unification of humankind. Real social progress, Bahá'u'lláh taught, waits upon attainment of this new level in the development of human civilization: "The well-being of mankind, its peace and security are unattainable unless and until its unity is firmly established."[30] Bahá'u'lláh held that political action, which is necessarily partisan and divisive in nature, cannot hold the answers to problems that are universal in their very essence. All political instruments, he pointed out, are limited and particular, whether they be national, racial, cultural, or ideological.

The Bahá'í principle of noninvolvement in politics does not prevent Bahá'ís from taking public positions on purely social and moral issues, when these issues are not part of any partisan political debate. Indeed, over the years Bahá'ís have been at the forefront of action on several social issues such as racial equality and nondiscrimination.

The principle of noninvolvement in politics is closely related, both in belief and practice, to the Bahá'í teaching of loyalty to government. Bahá'u'lláh called upon his followers to obey the government in power at a given time, and to refrain strictly from any attempts to subvert or to undermine it. Should the government of a nation change, the Bahá'í community must, in the same spirit of faithfulness, give its loyalty to the new administration, in every fashion consistent with the principle of nonpolitical involvement.[31]

## THE UNDERLYING REQUISITE OF BAHÁ'Í COMMUNITY LIFE: CONSULTATION

Underlying all the laws and community structures in the Bahá'í Faith is a group decision-making process called "consultation." Essentially, Bahá'í consultation involves a frank but loving exchange of opinions by members of a group with a view towards the determination of the truth of some matter and the establishment of

---

[30] Cited by Shoghi Effendi in *World Order of Bahá'u'lláh*, p. 203.

[31] "In every country where any of this people reside, they must behave towards the government of that country with loyalty, honesty and truthfulness." Bahá'u'lláh, *Tablets of Bahá'u'lláh revealed after the Kitáb-i-Aqdas*, p. 22–23.

a genuine group consensus. It is no exaggeration to say that virtually every member of the Bahá'í Faith is a student of the process of consultation. Shoghi Effendi said on this subject:

The principle of consultation, which constitutes one of the basic laws of the Administration, should be applied to all Bahá'í activities which affect the collective interests of the Faith, for it is through cooperation and continued exchange of thoughts and views that the Cause can best safeguard and foster its interests. Individual initiative, personal ability and resourcefulness, though indispensable, are, unless supported and enriched by the collective experiences and wisdom of the group, utterly incapable of achieving such a tremendous task.[32]

Similar emphasis is placed on this principle in Bahá'í family life, and particularly in the relationship between husband and wife. Even in purely personal concerns, Bahá'ís are encouraged to seek consultation with others, wherever the circumstances seem so to indicate. The Universal House of Justice cautions, however, that:

It should be borne in mind that all consultation is aimed at arriving at a solution to a problem and is quite different from the sort of group baring of the soul that is popular in some circles these days, and which borders on the kind of confession that is forbidden in the Faith. . . . 'We are forbidden to confess to any person . . . our sins and shortcomings, or to do so in public, as some religious sects do. However, if we spontaneously desire to acknowledge we have been wrong in something, or that we have some fault of character, and ask another person's forgiveness or pardon, we are quite free to do so.'[33]

One of the best-known summaries of the Bahá'í pattern of consultation is to be found in a passage from 'Abdu'l-Bahá's writings which has become a working document for the Bahá'í national and local spiritual assemblies:

The first condition is absolute love and harmony amongst the members of the assembly. They must be wholly free from estrangement and must manifest in themselves the Unity of God, for they are the waves of one

---

[32] *Consultation: A Compilation, Extracts from the Writings and Utterances of Bahá'u'lláh, 'Abdu'l-Bahá, Shoghi Effendi and the Universal House of Justice*, p. 15.
[33] *Consultation*, pp. 22–23.

sea, the drops of one river, the stars of one heaven. . . . They must when coming together turn their faces to the Kingdom on High and ask aid from the Realm of glory. They must then proceed with the utmost devotion, courtesy, dignity, care and moderation to express their views. They must in every matter search out the truth and not insist upon their own opinion, for stubbornness and persistence in one's views will lead ultimately to discord and wrangling and the truth will remain hidden. The honored members must with all freedom express their own thoughts, and it is in no wise permitted for one to belittle the thought of another, nay, he must with moderation set forth the truth, and should differences of opinion arise a majority of voices must prevail, and all must obey and submit to the majority. It is again not permitted that any one of the honored members object to or censure, whether in or out of the meeting, any decision arrived at previously, though that decision be not right, for such criticism would prevent any decision from being enforced. . . . Should they endeavor to fulfill these conditions the Grace of the Holy Spirit shall be vouchsafed unto them, and that assembly shall become the center of the Divine blessings, the hosts of divine confirmation shall come to their aid, and they shall day by day receive a new effusion of Spirit.[34]

One other interesting feature of the consultation of Bahá'í spiritual assemblies is the deliberate aim of achieving unanimity of view. Majority decision-making is, therefore, regarded as a minimal requirement of Bahá'í administrative consultation:

The ideal of Bahá'í consultation is to arrive at a unanimous decision. When this is not possible a vote must be taken. . . . As soon as a decision is reached it becomes the decision of the whole Assembly, not merely of those members who happened to be among the majority.[35]

## CONCLUSIONS

The laws we have discussed above, and other fundamental laws and governing procedures of the Bahá'í Faith, represent a fiber of "tough-mindedness" which runs through the entire fabric of the new religion. Superficially, one might expect to find a preference

---

[34] Shoghi Effendi, *Bahá'í Administration*, pp. 22–23.
[35] *Consultation*, p. 21.

for vagueness and perhaps a lack of realism among the members of a faith focused on the goal of the unification of humankind and the creation of a new global society based on justice. Certainly the Bahá'í message is a visionary one, and certainly members of the Bahá'í community are caught up in this vision. On the other hand, they do not believe that the goal can be achieved without very great sacrifice and effort, both by individuals and by entire societies.

They believe that the achievement of a world order and a world civilization involves the creation of a new way of life which will discipline human nature to the larger purposes of God. This discipline must affect the most homely circumstances of life, as well as the larger concerns of society. The institution of marriage must be restored to its position as the foundation on which civilization can flourish. Personal life must be spiritualized through the disciplines of prayer, meditation, and service to others. Social habits such as backbiting, which strike at the very roots of human association, must be eliminated, and people must give up their fascination for such barren pursuits as partisan politics in favor of learning cooperation and the art of true consultation. New social structures involving a much greater degree of individual participation must be implemented. It is the contemporary failure to submit to these necessary (and inevitable) disciplines, and to implement these new structures, that Bahá'ís regard as surrender to wishful thinking and reliance on magical solutions for the world's critical problems. In the words of Bahá'u'lláh:

They whom God hath endued with insight will readily recognize that the precepts laid down by God constitute the highest means for the maintenance of order in the world and the security of its people. He that turneth away from them is accounted among the abject and foolish. We, verily, have commanded you to refuse the dictates of your evil passions and corrupt desires, and not to transgress the bounds which the Pen of the Most High hath fixed, for these are the breath of life to all created things. . . .

O ye peoples of the world! Know assuredly that My commandments are the lamps of My loving providence among My servants, and the keys of My mercy for my creatures. . . . Were any man to taste the sweetness of the words which the lips of the All-Merciful have willed to utter, he would, though the treasures of the earth be in his possession, renounce them one and all, that he might vindicate the truth of even one of His commandments, shining above the Dayspring of His bountiful care and loving-kindness.[36]

---

[36] Bahá'u'lláh, *Gleanings,* pp. 331–332.

# 9. The Bahá'í Community

From earliest times, communities have been created around religious beliefs. The early responses to the teachings of the Buddha, Jesus Christ, and Muhammad are particularly dramatic examples of how many thousands of persons were drawn into communities bound together by their faith, each organized on the basis of principles and priorities laid down by the founder. As these communities grew and proved themselves able to meet the needs of the members, they came to embrace millions of adherents, and eventually gave rise to new states and cultures.

This has been the role of religion at even the most primitive stages of human civilization. In his widely-read study, *The City in History,* the social philosopher Lewis Mumford said of the earliest forms of human settlement:

[They] have to do with sacred things, not just with physical survival: they relate to a more valuable and meaningful kind of life, with a consciousness that entertains past and future, apprehending the primal mystery of sexual generation and the ultimate mystery of death and what may lie beyond death. As the city takes form, much more will be added: but these central concerns abide as the very reason for the city's existence, inseparable from the economic substance that makes it possible. In the earliest gathering about a grave or a painted symbol, a great stone or a sacred grove, one has the beginning of a succession of civic institutions that range from the temple to the astronomical observatory, from the theater to the university.[1]

The process of community-building is well advanced in the Bahá'í Faith. During the first century of its existence, the Bahá'í community was primarily concentrated in Persia where, as a proscribed and much persecuted minority, it had little opportunity to

---

[1] Lewis Mumford, *The City in History;* p. 9.

experiment with the teachings of its founder. Once the teaching plans were implemented under the direction of Shoghi Effendi, however, and particularly as these plans became global in scope, the collective life of the believers began to manifest some of these "society-building" potentialities. Whether the Bahá'í Faith will ultimately become the inspiration and guiding force of a new advance in world civilization, as have other revealed religions, is something only time will demonstrate. The important fact to note is that, as a result of the activities of the faith over the past 140 years, a global Bahá'í community has come into existence and is now rapidly expanding. An understanding of the Bahá'í Faith must include an appreciation of this important development.

As we have already seen, the spiritual inheritance of the members of the Bahá'í community is impressive. The history of the community since 1844, with its martyrs, its sacrifices, its achievements, and its drama, can genuinely be called heroic. The Bahá'í message is equally powerful: Bahá'u'lláh's teachings deal with a vast range of human concerns and explore many of the most vexing issues in modern human thought. Few would deny, either, that the Bahá'í administrative order is a remarkable achievement, both in the way its principles are attuned to the faith's aims and in the success with which its institutions have been established in the precise form planned by the founder. If one considers the history, the teachings, and the Bahá'í administration as Bahá'u'lláh's legacy to his followers, the new faith has begun its life with great advantages.

What have the heirs of Bahá'u'lláh done with this inheritance? What kind of community have they thus far been able to create as the result of their efforts to emulate the heroes of their faith, to understand the founder's purpose and message, and to organize their collective life on the administrative pattern laid down by him and by his appointed successors?

It may be helpful to begin with an examination of the physical size of the community and the kind of expansion that has occurred since its inception. While precise statistics are not available, there appear to be just over 3 million Bahá'ís around the world, of whom nearly half live in one or other of the two largest national communities: India and Iran. The total figure is not large when one considers the size of other religious movements that are roughly contemporary with the Bahá'í Faith.[2]

The significance of the growth emerges only as one examines the nature of the expansion that has occurred. It has been widespread. Today there are 30,000 elected local spiritual assemblies, functioning in over two hundred independent states and major territories; and there are more than 100,000 centers where Bahá'ís, or Bahá'í groups, reside. It is estimated by the Bahá'í International Community that this membership represents over two thousand different ethnic and tribal minorities, many of whom live in remote areas of the world: Pacific islands, Arctic settlements, jungle villages, and the Andean highlands. In their efforts to educate and organize the highly diversified communities entrusted to their care, the 143 national spiritual assemblies that have so far been established have translated and published Bahá'í prayers and literature in over six hundred and sixty languages.

That a relatively small religious community should be cosmopolitan, widespread, and highly organized at so early a stage in its history is an extraordinary accomplishment. The same may be said of the community's success in establishing its credentials in the eyes of civil authorities. Far from rejecting "the world" and the institutions that govern it, the Bahá'í community has deliberately pursued a close relationship with civil authorities as an integral part of its development. Through continuous efforts in a series of global development plans, Bahá'í spiritual assemblies at both the local and national levels have become legally incorporated in the majority of countries where the faith has been established. The

---

[2] The details of the expansion can be traced in *The Bahá'í Faith, 1844–1952;* as well as in *The Bahá'í World: A Biennial International Record,* vol. 7, 1936–1938; *The Bahá'í World: A Biennial International Record,* vol. 8, 1938–1940; *The Bahá'í World: A Biennial International Record,* vol. 9, 1940–1944; *The Bahá'í World: A Biennial International Record,* vol. 10, 1944–1946; *The Bahá'í World: A Biennial International Record,* vol. 11, 1946–1950; *The Bahá'í World: A Biennial International Record,* vol. 12, 1950–1954; *The Bahá'í World: An International Record,* vol. 13, 1954–1963; *The Bahá'í World: An International Record,* vol. 14, 1963–1968; *The Bahá'í World: An International Record,* vol. 15, 1968–1973; and *The Bahá'í Faith, Statistical Information, 1844–1968.*

Bahá'í marriage ceremony has secured formal recognition under a great many civil jurisdictions and, in various parts of the world, Bahá'í holy days are beginning to gain similar status to that which is accorded those of other major faiths in businesses, schools, and government offices.

In the United Nations, the Bahá'í International Community has steadily expanded the status accorded to it as a consulting member of various nongovernmental councils. Its representatives participate in the wide range of international conferences called by the various organizations and agencies of the U.N. family, thus gaining not only a forum for the faith's universal ideals, but also an opportunity for the Bahá'í community to directly participate in laying the foundations of international accord.[3]

Much attention is given to assuring that, to the extent circumstances permit, the general public in all parts of the world is made aware of the existence of the faith and the nature of its teachings. Publishing trusts in various countries print and distribute a great variety of Bahá'í literature, ranging from compilations of the writings of Bahá'u'lláh to scholarly commentaries, popular books, newsletters, and magazines. Other media are also extensively utilized: films, television programs and spot announcements, radio broadcasts, newspaper articles and advertisements, pamphlets, posters and manuals, correspondence courses, exhibitions, lecture series, and winter and summer schools. The objective of all this activity is to assure that, in time, every person on earth will come in contact with the message of Bahá'u'lláh.

One Bahá'í institution that has played a particularly prominent role in this program of public education is the house of worship. Today there are Bahá'í houses of worship on every continent, and a great many additional sites have been purchased around the world for future construction of these edifices, which are intended to play

---

[3] During the Five-Year Plan (1974–1979), for example, the Bahá'í International Community participated in thirty-five United Nations conferences and congresses around the world, in seventy-two regular sessions of the Economic and Social Council or its related bodies, and in the special session of the General Assembly devoted to the study of disarmament.

a central role in Bahá'í community life. Around each, in time, will be constructed other agencies such as schools or colleges, hostels, homes for the aged and administrative centers. At the present time, the houses of worship are not principally used for Bahá'í community services. Rather, they are opened as places where individuals of all religious backgrounds (or those professing no particular faith) meet in the worship of the one God. Services are nondenominational and consist of readings and prayers from the scriptures of the world's faiths, with no sermons or other attempts to cast these teachings in a mold of specifically Bahá'í interpretation. Selections are often set to music and sung by trained a capella choirs. The only requisite architectural features of a house of worship are that it have nine sides and a dome, symbolic of Bahá'í acceptance of all religious traditions and representative of the fact that, although the participants may enter by different doors, they assemble together in recognition of one Creator.

In many ways, the houses of worship are expressive of the attitude the Bahá'í Faith takes towards its relationship with the rest of society. The temples are open structures, filled with light. They are designed to express the Bahá'í commitment to unity in diversity and to demonstrate the practicality of the principle. In the case of the "Mother Temple of the West" located in Wilmette, Illinois, the architect integrated several major architectural traditions and wove together in his design the symbols of several of the major revealed religions. In his own words:

When man-made beliefs are rooted out of all religions, we find only harmony. Today, however, religion is foundering so much in superstitions and human theories that it has to be defined in a new form in order to become pure and spotless once more. It is the same in architecture. . . . Now, in this new concept of the Temple is woven, in a symbolical form, the great Bahá'í teaching of unity—unity of all religions and of all mankind. We find there combinations of mathematical lines, symbolizing those of the universe and in their complex merging of overlapping circles, circles within circles, we can describe the merging of all religions into one.[4]

---

[4] Cited in Louis Bourgeois, *Un Homme et Son Oeuvre.*

In the architecture of the houses of worship can also be seen the Bahá'í community's optimism. Bahá'ís confidently expect that the generality of humankind will eventually become followers of Bahá'u'lláh's teachings. They believe that, as the crises of the present age deepen, men and women everywhere will be moved to search more seriously for truth; and if the message of Bahá'u'lláh is properly presented, those who seek will respond to its precepts in ever-increasing numbers. In their openness of design, their integration of various architectural traditions, and their services free from sermons and ritual, the Bahá'í houses of worship powerfully express this spirit of optimism.

Thus far the optimism of the Bahá'í community seems fully justified. The Bahá'í Faith is now one of the world's most rapidly growing religious systems. In April 1979 the Universal House of Justice announced that the latest in the series of international teaching plans, the five-year plan launched in 1974, had been successfully completed. Many of its goals were surpassed, particularly with respect to the number of spiritual assemblies to be formed and the number of localities to be opened. It was estimated that the number of believers rose by over 40 percent during that five-year period.

Whereas the most rapid growth during the previous nine-year plan had occurred in Africa and Latin America, a marked lead had now been taken by Bahá'í communities in Asia and the Pacific islands. Encouraged by these results, the Universal House of Justice announced the immediate launching of a new seven-year plan to be completed by spring 1986.[5] By the time Bahá'í delegates from around the world gathered in Haifa for their 1983 international convention, this new undertaking was also exceeding its objectives.

The scope of the international Bahá'í community and the nature of the expansion that has characterized it have been briefly surveyed. More difficult is an examination of the internal life of the community. The most direct approach is to attempt to view it through the experiences of its members. How does one become a Bahá'í? What

---

[5] The details of the achievements of the five-year plan are outlined in *The Five Year Plan, 1974–1979: Statistical Report*.

features particularly stand out in the experience of a person who joins the Bahá'í Faith at this time in its history?

Obviously, the answers will vary from individual to individual. Moreover, there are likely to be significant differences of emphasis and priority in the various regions of the world, causing relative differences in the experiences of the membership. Nevertheless, the history of the Bahá'í Faith, its teachings, and the unfolding administrative order represent a total context that is essentially the same throughout the world, and this must inevitably evoke certain consistent responses from those who embrace it, whatever their ethnic origins.

With respect to the qualifications for Bahá'í membership, the Universal House of Justice has written:

The prime motive should always be the response of man to God's Message, and the recognition of His Messenger. Those who declare themselves as Bahá'ís should become enchanted with the beauty of the teachings, and touched by the love of Bahá'u'lláh. The declarants need not know all the proofs, history, laws, and principles of the Faith, but in the process of declaring themselves they must, in addition to catching the spark of faith, become basically informed about the Central Figures of the Faith, as well as the existence of laws they must follow and an administration they must obey.[6]

For those born into and raised by a Bahá'í family, the process of formal enrollment is fairly direct. While the Bahá'í teachings condemn dogmatism in child-raising, Bahá'í children are raised as members of the community. They participate in most of the events of the Bahá'í calendar, study Bahá'í history and the teachings of Bahá'u'lláh, as well as the other great world religions, and are encouraged to live by the standards of Bahá'í life appropriate to their age.[7] The emphasis the Bahá'í teachings place on contemporary social issues no doubt contributes to encouraging Bahá'í youth to continue their spiritual and intellectual search within the Bahá'í Faith. Nevertheless, they are free to reject such membership if they

---

[6] Cited in the Universal House of Justice, *Wellspring of Guidance*, p. 32.

[7] See *Bahá'í Education: A Compilation, Extracts from the Writings of Bahá'u'lláh, 'Abdu'l-Bahá, and Shoghi Effendi.*

wish. On reaching the "age of consent," which in the Bahá'í community is fifteen years of age, youths assume responsibility for their own individual spiritual development. At approximately this age, youths indicate whether or not they regard themselves as Bahá'ís and will continue to particiate in the Bahá'í community life.

In the case of those who come into the faith as adults, the decision to join the community is most frequently reached as a result of informal associations with believers. The community's wide range of information activities regularly attract thousands of interested inquirers to contact members of the faith. Through small study group meetings or more formally arranged presentations, inquirers are given the teachings and objectives of the Bahá'í Faith as closely as their inclinations prompt them. At some point, they may either spontaneously inquire about membership or they may be invited by Bahá'ís to consider it. Should they request membership, application is made to the local spiritual assembly of the area; if that institution is satisfied that the applicants understand the implications of membership and are prepared to assume the responsibility of living according to Bahá'u'lláh's teachings, they are enrolled. There are no rituals or pledges, but the event may be the occasion for an informal celebration.

Once enrolled as a member of the Bahá'í community, the new believer is caught up in two simultaneous processes: personal spiritual development, and the struggle of a very young community to understand and express the ideals expounded in the teachings of its founder. Prayer, meditation, fasting during the designated period of the year, abstention from the use of drugs and alcohol, and the struggle to avoid criticism and backbiting are the major elements of an explicit pattern of individual discipline. Likewise, the Bahá'í community is embarked on a long-term program of growth and expansion which demands concerted effort and an attention to priorities and goals. The thrust of Bahá'í belief and practice emphasizes the reciprocal relationship between the individual believer and the Bahá'í community.

The two challenges come together because of the emphasis the Bahá'í Faith places on service. Bahá'u'lláh taught that the highest expression of human nature is "service." Inner growth, "becoming one's true self," occurs as one serves the ideal of the unification of humankind. The aim of all personal spiritual discipline is to free the soul from a preoccupaton with itself, deepen the sense of identification with the whole of humanity, and focus energy on discovering ways to serve the needs of others. The activities of the Bahá'í community provide the individual a broad scope for such service. In the absence of a clergy, the affairs of the community are organized so as to encourage maximum participation by its entire membership.

Participation is particularly encouraged in efforts to promote the expansion of the faith. Bahá'u'lláh said that the greatest service which anyone can render in this day is to "teach the Cause of God."[8] Each individual Bahá'í is encouraged to share the task of taking the message of Bahá'u'lláh to the many people who, Bahá'ís believe, can be receptive to it. The time, 'Abdu'l-Bahá warned, is short. The crises that grip present-day society will deepen, and bring steadily more suffering and eventual destruction to existing institutions. An alternative way of life must be developed within Bahá'í communities, and this can only be done by vastly increasing the numbers in all lands who have responded to the call of Bahá'u'lláh and committed themselves to putting his teachings into effect.[9]

Not surprisingly, most newly enrolled members are eager to respond in whatever way they can to this appeal. They have found something which has given them great reassurance and purpose and they want to share it with others. Despite the strong emphasis on teaching, however, proselytism is explicitly forbidden.[10] Bahá'ís, therefore, face a challenge to find ways of sharing their beliefs that do not infringe on the privacy of others or offend the customs of the society in which they reside. The result has been to

---

[8] See the compilation entitled *The Individual and Teaching, Raising the Divine Call, Extracts from the Writings of Bahá'u'lláh, 'Abdu'l-Bahá, and Shoghi Effendi.*

[9] Bahá'u'lláh, *Gleanings,* p. 277.

[10] "If ye be aware of a certain truth, if ye possess a jewel, of which others are deprived, share it with them in a language of utmost kindliness and good will. If it be accepted, if it fulfil its purpose, your object is attained. If any one should refuse it, leave him unto himself, and beseech God to guide him. Beware lest ye deal unkindly with him." Bahá'u'lláh, *Gleanings,* p. 289.

generate a great deal of experimentation, varying widely from one part of the world to another and from individual to individual.

It is difficult to generalize regarding the nature of Bahá'í teaching activities. In most Western countries, Bahá'ís teach as individuals or as families, through the normal associations of daily life: conversations with neighbors, friends, and fellow workers; acquaintanceships that arise out of shared interests in public service projects; study courses or recreational activities; and encounters at Bahá'í events that are open to the public. In many other areas of the world, religion is the focus of much greater general interest and entire communities may become involved in discussing the new spiritual teachings. Large-scale enrollments in the Bahá'í Faith have occurred in Central Africa and South America, through visits by teams of Bahá'ís who combine musical and dramatic presentations with talks or study courses on the faith. In some social settings, the initiative may come from the prospective listeners. North American Bahá'ís have found themselves invited to speak to the congregations of black churches in the southern states or to "share the Bahá'í message" in presentations made at Native American pow wows in the Canadian prairies. Bahá'í academics in North America, in India, in the emerging nations of the Pacific, or in the Caribbean, may find themselves invited to lecture in colleges and universities on the teachings of their faith.

The most common method used in spreading the teachings of Bahá'u'lláh, however, is the "fireside." The term originated with the early Bahá'í group in Montreal, Canada, although the activity was already going on in a number of centers.[11] It describes small study groups held at regular intervals in private homes, to which friends and acquaintances are invited. This informal activity has been a prolific source of new members. It allows inquirers to explore the Bahá'í concepts, laws, and teachings at their own pace, free from the concern that their private spiritual search may be "on

---

[11] The authors are indebted for this information to Mrs. Rúḥíyyih Rabbani, widow of the late Guardian of the Bahá'í Faith, whose mother organized the original firesides in Montreal. The widespread use of the term no doubt owes much to its incorporation in the Guardian's correspondence.

display," as might be the case in an open meeting. The arrangement also strengthens ties that continue after a new member has joined the Bahá'í community, and permits the Bahá'í teacher to assist his or her integration into the community.

A special form of teaching is the service Bahá'ís call "pioneering." As there is no clergy, neither are there professional missionaries who carry the Bahá'í teachings to new localities. Rather, the Bahá'í Faith expands as a result of the initiative taken by thousands of its followers who, individually or in families, leave their homes to settle in new places. Pioneers are expected to support themselves through their trade or profession and to perform their Bahá'í services in their free time. Jobs are changed, houses are sold and new ones found, second languages are learned, and many other aspects of day to day life are reordered for the sole purpose of introducing the Bahá'í Faith to some new town, district, or territory.

Pioneering may also involve moving to an entirely different country where the faith is not yet firmly established. In each global teaching plan, the Universal House of Justice identifies a list of countries which need the assistance of community workers from elsewhere and specifies the number required. In many of the plans, specific goals are assigned to the various national Bahá'í communities; not infrequently three or four different countries may be called upon to send pioneers to the same country or region. As a result, a goal center in Finland or Haiti may have received pioneers from Iran, France, Japan, and the United States. Entirely apart from the resources these new arrivals represent, the host community's experience of the Bahá'í principle of "unity in diversity" is greatly enriched (as is, no doubt, the experience of the pioneers arriving from abroad).

In this as in all its activities, therefore, the Bahá'í community depends directly on the initiative and responsibility undertaken by individual believers. No agency monitors the extent to which any person discharges his or her obligation to teach the faith. While a spiritual assembly may intervene if a particular individual's teaching activities seem inappropriate in some way, the response to the call of teaching is decided upon by the believer in his or her own conscience. This is equally true of pioneering, a service considered to be a great privilege. Each month, the pioneering and teaching needs are shared with the members of each local Bahá'í community at the nineteen-day feast, as well as at conferences and through the community's various publications. The initiative must come from within the heart of the individual believer and from the consultation of the Bahá'í family. The pioneer or pioneer family then approaches the administrative agencies of the faith to consult on specific projects and goals.

Voluntary participation is also the key to the financing of the Bahá'í Faith's many programs. At the beginning of the Bahá'í year, each local or national spiritual assembly decides on the budget required to carry out the projects for that particular year, whether related to teaching goals, property purchase and development projects, administrative expenses, or community services. These needs are then announced to the Bahá'í community in the same manner as are the teaching and pioneering needs. The professional "fund-raising" often associated with religious and charitable organizations is not permitted in a Bahá'í community. Only general appeals may be made; individual canvassing is prohibited. All contributions are voluntary, and Shoghi Effendi strongly condemned anything suggestive of psychological manipulation.[12] Moreover, the contributions are kept confidential between the individual or family and the treasurer of the institution to whom the contribution is made.

Bahá'ís consider the opportunity of contributing to the Bahá'í Fund as a spiritual privilege reserved for those who have recognized Bahá'u'lláh. Consequently, no contributions in any form for the advancement of the Bahá'í Faith can be accepted from persons who are not registered Bahá'ís. Not infrequently, Bahá'í assemblies have donations pressed on them by non-Bahá'ís who are appreciative of one or another of the community's programs. In such instances, the donors are urged to divert the funds to a public charity. In the case of anonymous donations, the Bahá'í administration puts the contri-

---

12 *Bahá'í Funds and Contributions,* p. 11.

butions into a public charity. Only with regard to programs that serve the social, economic, or educational needs of society in general can Bahá'í agencies accept and use funds from non-Bahá'í sources. This policy heightens the individual members' feeling of identification with and personal responsibility for the work undertaken by the community.[13]

The administration of the affairs of the Bahá'í community also offers many opportunities for the individual's response to the Bahá'í ideal of service. The fact that the Bahá'í Faith is a layman's religion impresses itself on new members very soon after enrollment. They realize that they have joined a community, not a congregation. The members of the community perform not only the more humble tasks of "service functions," but are also fully responsible for the decision-making process, for planning, and for serving as formal representatives of the community.

New members of the community quickly come to realize that their adopted faith is in its formative stages. There is not only a great deal of room for experimentation, within the broad outlines laid down by the Bahá'í writings and under the ongoing guidance of the Universal House of Justice; but there is also an acute need for this experimentation, in order to assure that the rapidly evolving community can achieve its amibitious goals. If the new believer has specific talents, these may soon be put to use. He or she may be asked to teach a children's class, to design newspaper advertising, to serve on a delegation to the mayor of the city or to a government commission, to host a nineteen-day feast, to assist in planning a regional conference, to take part in a musical or dramatic event, to run a projector, build a display, type correspondence, assist with bookkeeping, set up a small library, or any one of a variety of other

---

[13] The Bahá'í approach to financing the faith is summed up in a letter from Shoghi Effendi sent to the National Spiritual Assembly of the Bahá'ís of the United States in 1942: "We must be like the fountain or spring that is continually emptying itself of all that it has and is continually being refilled from an invisible source. To be continually giving out for the good of our fellows undeterred by the fear of poverty and reliant on the unfailing bounty of the Source of all wealth and all good: this is the secret of right living." Cited in *Bahá'í Funds and Contributions*, p. 16.

community activities. To respond to the question: "Why are we not doing such-and-such?" the answer more often than not is: "Because up until now there's been no one with the time or ability required to undertake it."

An active social life is a prominent feature of the Bahá'í community. Reference was made in chapter 8 to the nineteen-day feast that forms the basis of Bahá'í social community life at the local level, and to the importance which the Bahá'í writings attach to all aspects of this gathering. The regional and national conventions are also occasions for consultation on the affairs of the community, and at the same time involve a great deal of socializing among the believers of the region or the country.

In addition, the community regularly holds conferences of all kinds. Each global teaching plan includes arrangements for a number of international conferences in major centers. These are well-attended events, with Bahá'ís coming in from many parts of the world to spend three to five days celebrating recent teaching achievements, studying current trends and needs, and acquainting themselves with new literature, audio-visual resources, and other aids to community development. The Hands of the Cause (see chapter 8) are often featured speakers at these events, as are leading Bahá'í scholars in various fields. The conferences also provide an opportunity for Bahá'ís to experience firsthand the range of cultures represented in the worldwide Bahá'í community through dramatic, musical, and other artistic presentations.[14]

This pattern is followed, to the extent resources permit, at the national and regional levels as well. As a result, Bahá'ís generally benefit from an unusual opportunity to get to know one another. The amount of traveling these events entail tends to further provide members with an increased exposure to the customs and social patterns of other societies than would otherwise be the case. For many, no doubt, it also provides the occasion for informal teaching of the faith, and makes the possibility of an eventual pioneer project

---

[14] During the current seven-year plan, international conferences were held in Montreal, Canada; Quito, Ecuador; Lagos, Nigeria; Canberra, Australia; and Dublin, Ireland.

both more attractive and less intimidating to the individual or family who may be considering it.

No Bahá'í institution contributes more intensely to the spiritual and social enrichment of the believers' experience than pilgrimage. Bahá'u'lláh encouraged each of his followers to try, at least once during a lifetime, to undertake a nine-day pilgrimage to the World Centre of the Bahá'í Faith in Haifa, Israel. Increasing numbers of believers respond to this injunction, so many in fact that, for the past several years, there has been a waiting period.

The pilgrimage is considered one of the high points of any Bahá'í's life. He or she arrives in Haifa as one of a group of eighty or so believers from all parts of the world. For nine days the group visits the holy places in and around Haifa and Acre. Alone or in small groups they spend time in the shrines of Bahá'u'lláh, the Báb, and 'Abdu'l-Bahá. They may visit the homes inhabited by the founder of their faith during his exile and imprisonment in the Holy Land, and devote part of a day to touring the magnificent Archives Building where the original Bahá'í writings may be examined and articles sacred to the memory of the central figures of the faith and its early heroes and martyrs may be viewed. Portraits of the Báb and Bahá'u'lláh, not otherwise on display, are also available for viewing.[15] The close and still relatively informal bonds that unite the Bahá'í community at this early stage in its growth are enhanced by a reception given by the Universal House of Justice to each group of pilgrims, and the opportunity the individual believers may have for an informal association with the members of this supreme institution of their faith.

For the pilgrims, the experience is usually intense. Bahá'ís believe that in many respects the pilgrimage represents one's nearest approach in this life to the World of God. In the words of a highly respected Bahá'í writer, the former Anglican archdeacon, George Townsend: "God has passed by" in the revelations of the Báb and Bahá'u'lláh. At Haifa and at Acre, the believer is in contact with the

---

[15] Shoghi Effendi discouraged the display of portraits of the Báb and Bahá'u'lláh, except during the brief pilgrimage viewings, so as to avoid their becoming objects of veneration.

most intimate traces of this divine passing, and the experience brings his or her mind and heart to intensely concentrate on the fundamental truths of the Bahá'í revelation.

The pilgrimage also provides individuals with an opportunity to further enrich their social understanding of the global community of which they are members. To spend nine days in close association with people from many different cultures is a chance that is available only to a relatively small number in modern society. To do so in an environment reminiscent of a shared history of tragedy, sacrifice, and achievement is to intensely experience the "global family" the revelation of Bahá'u'lláh has brought into being. In addition, the pilgrimage is often an occasion for Bahá'ís to undertake travel-teaching projects in other parts of the world, to visit friends who are pioneering overseas, and to explore firsthand the possibilities of undertaking such a project themselves.

Along with moral and spiritual training of this kind, Bahá'u'lláh placed great emphasis on education in the arts and sciences. Bahá'ís are urged not only to assure the best possible education for their children, but also to take advantage of educational opportunities in society for their own continuing development.

Knowledge is as wings to man's life, and a ladder for his ascent. Its acquisition is incumbent upon everyone. The knowledge of such sciences, however, should be acquired as can profit the peoples of the earth, and not those which begin with words and end with words. Great indeed is the claim of scientists and craftsmen on the peoples of the world.[15]

From its earliest days, the Bahá'í community in Persia took this injunction very seriously. As a result, after the passage of three or four generations, the community has reached a point where its members represent an important percentage of the educated class in present-day Iran, although they number only about 300,000 in that country.[16] In a country where the literacy rate has hovered under 40

---

[15] Bahá'u'lláh, *Epistle to the Son of the Wolf*, pp. 26–27.

[16] The achievement has had unexpected and unwelcome consequences during the recent political upheavals in Iran. Representing so significant a segment of the educated classes, many Bahá'í families had built successful careers in the civil service, the professions and in business and industry. This very prominence,

percent, the Bahá'í community has enjoyed a literacy rate of over 90 percent.

The Iranian example is being followed by Bahá'ís around the world, to whatever extent local facilities make possible. One of the specific tasks that recent international teaching plans have assigned to local and national spiritual assemblies has been the provision of counseling for Bahá'í youth to assist them in planning their education so as to be of maximum service not only to their faith, but to humankind.[17] Many Bahá'í summer and winter schools offer programs of this type. They also take advantage of whatever time qualified speakers can make available to conduct courses relating to contemporary knowledge in the various disciplines to the teachings of the Bahá'í writings. The example of mature scholars who have successfully integrated science and faith in their own intellectual lives no doubt serves as a strong stimulant to young believers to follow their example.[18]

Where public schooling is inadequate or unavailable, local Bahá'í communities begin educational programs of their own, particularly at the elementary level. In India, the National Spiritual Assembly operates several full-time Bahá'í schools offering courses at the primary, secondary, and technical training levels. Correspondence courses for adults as well as for children and youth are a major activity in many other national Bahá'í communities. During the last international Plan thirty-seven different national spiritual assemblies indicated that they had instituted similar programs.

---

however, attracted the hostility of revolutionary elements. With cruel irony, the Bahá'ís found themselves accused of "profiting" from the former régime, despite the systematic discrimination against them under the two Pahlavi shahs and despite their record of total abstention from partisan politics.

[17] The Iranian Bahá'ís have set an example for other communities with heavy pioneering responsibilities by encouraging their youth to pursue courses of study which will make it especially easy for them to find work in developing countries: in medicine, in nursing, in engineering, in technical education, in agricultural sciences, and so forth.

[18] In 1974 a group of Bahá'í students and university professors formed the Association for Bahá'í Studies (ABS). It has since established the Centre for Bahá'í Studies in Ottawa, Canada, with national affiliates around the world. The principal aim of the Association is to develop courses and resource materials for the study of the Bahá'í Faith in institutions of higher learning.

An aspect of education that has received marked attention from the earliest days of Bahá'í history is the aesthetic. Bahá'u'lláh designated art a form of worship to God, and the physical beauty of Bahá'í shrines, temples, and gardens is one of the dominant impressions observers carry away from their contacts with the Faith. Shoghi Effendi emphasized that it will be a matter of centuries before anything that might be called "Bahá'í art" may be expected to appear. It is only when a revelation has fully blossomed into a new civilization that new art forms emerge which may be specifically identified with it. At the same time, there is no doubt that the work of contemporary artists who are Bahá'ís has been affected by Bahá'u'lláh's appeals for unity, harmony, openness, and optimism. The American Bahá'í artist, Mark Tobey—one of the most renowned painters of the twentieth century—said of this influence on his work:

This universal Cause of Bahá'u'lláh which brings the fruition of man's development, challenges him and attracts him to see the light of this day as the unity of all life; [it] dislodges him from a great deal of automatic and environmental inheritance; [it] seeks to create in him a vision which is absolutely necessary for existence. The teachings of Bahá'u'lláh are themselves the light with which we can see how to move forward on the road of evolution.[19]

Regarding the relationship of art to the future world civilization, Tobey added:

Of course we talk about international styles today, but I think later on we'll talk about universal styles . . . the future of the world must be this realization of its oneness, which is the basic teaching as I understand it in the Bahá'í Faith, and from that oneness, will naturally develop a new spirit in art, because that's what it is. It's a spirit and it's not new words and it's not new ideas only.[20]

Bahá'í musicians have been similarly influenced. Indeed, 'Abdu'l-

---

[19] Cited by Arthur Dahl in "The Fragrance of Spirituality: An Appreciation of the Art of Mark Tobey," in *The Bahá'í World: An International Record,* vol. 16, 1973–76, pp. 638–645. Tobey attracted another internationally famous artist to the Faith, the British potter Bernard Leach.
[20] Ibid., p. 644.

Bahá devoted a great deal of attention to encouraging the Bahá'í communities to make good use of those individuals possessing musical talents:

The art of music is divine and effective. It is the food of the soul and spirit. Through the power and charm of music the spirit of man is uplifted. It has wonderful sway and effect in the hearts of children, for their hearts are pure and melodies have great influence in them. The latent talents with which the hearts of these children are endowed will find expression through the medium of music. Therefore you must exert yourselves to make them proficient; teach them to sing with excellence and effects. It is incumbent upon each child to know something of music . . .[21]

Such, then, are some of the features of the life of the Bahá'í community which has taken up the legacy of the history, the teachings, and the administrative institutions bequeathed to it by Bahá'u'lláh. It has been established in most of the countries and territories on earth; it is representative of a cross-section of humanity; and it remains devoted to the mission entrusted to it by 'Abdu'l-Bahá: "the spiritual conquest of the planet." The process of its expansion involves its individual members in various types of participation, social interaction and personal development. This interaction and subsequent spiritual growth produce a sense of "global family" and provide the community with a new identity, distinct from that of other religious traditions.

Bahá'ís see this community as not merely a collective, but as an organic whole. The writings of 'Abdu'l-Bahá and Shoghi Effendi are studded with the language of biological analogy: "efflorescence," "evolution," "germ," "seed," "organic development," "nucleus," "generating influence," "assimilation." Bahá'ís are encouraged to see themselves individually as parts of a living, growing organism whose life systems are the laws, teachings, and institutions created by Bahá'u'lláh. The Universal House of Justice has emphasized that the development of the individual's capacities and

---

[21] 'Abdu'l-Bahá, cited in *Bahá'í Writings on Music*, p. 6.

sense of identification with the Bahá'í teachings depends upon his or her ability to fully participate in the life of the community:

In the human body, every cell, every organ, every nerve has its part to play. When all do so the body is healthy, vigorous, radiant, ready for every call made upon it. No cell, however humble, lives apart from the body, whether in serving it or receiving from it. This is true of the body of mankind in which God "has endowed each humble being with ability and talent," and is supremely true of the body of the Bahá'í world community, for this body is already an organism, united in its aspirations, unified in its methods, seeking assistance and confirmation from the same Source, and illumined with the conscious knowledge of its unity. . . . The Bahá'í world community, growing like a healthy new body, develops new cells, new organs, new functions and powers as it presses on to its maturity, when every soul, living for the Cause of God, will receive from the Cause, health, assurance and the overflowing bounties of Bahá'u'lláh which are diffused through His divinely ordained Order.[22]

Moreover, Bahá'ís believe that the life of their community provides a model for the unification of humankind, a model which should encourage all those interested in this ideal, regardless of whether or not they themselves become Bahá'ís. In July 1976, on the fortieth anniversary of the World Congress of Faiths held in Canterbury, England, the Bahá'í spokesman concluded his presentation with the following:

If I may then sum up: . . . there now exists a promising, operating model for the spiritually-based world society which this Congress was founded to seek. The model is a global community which, far from seeing itself as already complete or self-sufficient, is embarked on an infinite series of experiments at the local, national and international levels in its efforts to realize the vision of mankind's oneness which it finds in the Writings of its Founder and of all the Messengers of God. In this great undertaking all people of goodwill are free to participate.

I . . . draw your attention especially to a number of notable features which the model demonstrates: universality, unity, a relevant and effective moral system, a common history, a coherent administrative framework, and an embrace which accepts all the varieties of human life. For a

---

[22] The Universal House of Justice, *Wellspring of Guidance*, pp. 37–38.

global community to manifest these features at this critical stage in history seems to me the most significant development which could come to our attention. For its existence is, so far as I am aware, the first convincing evidence that the goal we seek here is fully realistic and eminently attainable within the foreseeable future. No matter how limited in size or self-restricted in influence the model may be, such a phenomenon deserves the most able and most disinterested study mankind can bring to it.[23]

---

[23] Douglas Martin, "Bahá'u'lláh's Model for World Unity," in *Bahá'í World, 1973–1976* vol. 16, p. 685.

# 10. The Challenges of Success

In the Introduction, we noted an opinion tentatively advanced by Edward Granville Browne, one of the first Western scholars to encounter the Bahá'í Faith in Persia in the nineteenth century. Browne expressed his belief that the young faith probably represented the beginnings of a new world religion. It appeared to him to offer a unique opportunity for scholars to examine in detail just how a new religion comes into being.[1] As a result of his initial investigations, Browne devoted much of his time over the next three decades to a careful study of Bahá'í origins; he produced several critical commentaries and published some English translations of major pieces of Bábí and Bahá'í literature.

These efforts were not universally appreciated by Browne's contemporaries. Although his work attracted the sympathetic support of some of his colleagues, others felt that he was giving disproportionate attention to what they saw as merely a reform movement within the Islamic religion.[2] In the influential scholarly journal *The Oxford Magazine,* one reviewer went so far as to denounce Browne's Bahá'í studies as an "absurd violation of historical perspective."[3]

The history of the hundred years since Browne took up his study of the Bahá'í Faith has vindicated his initial judgment. Slowly but certainly, a new and independent religious system has taken shape and become established in virtually every part of the world, a system distinct from the Islamic milieu from which it emerged. It is no longer surprising to find modern authorities on

---

[1] E. G. Browne, *A Traveller's Narrative,* p. viii.

[2] See, for example, E. Denison Ross, "Babism" in *Great Religions of the World,* pp. 189–216. Ross was a British orientalist and an academic friend of Browne.

[3] Cited by E. G. Browne in his introduction to Myron H. Phelps, *Life and Teachings of Abbas Effendi* p. xiii, f.n. 1.

comparative religion, such as historian Arnold Toynbee, including the Bahá'í Faith with Islam and Christianity as one of the world's independent religions.[4] The same opinion has been expressed, although in a rather different spirit, by official spokesmen for Islamic institutions. As early as 1924, a Sunni Appellate Court sitting in Beba, Egypt, concluded in a test case submitted to it for judgment, that: "The Bahá'í Faith is a new religion entirely independent [of Islam]. . . . No Bahá'í, therefore, can be regarded as a Muslim or *vice versa*, even as no Buddhist, Brahmin or Christian can be regarded a Muslim."[5]

Bahá'ís believe that this new independent faith has the capacity to unite the peoples of the world and will, in the distant future, make possible the birth of a global civilization. It will do so, they emphasize, as their community is able to respond to the tests created by its own success. The question of tests, in the Bahá'í meaning of the term, needs special comment.

Tests, Bahá'u'lláh taught, are essential to human growth. If we are not tested, 'Abdu'l-Bahá said, the capacities latent within us, and which are our eternal endowment, will never develop:

Were it not for tests, genuine gold could not be distinguished from the counterfeit. Were it not for tests, the courageous could not be known from the coward. . . . Were it not for tests, the intellects and faculties of the scholars in the great colleges could not be developed.[6]

This concept applies also to the development of the Bahá'í community itself. Shoghi Effendi wrote:

Indeed, the history of the first hundred years of its evolution resolves itself into a series of internal and external crises, of varying severity, devastating in their immediate effects, but each mysteriously releasing a corresponding measure of divine power, lending thereby a fresh impulse to its unfoldment, this further unfoldment engendering in its turn a still graver calamity, followed by a still more liberal effusion of celestial grace en-

---

[4] See Foreword, fn. 1.
[5] Cited in Shoghi Effendi, *God Passes By*, p. 365.
[6] 'Abdu'l-Bahá, *The Divine Art of Living*, p. 91.

abling its upholders to accelerate still further its march and win in its service still more compelling victories.[7]

Before concluding our study, therefore, it will be helpful to consider the new kinds of tests the Bahá'í Faith is now beginning to encounter as an established religion with growing recognition. As the faith approaches the hundredth anniversary of its founder's passing, the principal challenges facing the Bahá'í community include (1) maintaining a unified community; (2) achieving universal participation; (3) coping with increasing opposition; and (4) establishing a Bahá'í way of life as a model that will serve the emergence of world civilization.

The single most important endowment of the Bahá'í Faith is its unity. One of the primary goals of the Bahá'í community is to help humankind to bring about the unification of the human race. In the eyes of a highly skeptical age, therefore, the faith's most interesting credential is the fact that it has passed safely through the first critical century of its history with the unity of its community firmly intact (i.e., it has not divided into sects).[8] Alone, this achievement distinguishes it among the religions of the world, as there is no other significant religious movement of which the same can be said. Time and again, in all forms of religious association, the process of schism has taken hold in the early, most vulnerable stages; and the originating impulse has had to continue its work through the efforts of often contending sects and denominations.

For earlier world religions, the problem was somewhat less critical. Other concerns had first claim on the energy and attention of the believers. In the case of the Bahá'í Faith, however, unity is the hallmark of its claim to divine origins. Bahá'u'lláh condemned in the strongest terms any attempt to introduce the virus of party

---

[7] Shoghi Effendi, *God Passes By*, p. xiii.

[8] As the stories of Muḥammad-'Alí and Ibrahim Kheiralla (see chapter 4) indicate, the success of the Bahá'í community in avoiding schism has not been due to any lack of attacks on its fundamental unity. In addition to these two contemporaries of 'Abdu'l-Bahá, the history of the Bahá'í Faith since the death of Bahá'u'lláh in 1892 has seen several attempts by prominent members of the Bahá'í community to detach segments from it and set up factions loyal to themselves. None of these efforts, however, attracted the support of any significant number of Bahá'ís, and most perished with the deaths of those individuals who initiated them.

or factionalism into the community.[9] There are no "liberal," "orthodox," or "reformed" Bahá'ís. There are only Bahá'ís, members of a single, organically unified community.

What will happen now that the faith has begun very rapidly to expand its membership around the world, among cultures and peoples radically different from one another? Will it be able to maintain the same degree of unity when some regional communities are decades ahead of others in the integration of some of the faith's teachings into their social structure, while remaining decades behind others in terms of available resources and administrative sophistication? Today we live in an era of bitterly intense political pressures. Will the Bahá'í communities in countries currently being torn apart by ethnic and cultural rivalries be able to continue to expand their membership by attracting people from these numerous contending backgrounds? The authority of the Universal House of Justice is vital to the faith's unity. Will it be able to maintain Bahá'í discipline in a highly diversified and rapidly growing religious community during a time of such widespread social breakdown? For that matter, will the Bahá'í community be able to maintain unity of belief by focusing on the interpretations of the teachings of Bahá'u'lláh which have been provided by the central figures of the Bahá'í revelation, including the Guardian, Shoghi Effendi?

In one respect, the Bahá'í community is obviously far better

---

[9] In his *Will and Testament*, 'Abdu'l-Bahá (pp. 12–13) called upon the Hands of the Cause to immediately expel from the faith any individual who was deemed to be deliberately attempting to subvert the unity of the community. The test is to determine the individual's attitude toward the central institutions established in the Covenant of Bahá'u'lláh: "The sacred and youthful branch, the guardian of the Cause of God, as well as the Universal House of Justice, to be universally elected and established, are both under the care and protection of the Abhá Beauty [i.e., Bahá'u'lláh], under the shelter and unerring guidance of His Holiness, the Exalted One [i.e., the Báb] . . . whatsoever they decide is of God. Whoso obeyeth him not, neither obeyeth them, hath not obeyed God. . . ."

'Abdu'l-Bahá made it clear that he was not speaking here of differences of opinion or failures in personal behavior, but rather of deliberate efforts to create a schism by denying the authority established in the Bahá'í writings. He termed one who does this a "covenant-breaker" and asserted that such a person could no longer claim to be a Bahá'í or to have any connection with the Bahá'í community.

equipped to meet these challenges today than was ever the case in the past. No one with a reasonably good understanding of the Bahá'í teachings and history could plead confusion regarding the position of the Universal House of Justice as the sole legislative authority for the community. The documentation is complete and has been widely published; the entire body of believers participates in the election of this institution along the lines laid down by Bahá'u'lláh; and the Universal House of Justice itself has guided the development of the global community through successive global teaching plans in which all of the other agencies of the community have carried out the roles assigned to them by the House.

Any vulnerability the faith may have at this point in its history is related rather to the Bahá'í community's rapid expansion and to the uncertain world situation. In recent years, scores of thousands of new believers have joined the faith annually, and this continuous increase in membership now seems to be further accelerating. This is particularly true in the Third World. Large sections of the global community consist of new members who have come into the faith because of an "intuitive" recognition of Bahá'u'lláh as the Messenger of God, and because of the attraction exerted by the spirit and the practical example of Bahá'í unity.

Many of these new believers are illiterate, and consequently the consolidation of the growing community depends heavily on a network of travel and communications which becomes daily more disrupted through uncontrollable world events. Both 'Abdu'l-Bahá and Shoghi Effendi predicted that a time would come when, owing to the effects of a general social disruption and eventual complete breakdown, communications with the World Centre of the faith would be temporarily interrupted (as, indeed, they were during World War I and World War II), from time to time and perhaps over significant periods of time. Will the infant Bahá'í administration be able to maintain the present unity of belief and action during such periods?

The Bahá'ís are confident that it will. For them, the Covenant of Bahá'u'lláh holds an absolute assurance that God will continue to preserve the unity of his community as he has done through the vicissitudes of the past years. Certainly, the agencies of the faith possess the scriptural authority required to revoke the membership of any individual or group of individuals who, after counseling and warning, attempt to create a schism. Nevertheless, one thing is evident: the Bahá'í community is now moving into a stage in its development where its painstakingly preserved unity will be further subjected to powerful stresses.

A second challenge facing the community today is to secure the participation of the mass of its members in the work of the faith. At first glance, the issue hardly seems one which should preoccupy the members of this faith. The Bahá'í community is a lay organization (i.e., without a clergy); one of its distinguishing characteristics is the extent to which its members, from the highly placed to the most humble, are already involved in the conduct of its affairs.

This feature is not, however, merely a gratifying adjunct to its life. It is essential to its survival and growth. The *raison d'être* of the Bahá'í Faith is to build a new kind of society that can become the model for a global civilization. It will succeed, at least in the eyes of its founder and its adherents, only as it moves steadily along the path to the accomplishment of this mission. Such progress depends on the mobilization of enormous human and material resources. For a community so small, relatively speaking, these resources can be made available only through the willingness of all or the vast majority of the membership to take an active part in the community's programs. It was no doubt with such considerations in view that the Universal House of Justice set "universal participation" as one of the twin goals of its first global plans the first of which was launched in April 1964, a year after its first election.[10] Elaborating on this theme, the Universal House of Justice published the following statement:

. . . the participation of every believer is of the utmost importance, and is a source of power and vitality as yet unknown to us. . . . If every believer will carry out these sacred duties, we shall be astonished at the accession

---

[10] Universal House of Justice, *Wellspring of Guidance,* p. 25.

of power which will result to the whole body, and which in turn will give rise to further growth and a showering of greater blessings on all of us.

The real secret of universal participation lies in the Master's [i.e., 'Abdu'l-Bahá's] oft-repeated wish that the friends should love each other, constantly encourage each other, work together, be as one soul in one body, and in so doing become a true, organic, healthy body animated and illumined by the Spirit.[11]

This appeal has obvious applications to the life of the Bahá'í community in the Western world. In the younger communities of Africa, South America, Asia, and the Pacific, where the faith was introduced primarily by pioneers and teachers from Iran and North America, the call for universal participation has still another dimension: in these lands, the challenge is for the large indigenous memberships of the Bahá'í community to assume full responsibility for the administration of the faith in their countries, and for its development along lines appropriate to the particular cultural environment.

The Bahá'í community, as a whole, has already made impressive progress in this direction. Early photographs of the national spiritual assemblies from a number of these areas (indeed, even from some of the smaller European nations) showed a high percentage of foreign pioneers. This has now completely changed. There are few, if any, national communities where the affairs of the faith are not fully in the hands of believers indigenous to those parts of the world. Control of the administration of the Baha'i community is, however, only the first step. The challenge now is for the indigenous membership of these large Bahá'í communities to assume full responsibility for the many detailed activities required by the global plans devised by the Universal House of Justice: creating schools and community centers, organizing economic development projects, and pressing ahead with the establishment of closer ties with civil government authorities at all levels.

Nowhere is the challenge to participation greater than in the work of spreading the Bahá'í message. Although the present rate of membership growth would be considered impressive by most

---

[11] Universal House of Justice, *Wellspring of Guidance*, p. 38.

religious bodies, it falls far short of generating the millions of supporters needed to realize Bahá'u'lláh's vision for his community.
Clearly, this is because only a small minority of the Bahá'ís are as
yet directly engaged in teaching the faith to others. In part, this may
be an effect of the Bahá'í prohibition against aggressive proselytism,
a principle whose value few observers would wish to dispute. Since
many Bahá'ís are successfully attracting others without violating
this principle, however, it seems evident that much greater participation is the real issue.

In short, the present situation opens up opportunities for the
increased active participation by thousands of Bahá'ís who might
otherwise have remained mere passive members of the community.
Will this actually occur? Or will the attractions and pressures of
political and economic issues divert the energies of the more able
believers from the faith's programs, as has happened with the membership of a number of other religious organizations? Can the indigenous members of the larger national communities adapt the
pattern of Bahá'í life imported by foreign pioneers in a way that
meets their regional needs while remaining faithful to Bahá'u'lláh's
vision? Can they generate the human resources which the international Bahá'í community so urgently requires to carry out its ambitious programs?

Such challenges as those discussed above are the kind of positive stimulation on which healthy organisms tend to thrive. Other
challenges are less attractive. There are people who are deeply opposed to the expansion of the Bahá'í Faith and, in some cases, bent
on its destruction. Bahá'ís, generally, are disinclined to dwell on the
subject, but it is one which is addressed vigorously in the writings
of their faith. Shoghi Effendi, for example, said:

How can the beginnings of a world upheaval, unleashing forces that are so
gravely deranging the social, the religious, the political, and the economic
equilibrium of organized society . . . fail to produce any repercussions on
the institutions of a Faith of such tender age whose teachings have a direct
and vital bearing on each of these spheres of human life and conduct?

Little wonder, therefore, if they [the Bahá'ís] . . . find that in the midst
of this whirlpool of contending passions their freedom has been curtailed,

their tenets contemned, their institutions assaulted, their motives maligned, their authority jeopardized, their claim rejected.[12]

Such attacks, to one degree or another, have marked the entire century and a third of the young religion's life. Recently, they have begun to grow in seriousness and to demand an energetic and unified response from the international Bahá'í community. In several Muslim countries, opposition has taken the form of overt campaigns of suppression, and in Iran, the land of the Bahá'í Faith's birth, the result has been human suffering on a vast scale.

The principal offense of the Bahá'í Faith in the eyes of the Shiah Muslim clergy in Iran is its very existence. Fundamentalist Muslim theology regards Muhammad as the last messenger whom God will send, and Islam as the final religion for all humankind. In this view, therefore, it is literally impossible for any new religion to come into existence. Forced to deal with the fact that the Bahá'í Faith not only exists but is rapidly expanding, fanatical Muslims, particularly in Shiah Iran, have sought to picture it variously as a "heresy," "a political movement," or "a conspiracy against Islam," and regard the extirpation of the faith as a service to God.

Under the regime of the shahs, and in response to this pressure from the clergy, the Bahá'í Faith was denied the civil recognition accorded to the beliefs of the other three religious minorities in the country: Jews, Christians, and Zoroastrians. Since civil rights in Iran were dependent on the formal recognition accorded to one's religious faith, this meant that the more than 300,000 Bahá'ís, who outnumber the other three minorities combined, had no recourse to the protections of civil law.

The result was to expose Bahá'ís to whatever injuries the ill-disposed among the Muslim majority decided to visit upon them. Bahá'í cemeteries were frequently desecrated by organized mobs, Bahá'í children were commonly humiliated in class as "dirty Bábís," Bahá'ís were denied employment in several branches of the civil service, and many members of the Faith were beaten, raped, and even killed in occasional outbursts of fanaticism aroused by the

---

[12] Shoghi Effendi, *Advent of Divine Justice*, p. 2

Shiah Muslim clergy. Occasionally, in order to distract public attention from political or economic concerns, the Shah's regime would itself initiate persecution of the Bahá'ís as scapegoats. In 1955 one such organized persecution required the intervention of the United Nations.[13]

Following the Islamic revolution in early 1979, the situation worsened.[14] Under the direction of Shiah clergy now in control of the new government, Bahá'í properties were seized, Bahá'í shrines were occupied by armed Muslim bands and largely destroyed, the faith's cemeteries were bulldozed, members of the community were driven from their jobs and had their pensions canceled and their savings expropriated, and Bahá'í children throughout Iran were expelled from school. The new Islamic Constitution, adopted in the fall of 1979, made the exclusion of the Bahá'ís from any civil rights even more explicit than had the old imperial constitution.

In the summer of 1980 revolutionary committees began arresting the members of the local and national Bahá'í Assemblies, as well as other prominent believers, and sentencing them to death. Although an effort was made by the regime's spokesmen outside Iran to represent these killings as the execution of "spies," the indictments were explicit in identifying the victims' Bahá'í beliefs and memberships as the "crimes" for which they had been sentenced, and each was offered his or her life in return for conversion to Islam. The executions and other acts of persecution against Bahá'ís were openly reported in the government-controlled press in

---

[13] For a full discussion of the persecutions during the Pahlavi period see Douglas Martin, "The Bahá'ís of Iran under the Pahlavi Regime, 1921–1979," in *Middle East Focus*, vol. 4, no. 6, 1982, pp. 7–17.

[14] The new regime's views were expressed by Ayatollah Khomeini in an interview with Professor James Cockroft of Rutgers University in December 1978, published in the U.S. journal of public affairs, *Seven Days*, 23 February 1979, p. 20. The transcript of the interview was approved by the Ayatollah and his aide, Dr. Ibrahim Yazdi:

*Question:* "Will there be either religious or politcal freedom for the Bahá'ís under an Islamic government?"

*Answer:* "They are a political faction; they are harmful; they will not be accepted."

*Question:* "How about their freedom of religion—religious practice?"

*Answer:* "No."

Iran as the suppression of "the Bahá'í heresy."[15] Finally, in August 1983, the Islamic regime formally banned all Bahá'í religious, educational, and charitable institutions in Iran. In obedience to the Bahá'í principle of submission to civil authority in such matters, the National Spiritual Assembly of the Bahá'ís of Iran disbanded all local spiritual assemblies and then announced its own dissolution. Despite this compliance, the authorities began imprisoning all former members of the disbanded assemblies, in effect making the decree retroactive. The United States Congress heard firsthand evidence that the prisoners were systematically tortured to secure recantations and confessions of "espionage."

The Bahá'í response to these attacks has taken two forms. When repeated appeals to the successive Iranian revolutionary regimes met with no response, a concerted effort was made to secure international intervention. Beginning with a unanimous resolution in the summer of 1980 by the Canadian Parliament, several national governments began pressing Iran to halt the campaign of terror. The European Parliament followed suit in the fall of 1980, and a succession of hearings by agencies of the United Nations led to a series of annual resolutions, one of which, in March 1984, established a mandate for investigation by the Secretary General. The Congress of the United States has twice denounced the persecution in particularly strong terms. This pressure, coupled with widespread publicity given by world media to the Iranian Bahá'ís' ordeal, may have succeeded in imposing some restraint in Iran. The wholesale massacres which were at one time threatened by the more extremist elements of the Shiah Muslim clergy, have so far not taken place.[16]

In the long run, however, the most significant response will

---

[15] In an interview with the government-controlled newspaper, *Khabar-i-Junúb,* Shiraz, Feb 22, 1983, the Islamic religious judge who sent ten Bahá'í women and teenage girls to the gallows in that city said: "Before it is too late Bahá'ís must recant Baha'ism. Otherwise the Islamic Nation will soon . . . fulfill the prayer mentioned in the Qur'án: 'Lord, leave not on earth a single family of infidels.' " For a documented examination of the persecution, see *The Bahá'ís in Iran, A Report on the Persecution of a Religious Minority.*

[16] For a fuller discussion of both the persecution under the Islamic regime and the Bahá'í response to it, see Douglas Martin "The Bahá'ís of Iran under the Islamic Republic, 1979–1983," in *Middle East Focus,* vol. 6, no. 4, pp. 17–27, 30–31.

likely be that of the Iranian Bahá'í community itself. Despite the attacks of the mullas, the Iranian Bahá'ís have maintained their attitude of respect for Islam. To them, the criticism that their faith might be antagonistic to Islam appears to be particularly unjustified. They have pointed out that, in becoming Bahá'ís, great numbers of believers from Christian, Jewish, Buddhist, or Hindu backgrounds have also accepted the divine character of Islam and its Prophet.

The community has also given conclusive evidence of its adherence to the Bahá'í principle of respect for civil government and avoidance of involvement in partisan politics. Although the most abused minority in present-day Iran, Bahá'ís have refused to take part in the various civil upheavals by which the political enemies of the Islamic regime have sought to bring about its demise. Indeed, they initially refrained from appealing for international intervention during the first year of the current persecution, out of a willingness to give the regime a chance to correct the abuses that were occurring. The same policy, which Bahá'ís believe will be a long-term protection for their Faith, had consistently been followed under the Pahlavi dynasty.

From a purely objective point of view, the current ordeal in Iran may be said to have had important benefits for the religion, however agonizing the cost. The worldwide attention given to efforts to alleviate the suffering of Bahá'ís has entailed a massive education of government officials, academics, the media, and the general public in many lands about the nature of the Bahá'í Faith and its aims and teachings. The very nature of the issues involved has tended to throw into clear relief the peaceful and progressive character of the Bahá'í community. For Bahá'ís outside Iran, the experience of arising together to defend their fellow believers against an unprovoked and barbarous assault has no doubt had a powerful consolidating effect on the faith of its highly diverse membership. Above all, the heroic capacity for self-sacrifice demonstrated by the Iranian believers has served as convincing proof that the faith's original spiritual impulse has in no way abated. Once again, the ancient adage that "the blood of the martyrs is the seed of the faith" is being demonstrated, this time before the television cameras of the world.

Persecution of Bahá'ís has not been limited to Muslim societies. Like many other religions the Bahá'ís have also encountered hostility from totalitarian regimes. In Nazi Germany the faith was officially banned and its activities forbidden. This was primarily because of the Bahá'í teachings of racial oneness. In communist countries, suppression has been almost as complete. Marxist theory, which denies the existence of God and of a rational soul, and which seeks to account for all of humankind's social history through a philosophy of materialism, "defined" the Bahá'í Faith out of existence without examination. There was no more room for a new revelation from God in the Marxist cosmography than for earlier ones. In Soviet Russia, a great many Bahá'ís were arrested and eventually exiled to Siberia; the institutions of the faith were dissolved; its literature and archives were seized; and a ban was placed on all of its teaching activities. The Bahá'í house of worship in Ishqábád, the first ever erected, was confiscated for government use.[17] Today, the degree of suppression varies from one communist country to another, but in all cases there have been severe restrictions imposed on the Bahá'í community's continued existence.[18]

As a result of this politico-philosophical rejection of the spiritual foundations of the faith, there has been little opportunity for Bahá'ís to enter into discussions with communist governments. This circumstance may change as antireligious measures in communist states gradually ease. Certainly, there would appear to be no objective reason why the Bahá'í Faith should be seen as a political threat.[19] The community has scrupulously avoided identification with the diplomatic policies of any nation or group of nations,

---

[17] It had been built in the late nineteenth century. The Soviet authorities eventually demolished it.

[18] Shoghi Effendi, *God Passes By*, pp. 361–362, summarizes the experience of the Bahá'í community under Nazi and Communist regimes.

[19] Bahá'ís are required to obey a communist government as they would any other, although Shoghi Effendi is explicit in ranking communism itself with racism and nationalism as ideologies harmful to human progress: Shoghi Effendi, *The Promised Day Is Come*, p. 117.

investing its energies instead in the work of the United Nations and its complex of organizations and agencies.

As the Bahá'í community continues to expand, Bahá'í scholars seek to apply Bahá'u'lláh's teachings to economic issues. Increasingly, they will find themselves drawn into dialogue with spokesmen of the various schools of socioeconomic thought, including those influenced by Marxist theory. Without doubt, this encounter will stimulate new developments in Bahá'í community life and thought. Bahá'ís hope that it will not also excite new kinds of opposition.

Finally, the Bahá'í Faith has sustained a persistent onslaught from various representatives of traditional Christianity, particularly from returning missionaries.[20] No area of Christian missionary work has been so barren and so discouraging as the Islamic Near and Middle East. Over seventy years ago Edward Granville Browne pointed out that a number of Christian missionaries who had witnessed the failures of their efforts had begun to resent the successes of the Bahá'í teachers who were working in the same areas. This antagonism was exacerbated as the Bahá'í Faith began to make significant progress in Western countries as well, among persons of Christian background. The response of the missionaries was to join with their Muslim counterparts in publishing bitter attacks on Bahá'í motives and practices. A faith which had been the object of barbarous persecutions in the East now found itself subject in the West to gross distortions of its history and teachings and efforts to represent it as hostile to Christianity.[21]

Today, Christian ecclesiastics who oppose the Bahá'í Faith tend

---

[20] See, for example, S. G. Wilson, *Bahá'ism and Its Claims*; J. R. Richards, *The Religion of the Bahá'ís*; W. M. Miller, *Baha'ism Its Origins and Teachings*, New York, Chicago, Fleming H. Revell company, 1931; R. P. Richardson, numerous articles, including "The Persian Rival to Jesus . . . ," August 1915 and "The Precursor, The Prophet and The Pope," October 1915, *Open Court*, a journal of comparative religions.

[21] Robert Richardson, "The Precursor, The Prophet and The Pope", in *Open Court*, vol. XXX, November 1916, p. 626, says, for example, of the Bahá'í belief that the Manifestation of God is infallible: "This doctrine, which can be characterized only as the most pernicious religious principle that any human being has ever dared to set forth—the very principle which actuated the religious sect known as the Assassins—had been consistently adhered to by Bábís and Bahá'ís through thick and thin."

to attack it on historical rather than theological grounds. Representing themselves often as disinterested scholars who encountered the Bahá'í Faith during their studies of comparative religion, these writers have sought to portray the faith as a form of religious conspiracy conceived by a succession of individuals of questionable moral character.[22] While their use of documentation and other forms of historical evidence would be dismissed by scholars, it is likely that the authors achieve a degree of the success they seek. The academic packaging gives such works an air of thoroughness and authority which may well deceive many general readers who lack a basis upon which to assess the material.

Such attacks on their faith represent a special kind of challenge for Bahá'ís. Not surprisingly, most are strongly disinclined to involve themselves in religious controversy. Apart from whatever natural distaste they may have for such involvement, the Bahá'í teachings strongly discourage disputation and retaliation. In the words of 'Abdu'l-Bahá:

> Recognize your enemies as your friends and consider those who wish you evil as the wishers of good. You must not see evil as evil and then compromise with your opinion, for to treat in a smooth, kindly way one whom you consider evil or an enemy is hypocrisy and this is not worthy nor allowable. No! You must consider your enemies as your friends, look upon your evil-wishers as your well-wishers and treat them accordingly. Act in such a way that your heart may be free from hatred.[23]

For the most part, therefore, Bahá'ís have left the task of responding to criticism of their faith from disgruntled Christian clergymen to Bahá'í institutions. Where attacks have included attempts to misrepresent the faith in the media, Bahá'í assemblies have responded with public statements drawing attention to responsible scholarly sources. With religious fundamentalism on the rise in many parts of the world, however, opposition to the Bahá'í vision

---

[22] An example is a book by the long-standing missionary opponent of the Bahá'í Faith, Reverend William Miller, *The Bahá'í Faith, Its History and Teachings*. For a Bahá'í commentary, see Douglas Martin, "The Missionary as Historian" in *World Order*, vol. 10, no. 3, 1976, pp. 43–63.

[23] Cited in H. Colby Ives, *Portals to Freedom*, p. 169.

of humankind's future on the part of certain elements among the Christian clergy can only be expected to increase.

Opposition represents a challenge that will assume new forms and dimensions as the activities of the Bahá'í community expand and attract greater public attention. The spirit in which the Bahá'ís meet these new attacks and their response to the issues will have a profound effect on the emerging international image of their faith and on the quality of life within their own membership.

The maintenance of unity, the response to opposition, and the involvement of the great majority of the members of the community in its work of expansion would not, in themselves, fulfill Bahá'u'lláh's purpose. Nor would they be likely to convince humankind in general that the Bahá'í revelation holds the answers to humanity's future. This will happen only if an increasingly skeptical age observes among Bahá'ís the features of a new and more attractive way of life. In an often-quoted statement, Shoghi Effendi said:

One thing and only one thing will unfailingly and alone secure the undoubted triumph of this sacred Cause, namely, the extent to which our own inner life and private character mirror forth in their manifold aspects the splendour of those eternal principles proclaimed by Bahá'u'lláh.[24]

There is little doubt that the Bahá'í community provides an attractive alternative to much of what imposes itself on the attention of modern society. From its earliest days, the character of the members of the faith has generally won admiration and praise from observers. Edward Granville Browne made the following observation in the late nineteenth century:

I have often heard wonder expressed by Christian ministers at the extraordinary success of Bábí [i.e., Bahá'í] missionaries, as contrasted with the almost complete failure of their own. . . . The answer, to my mind, is plain as the sun at midday. [There follow some comments critical of certain aspects of Christian sectarianism]. . . .

To the Western observer, however, it is the complete sincerity of the Bábís, their fearless disregard of death and torture undergone for the sake

---

[24] Shoghi Effendi, *Bahá'í Administration*, p. 66.

of their religion, their certain conviction as to the truth of their faith, their generally admirable conduct towards mankind, and especially toward their fellow-believers, which constitute their strongest claim on his attention.[25]

Present-day observers tend to be equally complimentary about the community. A practical demonstration of full racial integration, a consistent avoidance of religious controversy or criticism of other faiths, a freedom from the taint of moral and financial scandal too often associated with modern-day religious movements, the spread of the Bahá'í message without recourse to aggressive proselytism, and a general reputation for hospitality which the community has gained—each of these has helped to lay the foundations of widespread respect.

Again, however, the augmenting crises in human affairs today present awesome challenges to the Bahá'í community's claim to represent a model for radical social change. In Western countries, the public will be watching to see whether, for example, Bahá'í marriages and family life represent a new beginning: whether the teachings of Bahá'u'lláh give hope that the general trend toward the disintegration of this basic social building block can be reversed. In Africa, tribalism continues to frustrate the efforts of political and religious movements alike to provide an appropriate identity around which a different type of society can be organized. Do the Bahá'í communities in those countries show signs of meeting this challenge? In many Asian cultures, despite concerted programs of education, women remain in the essentially inferior social position they have occupied throughout the centuries. While Bahá'í communities have made great strides in breaking this pattern, can Bahá'u'lláh's teachings on the equality of the sexes so permeate these communities as to open up to Bahá'í women the transformational role in society which he envisioned for them?

Finally, can the Bahá'í community demonstrate the relevance of its beliefs to the economic problems that are crippling the social and spiritual life of mankind? Already, in several Third World countries,

---

[25] E. G. Browne, in his introduction to Myron H. Phelps, *Life and Teachings of 'Abbás Effendi,* pp. xv–xx.

there are areas where Bahá'ís are becoming a majority of the local inhabitants and where their local assemblies are directly facing this challenge. At the 1983 international convention, the Universal House of Justice announced the creation of a new Office of Social and Economic Development. Bahá'í communities have been encouraged to begin "at the grassroots level" a host of projects that will draw on the social and economic principles to be found in Bahá'u'lláh's writings. Clearly, the community sees itself engaged in a process of learning through experimentation in economic affairs, rather than as offering an ideological system. These efforts will be an aspect of Bahá'í life that will attract particularly sharp scrutiny in the difficult years that lie ahead.

Such challenges will test to the utmost Bahá'í heroism and enthusiasm in the closing years of the twentieth century. Particularly will they test the potential of the global Bahá'í community as a new social model. In the years immediately ahead the followers of Bahá'u'lláh will have ample cause to ponder deeply the statement in which the founder of their faith drew the distinction between his mission and that of an earlier Manifestation of God:

Verily He [Jesus] said: "Come ye after Me, and I will make you to become fishers of men." In this day, however, We say: "Come ye after Me, that We may make you to become the quickeners of mankind."[26]

No observer of the Bahá'ís' struggle will fail to note that their faith enjoys one enormous advantage unknown to any previous period of its history. The world appears at last ready to listen. The rising rate at which people in many parts of the world are becoming Bahá'í tells only a part of the story. Equally important is the growing acceptance outside the community of the diagnosis of the human condition found in Bahá'u'lláh's writings. With the spreading loss of faith in technology, in the transforming power of wealth, and even in the efficacy of political action, there is a deepening conviction in many quarters that fundamental social change depends upon some form of spiritual and moral transformation. Expressed another way, there is an emerging consensus among many thinkers

---

[26] Cited in Shoghi Effendi, *Promised Day Is Come*, p. 120

that the "global village" made possible by science and technology will be one that human beings can live in only if some universal system of values can generate unity of purpose. Aurelio Peccei, in his last presidential address to the Club of Rome, meeting in Budapest, put the matter succinctly:

Thanks to the extraordinarily great progress made by our techno-scientific and industrial capacity, we have accumulated the elements and forged the instruments of fantastic power; yet we have not acquired a clear vision and comprehension of how much all this progress has enhanced our position and enlarged our responsibilities on earth. . . .

We must therefore construct a philosophy of life adapted to our times, building it around "pillars of wisdom" which necessarily must be consistent with the character and imperatives of this age.[27]

A host of social scientists, political philosophers, and economists echo both his conviction that belief is fundamental to social order and that, in Bahá'í terms, "the earth is one economy."[28] By 1980 the influential study produced by the Brandt Commission was warning that the restructuring of our system of values had become a matter of survival itself.[29] A flood of literature by social commentators like Alvin Toffler, Marilyn Ferguson, Fritjof Capra, and John Naisbitt has made certain that the message and its metaphysical implications have been communicated to a popular readership.[30] International conferences on the future, extensively covered by the media, have focused public attention on spiritual questions that once concerned only theologians.

---

[27] Aurelio Peccei, "Food Prospects . . . ," *Globe and Mail,* Toronto, Oct. 20, 1983, p. 11.

[28] See, for example, Robert L. Heilbronner. *Beyond Boom and Crash* New York: W. W. Norton, 1978; Michio Morishima. *Why Has Japan Succeeded? Western Technology and the Japanese Ethos,* Cambridge: Cambridge University Press, 1982; Barbara Ward. "A Global Marshall Plan" in *Dialogue for a New Order,* edited by Haw Khadija, New York: Pergamon, 1980.

[29] The Brandt Commission. *North-South: A Program for Survival.* Cambridge: M.I.T. Press, 1980.

[30] See, for instance, Fritjof Capra. *The Turning Point* New York: Bantam Books, 1982; Marilyn Ferguson. *The Aquarian Conspiracy* Los Angeles: J. P. Tarcher, 1980; Hazel Henderson. *Creating Alternative Futures* New York: Berkley Windhover Books, 1978; John Naisbitt. *Megatrends* New York: Warner Books, 1982.

If such views represent the direction humankind's search for security is taking, and if the Bahá'í Faith continues on the course it has so far unwaveringly followed, then one can readily believe that somewhere ahead lies that point of eventual convergence spoken of by Bahá'u'lláh over a century ago:

This is the Day in which God's most excellent favors have been poured out upon men, the Day in which His most mighty grace hath been infused into all created things. . . . Soon will the present-day order be rolled up, and a new one spread out in its stead.[31]

---

[31] Bahá'u'lláh, *Gleanings*, pp. 6–7.

# Appendix:
# Edward Granville Browne

The name of Edward Granville Browne has a special place in the history of the Bahá'í Faith's first century. While studying medicine at Cambridge in the 1880s, Browne became attracted to a field of research which he was to make his life's work: the literature and history of Persia. This in turn led him to investigate the Bábí movement, which he first encountered in the influential study by Joseph Arthur de Gobineau, *Les Religions et les Philosophies dans l'Asie Centrale*. A trip to Persia followed in 1887–1888, in consequence of which Browne set about the compilation and translation of major pieces of Bábí and and Bahá'í literature and the preparation of a number of scholarly studies in the field. Several of these were published under the auspices of the Royal Asiatic Society.

Browne's researches eventually took him to Palestine where, in 1890, he had the privilege of a series of four interviews with Bahá'u'lláh, two years before the latter's death. As idealistic as he was brilliant, Browne found himself irresistibly attracted by the heroic story of the new faith. The effects can be seen in reading the Introduction to his translation of 'Abdu'l-Bahá's *Traveller's Narrative*[1] and the lengthy paper entitled "Babism" published in *Religious Systems of the World*.[2]

Unhappily, as time passed, Browne's scholarly work became intertwined with late Victorian political preoccupations. Because of his great admiration for the Persian people, he longed to see them freed from the ignorance and despotism under which the

---

[1] Edward G. Browne *A Traveller's Narrative written to illustrate The Episode of the Báb.*

[2] Edward G. Browne "Babism" in *Religious Systems of the World, a contribution to the study of comparative religion.*

dual regime of the Shiah clergy and the Qájár dynasty kept them. Consequently, he became an advocate of the so-called "Constitutional Movement" in Persia.[3] Browne raised money for the movement in Europe, spoke widely on its behalf, and made his home at Cambridge a way-station for Persian exiles. His liberal political sympathies were greatly intensified by nationalistic ones: the Constitutionalists were viewed in British imperialist circles as natural allies against Tsarist Russia which supported the Qájár Shahs.

Because Browne believed that the Bahá'í community (or "Bábí" community as he continued to call it) was the most cohesive progressive force in Persia, he looked to it to take the lead in bringing about political, as well as social change. To his intense disappointment, the Bahá'ís refused to be drawn into either domestic or international conflicts. The reason was Bahá'u'lláh's assumption of the prophetic role for which the Báb had prepared the way, and his refusal to compromise the universal nature of his message for partisan political ends. Browne's unhappiness is apparent in words he wrote about Bahá'u'lláh's statement on the oneness of humankind:

Bahá'ism, in my opinion, is too cosmopolitan in its aim to render much direct service to that revival [i.e., of Persian political life]. "Pride is not for him who loves his country," says Bahá'u'lláh, "but for him who loves the world." This is a fine sentiment, but just now it is men who love their country *above all else* that Persia needs. [italics added].[4]

Only one small handful of Bábís were prepared, indeed eager, to assume the political role which Browne had envisioned for them. These were the Azalís, who had by this time abandoned their erstwhile leader, Mírzá Yaḥyá, to his lonely exile on Cyprus, and had suddenly metamorphosed into political ideologists, journalists, and

---

[3] The Constitutionalists, a strange alliance of obscurantist Shiah mullas and radical secular politicians, were the forerunners of the revolutionary movement that eventually brought the Ayatollah Khomeini to power in 1979.

[4] English Introduction to *Nuqṭatu'l-Káf,* cited by Balyuzi, *Edward Granville Browne and the Bahá'í Faith,* p. 88.

underground agents.[5] In the process, they entered into intimate correspondence with Browne and became, as he said, his most trusted collaborators. It was these men, intensely ambitious for political careers and blocked by Bahá'u'lláh from using the Báb's legacy to this end, who provided Browne with the documents on which he based most of his later research.[6]

The effect was unfortunate, from the point of view of scholarship. The Azalí episode was of only passing significance in Bahá'í history, and key documents on which Browne placed great reliance proved, in time, to be spurious.[7] Particularly regrettable was the importance which Browne was induced to give to a strange document that he purportedly discovered in 1892 among the papers of the late Comte de Gobineau and that he later published under its esoteric Persian title *Kitáb-i-Nuqtatu'l-Káf* ("Book of the Point of K"). The full story is beyond the scope of this Note, but the subject deserves a brief glance because of the effect which Browne's decision had in temporarily derailing the study of Bahá'í origins.

Ostensibly a history of the Bábí movement, the *Nuqtatu'l-Káf* was attributed by Browne to a respected Bábí martyr, Hájí Mírzá Jání, who had been executed forty years earlier, in 1852, and who was known to have written a personal memoir of some of the events in which he was involved. Browne's sole authority for this attribution was Mírzá Yaḥyá, already discredited among most of his former associates; the manuscript itself bore no author's name.

---

5 The Azalís had refused to accept Bahá'u'lláh, and continued to refer to themselves as "Bábís". Most of them appear, however, to have abandoned all religious attachments in favor of radical political action in which their closest allies were, ironically, the same Shiah Muslim clergy who had instigated the earlier massacres of Bábís.

6 The two who took the lead in this were Aḥmad-i-Rúḥí and Áqá Khán-i-Kirmání, who had each married a daughter of Mírzá Yaḥyá. They appear to have regarded Browne's interest in Bahá'u'lláh as a threat to their political agenda. Thus the aim of the documents they generated was to represent Bahá'u'lláh as having usruped an authority that belonged in right to Yaḥyá. The extent of their influence can be seen in Browne's persistence in using the term "Bábí" to designate the community that had long since adopted the name Bahá'í.

7 See, for example, Hasan Balyuzi's discussion of two Azalí contributions in *Edward Granville Browne:* the "Hasht Bihisht," pp. 19–21, 33–34, 80–84; and the Persian Introduction to the Kitáb-í-Nuqtatu'l-Káf, pp. 70, 73–88.

Although excerpts from Jání's lost record do indeed seem to have been included, it should have been readily apparent to Browne that the martyr could not have been the author of the *Nuqṭatu'l-Káf.* Apart from other internal evidence, references are made in it to events which occurred in 1853-1854, over a year after Jání's death. Moreover, there is considerable reason to believe that the final version was put together some time in the late 1860's and a copy forwarded anonymously to Paris, either to Gobineau himself, or, after his death, to the Bibliothèque Nationale which had secured his collection of books. The collection is not mentioned in Gobineau's own book, *Les Religions et les Philosophies dans l'Asie Centrale* (published 1865) where it certainly would have been treated as a key source.[8] A prominent Bahá'í scholar who at one point had worked with a copy of the original Jání memoirs, Mírzá Abu'l-Faḍl Gulpaygani, denied flatly that the *Nuqṭatu'l-Káf* was the document in question.

Since the text of the *Nuqṭatu'l-Káf* contains extravagant praise of Mírzá Yaḥyá and seeks to deprecate the leadership which Bahá-'u'lláh is known to have exercised in events the book purports to describe, the manuscript may represent an attempt by partisans of Yaḥyá to reinforce the latter's fading role in the late 1860's. The bizarre character of some of the theological content, faithfully reflecting Yaḥyá's known views, lends further credence to this notion. Considerably more research will be required in order to unravel the mystery of the document's origins.

Browne, however, seized upon the *Nuqṭatu'l-Káf* as an authentic history of the events which so deeply interested him. Against all of the objective evidence, he appears to have been persuaded by his Azalí collaborators that the Bahá'í community had deliberately suppressed this early account because they wished to re-write Bábí history, in order to reinforce Bahá'u'lláh's claim. It is apparent from some of Browne's own references to the subject that he saw himself in the position of his contemporaries among spokesmen for the

---

[8] Precisely how the manuscript eventually entered the Gobineau collection remains mysterious; no evidence has yet come to light which would show that Gobineau himself ever had the item in his possession or was familiar with its contents.

so-called "Higher Criticism", biblical scholars who were simultaneously finding in the various Synoptic Gospels traces of sectarian
rivalries among the early Christians.[9]

Whatever the reason, the effect was to divert attention from
critical developments in the rise of the new religion. Perhaps sens-
ing this, Browne retained an association with the Bahá'í community to the last, corresponding with 'Abdu'l-Bahá, meeting him in
both London and Paris during his Western trip in 1911, and eventually contributing an obituary to the January 1922 issue of the *Journal
of the Royal Asiatic Society.* The latter described the late leader of
the Bahá'í Faith as one "who has probably exercised a greater influence not only in the Orient but in the Occident, than any Asiatic
thinker and teacher in recent times."

A valuable first step in assessing Browne's contribution to
Bahá'í history was taken in 1970 by the British-Iranian scholar
Hasan Balyuzi, under the title *Edward Granville Browne and the
Bahá'í Faith.* A full appreciation must await future studies which
will distinguish Browne's enduring scholarly achievements from
the more ephemeral political activities of his time. Whatever these
researchers reveal, the study of Bahá'í origins has been immensely
enriched by the balance of scholarship and sympathy which led a
distinguished Western authority to record so meticulously his firsthand experiences with the founders of the new faith.

---

[9] In this connection, Browne mentions the suggestion of one of his close friends
the British Foreign Service, Sir Cecil Spring-Rice, that relationship between Bahá-
'u'lláh and Yaḥyá was perhaps like that between Saint Paul and Saint Peter (with
reference to the former's usurpation of the primacy of the latter). In fact, as Browne
had earlier noted, the only meaningful analogy between the events of Christian and
Bahá'í history was that the Báb fulfilled a role for Bahá'u'lláh not unlike that which
John the Baptist had fulfilled in preparing the way for Jesus Christ. The only part
which a pursuit of this insight would have suggested for Mírzá Yaḥyá was that
played in Christian history by Judas Iscariot, an idea which would have had little
appeal for either Browne or his Azalí correspondents.

# Bibliography

## BOOKS

'Abdu'l-Bahá. *'Abdu'l-Bahá in Canada*. Compiled by the National Spiritual Assembly of the Bahá'ís of Canada. Toronto: National Spiritual Assembly of the Bahá'ís of Canada, 1962.

———. *Paris Talks, Addresses Given By 'Abdu'l-Bahá in Paris in 1911–1912*. London: Bahá'í Publishing Trust, 1912. 11th ed. 1969.

———. *The Promulgation of Universal Peace, Talks Delivered By 'Abdu'l-Bahá During His Visit to the United States and Canada in 1912*. Compiled by Howard MacNutt. Wilmette: Bahá'í Publishing Trust, 1922–1925. 2d ed. 1982.

———. *The Secret of Divine Civilization*. Translated by Marzieh Gail and Ali-Kuli Khan. Wilmette: Bahá'í Publishing Trust, 1957. 3d ed. 1975.

———. *Selections from the Writings of 'Abdu'l-Bahá*. Compiled by the Research Department of the Universal House of Justice. Haifa: Bahá'í World Centre, 1978.

———. *Some Answered Questions*. Collected and translated from the Persian by Laura Clifford Barney. Wilmette: Bahá'í Publishing Trust, 1930. 3d ed. 1981.

———. *Tablets of 'Abdu'l-Bahá 'Abbás*. Vol. 1. Chicago: Bahá'í Publishing Society, 1909.

———. *Tablets of the Divine Plan, Revealed By 'Abdu'l-Bahá to the North American Bahá'ís*. Wilmette: Bahá'í Publishing Trust. Rev. ed. 1977.

———. *A Traveller's Narrative written to illustrate the Episode of the Báb*. Translated by E. G. Browne. A new and corrected ed. Wilmette: Bahá'í Publishing Trust, 1980.

———. *Will and Testament of 'Abdu'l-Bahá*. Wilmette: Bahá'í Publishing Trust, 1944. 2d ed. 1971.

Afnán, M. and Hatcher, W. S., "Western Islamic Scholarship and Bahá'í Origins," *Religion*, Vol. 15 (1985), forthcoming.

Algar, Hamid. *Religion and State in Iran, 1784–1906*. Los Angeles: University of California Press, 1980.

The Báb. *Selections from the Writings of the Báb*. Compiled by the Research Department of the Universal House of Justice and translated by Habib Taherzadeh *et al*. Haifa: Bahá'í World Centre, 1976.

*The Bahá'í Centenary 1844–1944*. Wilmette: Bahá'í Publishing Trust, 1944.

*Bahá'í Education: A Compilation, Extracts from the Writings of Bahá'u'lláh, 'Abdu'l-Bahá, and Shoghi Effendi*. Compiled by the Research Department of the Universal House of Justice. Toronto: Bahá'í Community of Canada, 1977.

*The Bahá'í Faith, Statistical Information, 1844–1968*. Haifa: The Universal House of Justice, 1968.

*Bahá'í Funds and Contributions*. Compiled by the Universal House of Justice. Toronto: National Spiritual Assembly of the Bahá'ís of Canada, 1970.

*The Bahá'ís in Iran, A Report on the Persecution of a Religious Minority*. New York: Bahá'í International Community, 1981. Rev. and updated 1982.

*Bahá'í Prayers, A Selection of Prayers revealed by Bahá'u'lláh, the Báb and 'Abdu'l-Bahá*. Wilmette: Bahá'í Publishing Trust, 1954. Rev. Ed. 1982.

*The Bahá'í World: A Biennial International Record*. Vol. 7, 1936–1983. Compiled by the National Spiritual Assembly of the Bahá'ís of the United States and Canada. New York: Bahá'í Publishing Committee, 1939.

*The Bahá'í World: A Biennial International Record*. Vol. 8, 1938–1940. Compiled by the National Spiritual Assembly of the Bahá'ís of the United States and Canada. Wilmette: Bahá'í Publishing Committee, 1942.

*The Bahá'í World: A Biennial International Record. Vol. 9, 1940–1944*. Compiled by the National Spiritual Assembly of the Bahá'ís of the United States and Canada. Wilmette: Bahá'í Publishing Committee, 1945.

*The Bahá'í World: A Biennial International Record*. Vol. 10, 1944–1946. Compiled by the National Spiritual Assembly of the Bahá'ís of the United States and Canada. Wilmette: Bahá'í Publishing Committee, 1949.

*The Bahá'í World: A Biennial International Record*. Vol. 11, 1946–1950. Compiled by the National Spiritual Assembly of the Bahá'ís of the United States and Canada. Wilmette: Bahá'í Publishing Committee, 1952.

*The Bahá'í World: A Biennial International Record*. Vol. 12, 1950–1954. Compiled by the National Spiritual Assembly of the Bahá'ís of the United States. Wilmette: Bahá'í Publishing Trust, 1956.

*The Bahá'í World: An International Record*. Vol. 13, 1954–1963. Compiled by the Universal House of Justice. Haifa: The Universal House of Justice, 1970.

*The Bahá'í World: An International Record.* Vol. 14, 1963–1968. Compiled by the Universal House of Justice. Haifa: The Universal House of Justice, 1974.

*The Bahá'í World: An International Record.* Vol. 15, 1968–1973. Compiled by the Universal House of Justice. Haifa: Bahá'í World Centre, 1975.

*Bahá'í Writings on Music.* No. 4 of a series issued by the Universal House of Justice. Oakham: Bahá'í Publishing Trust, n.d.

Bahá'u'lláh and 'Abdu'l-Bahá. *Bahá'í World Faith, Selected Writings of Bahá'u'lláh and 'Abdu'l-Bahá.* Wilmette: Bahá'í Publishing Trust, 1943. Rev. ed. 1956.

————. *The Divine Art of Living, Selections from Writings of Bahá'u'lláh and 'Abdu'l-Bahá.* Compiled by Mabel Hyde Paine. Wilmette: Bahá'í Publishing Trust, 1944. 4th rev. ed. 1979.

Bahá'u'lláh. *Epistle to the Son of the Wolf.* Translated by Shoghi Effendi. Wilmette: Bahá'í Publishing Trust, 1941. 2d ed. 1953.

————. *Gleanings from the Writings of Bahá'u'lláh.* Translated by Shoghi Effendi. Wilmette: Bahá'í Publishing Trust, 1939. 2d rev. ed. 1976.

————. *The Hidden Words of Bahá'u'lláh.* Translated by Shoghi Effendi. Wilmette: Bahá'í Publishing Trust, 1939.

————. *The Kitáb-i-Íqán, The Book of Certitude, revealed by Bahá'u'lláh.* Translated by Shoghi Effendi. Wilmette: Bahá'í Publishing Trust, 1931. 2d ed. 1950.

————. *Prayers and Meditations by Bahá'u'lláh.* Translated by Shoghi Effendi. Wilmette: Bahá'í Publishing Trust, 1938.

————. *The Proclamation of Bahá'u'lláh.* Haifa: Bahá'í World Centre, 1967.

————. *The Seven Valleys and the Four Valleys.* Translated by Marzieh Gail. Wilmette: Bahá'í Publishing Trust, 1945. 3d rev. ed. 1978.

————. *A Synopsis and Codification of the Laws and Ordinances of the Kitáb-i-Aqdas, the Most Holy Book of Bahá'u'lláh.* Compiled by the Universal House of Justice. Haifa: Bahá'í World Centre, 1973.

Balyuzi, H. M. *'Abdu'l-Bahá, The Centre of the Covenant of Bahá'u'lláh.* Oxford: George Ronald, 1971.

————. *The Báb, The Herald of the Day of Days.* Oxford: George Ronald, 1973.

————. *Bahá'u'lláh, The King of Glory.* Oxford: George Ronald, 1980.

————. *Edward Granville Browne and the Bahá'í Faith.* London: George Ronald, 1970.

Bourgeois, L. *Un Homme et Son Oeuvre.* Toronto: Bahá'í Centre Publication, 1973.

————. *The Bahá'í Temple: Press Comments, Symbolism.* Chicago: Louis J. Bourgeois, 1921.

Brown, Ira V., "Watchers for the Second Coming, the Millenial Tradition in America" in *Mississippi Valley Historical Review*, Vol. 39, No. 3, pp. 441–458.

Browne, E. G. "Babism" in *Religious Systems of the World, a Contribution to the Study of Comparative Religion.* Edited by W. Sheowring and C. W. Thies. London: Swan Sonneschein and Co., New York: Macmillan and Co., 1892.

————. *A Literary History of Persia.* Vol. IV, 1500–1924. Cambridge: 1924.

————. *Materials for the Study of the Bábí Religion Compiled by E. G. Browne.* Cambridge: Cambridge University Press, 1918.

————. *A Traveller's Narrative Written to Illustrate the Episode of the Báb.* Cambridge: Cambridge University Press, 1891.

Cole, J. R. *The Concept of Manifestation in the Bahá'í Writings, Bahá'í Studies.* Vol. 9. Ottawa: The Canadian Association for Studies on the Bahá'í Faith, 1982.

*Consultation: A Compilation, Extracts from the Writings and Utterances of Bahá'u'lláh, 'Abdu'l-Bahá, Shoghi Effendi, and the Universal House of Justice.* Compiled by the Research Department of the Universal House of Justice. Toronto: Bahá'í Community of Canada, 1980.

*The Continental Boards of Counselors.* Compiled by the National Spiritual Assembly of the Bahá'ís of the United States. Wilmette: Bahá'í Publishing Trust, 1981.

Corbin, H. *En Islam iranien; aspects spirituels et philosophiques.* Vol. 4. Paris; Gallimard, 1972.

Cross, W. R. *The Burned-over District, The Social and Intellectual History of Enthusiastic Religion in Western New York, 1800–1850.* New York: Cornell University, 1950. New York: Harper and Row, 1965.

Dahl, A. L. "The Fragrance of Spirituality: An Appreciation of the Art of Mark Tobey" in *The Bahá'í World: An International Record.* Vol. 16. 1973–1976. Compiled by the Universal House of Justice. Haifa: Bahá'í World Centre, 1978.

*The Five Year Plan, 1974–1979, Statistical Report.* Haifa: Bahá'í World Centre, 1979.

*A Fortress for Well-Being, Bahá'í Teachings on Marriage.* Wilmette: Bahá'í Publishing Trust, 1973.

Giachery, U. *Shoghi Effendi, Recollections.* Oxford: George Ronald, 1973.

Gobineau, Joseph Arthur le Comte de. *Les Religions et les Philosophies dans l'Asie Centrale*. Paris: Didier, 1865. Paris: Ernest le Roux, ed. 3d ed., 1900.

Hatcher, W. S. "Economics and Moral Values," *World Order*, Vol. 9, No. 2 (1974), pp. 14–27.

———. *The Science of Religion, Bahá'í Studies* Vol. 2. The Canadian Association for Studies on the Bahá'í Faith, Ottawa: 1980.

———. *The Concept of Spirituality, Bahá'í Studies*, Vol. 11, The Association for Bahá'í Studies, Ottawa: 1982.

Hatcher, W. S. and Afnán M.: See Afnán, M. and Hatcher, W. S.

*The Individual and Teaching, Raising the Divine Call, Extracts from the Writings of Bahá'u'lláh, 'Abdu'l-Bahá, and Shoghi Effendi.* Compiled by the Research Department of the Universal House of Justice. Toronto: Bahá'í Community of Canada, 1977.

Ives, H. C. *Portals to Freedom*. Oxford: George Ronald, 1973.

Johnson, Vernon Elvin, "The Challenge of the Bahá'í Faith" in *World Order*, Vol. 10, No. 3, p. 39.

Kunter, Dr. N., 12 August 1959 letter in *British Bahá'í Journal*, No. 141, p. 4.

*The Local Spiritual Assembly.* Compiled by the Universal House of Justice. Toronto: National Spiritual Assembly of the Bahá'ís of Canada, 1970.

Martin, J. D. "Bahá'u'lláh's Model for World Unity" in *The Bahá'í World: An International Record*. Vol. 16. 1973–1976. Haifa: Bahá'í World Centre, 1978.

———. "The Bahá'ís of Iran under the Islamic Republic, 1979–1983" in *Middle East Focus.* Toronto Vol. 6, no. 4, 1983.

———. "The Bahá'ís of Iran Under the Pahlavi Regime, 1925–1978" in *Middle East Focus.* Toronto Vol. 4, No. 6, 1981.

———. "The Missionary as Historian" in *World Order*. Vol. 10, no. 3, 1976.

Miller, W. M., *Baha'ism, Its Origins and Teachings.* New York and Chicago: Fleming H. Revell company, 1931.

———. *The Bahá'í Faith, Its History and Teachings.* South Pasadena: William Carey Library, 1974.

Momen, Moojan. *The Bábí and Bahá'í Religions*. Oxford: George Ronald, 1981.

Mumford, L. *The City in History, Its Origins, Its Transformations and Its Prospects.* New York: Harcourt, Brace and World, Inc., 1961.

Nabíl-i-A'zam (Muḥammad-i-Zarandí). *The Dawn-Breakers, Nabíl's Narrative of the Early Days of the Bahá'í Revelation.* Translated from the original Persian and edited by Shoghi Effendi. Wilmette: Baha'i Publishing Trust, 1932.

Nasr, S. H. *Ideals and Realities of Islam.* London: George Allen and Unwin Ltd., 1966. Boston: Beacon Press, 1972.

*The National Spiritual Assembly.* Compiled by The Universal House of Justice. Wilmette: Bahá'í Publishing Trust, 1972.

Nicolas, A. L. M. *Siyyid 'Alí-Muhammad Dit le Báb.* Paris: Librarie Critique, 1908.

―――. *Le Béyan Persan.* Translated from Persian by A. L. M. Nicolas. Paris: Librairie Paul Geuthner. 4 Vols. 1911–14.

Phelps, M. H. *Life and Teachings of Abbas Effendi.* New York and London: G. P. Putnam's Sons, 1903. New York: Knickerbocker Press. 2d rev. ed. 1912.

Rabbani, R. *The Priceless Pearl.* London: Baha'i Publishing Trust, 1969.

Ráfatí, Vahíd. *The Development of Shaykhí Thought in Shí'i Islam.* Los Angeles: University of California in Los Angeles, 1979.

Richards, J. R. *The Religion of the Bahá'ís.* London: S.P.C.K., 1932. New York: Macmillan Company, 1932.

Ross, E. D. *Great Religions of the World.* New York: Harper and Brothers Publishers, 1901.

Schaefer, U. *The Light Shineth in Darkness, Five Studies in Revelation after Christ.* Translated from the German by Hélène Momtaz Neri and Oliver Coburn. Oxford: George Ronald, 1977.

Shoghi Effendi. *The Advent of Divine Justice.* Wilmette: Bahá'í Publishing Trust, 1939. 3d ed. 1969.

―――. *Bahá'í Administration, Selected Messages 1922–1932.* Wilmette: Bahá'í Publishing Trust, 1928, 7th ed. 1974.

―――. *The Bahá'í Faith 1844–1952.* Wilmette: Bahá'í Publishing Trust, 1953.

―――. *Citadel of Faith, Messages to America, 1947–1957.* Wilmette: Bahá'í Publishing Trust, 1965.

―――. *The Dispensation of Bahá'u'lláh.* Wilmette: Bahá'í Publishing Trust, 1934.

―――. *God Passes By.* Wilmette: Bahá'í Publishing Trust, 1944. 3d ed. 1974.

―――. *High Endeavours, Messages to Alaska.* n.p. National Spiritual Assembly of the Bahá'ís of Alaska, 1976.

―――. *Messages to the Bahá'í World 1950–1957.* Wilmette: Bahá'í Publishing Trust, 1951. 2d ed. 1971.

―――. *Messages to Canada.* Toronto: National Spiritual Assembly of the Bahá'ís of Canada, 1965.

―――. *Principles of Bahá'í Administration.* London: Bahá'í Publishing Trust, 1950. 4th ed. 1976.

―――. *The Promised Day Is Come.* Wilmette: Bahá'í Publishing Trust, 1941. 3d ed. 1980.

———. *The World Order of Bahá'u'lláh, Selected Letters.* Wilmette: Bahá'í Publishing Trust, 1938. 2d rev. ed. 1974.

Ṭabáṭabá'í, 'Allámah Siyyid Muḥammad Ḥusayn. *Shi'ite Islam.* Translated and edited with introduction and notes by Seyyed Hossein Nasr. Albany: State University of New York Press, 1975.

Taherzadeh, A. *The Revelation of Bahá'u'lláh.* Oxford: George Ronald. Vol. 1, 1974; Vol. 2, 1977; Vol. 3, 1983.

———. *Trustees of the Merciful.* London: Baha'i Publishing Trust, 1972.

Universal House of Justice. *The Constitution of the Universal House of Justice.* Haifa: Bahá'í World Centre, 1972.

———. *Messages from the Universal House of Justice 1968–1973.* Wilmette: Bahá'í Publishing Trust, 1976.

———. *Wellspring of Guidance, Messages 1963–1968.* Wilmette: Bahá'í Publishing Trust, 1969. 2d ed. 1976.

Wagar, W. *The City of Man, Prophecies of a World Civilization in Twentieth-Century Thought.* Boston: Houghton Mifflin Company, 1963.

Ward, A. L. *239 Days, 'Abdu'l- Bahá's Journey in America.* Wilmette: Bahá'í Publishing Trust, 1979.

Widengren, Geo. "Iranian Religion" in *Encyclopedia Britannica* (Macropedia). Vol. 9. 15th ed. 1981.

Wilson, S. G. *Baha'ism and Its Claims.* New York: Fleming II. Revell Company, 1915.

## PERIODICALS

*British Bahá'í Journal*
*Middle East Focus*
*Mississippi Valley Historical Review*
*Open Court*
*Seven Days*
*Star of the West*
*World Order*

# Index

In cases where the Persian name begins with an honorific such as Siyyid, Mírzá, Shaykh, or Hájí, the proper name is given first followed by a comma and the honorific. Thus, Shaykh Ahmad-i-Ahsá'í is listed as Ahmad-i-Ahsá'í, Shaykh. However, during the Qájár period, the title Mírzá designated a prince whenever it followed a name. Therefore, in such cases the name appears here without a comma (e.g., Farhád Mírzá). The same is true from Turkish notables (e.g., Khurshid Páshá).